BREAK-THROUGH PROCESS REDESIGN

BREAK-THROUGH PROCESS REDESIGN

New Pathways to Customer Value

Charlene B. Adair ∗ Bruce A. Murray

amacom

American Management Association

New York • Atlanta • Boston • Chicago • Kansas City • San Francisco • Washington, D.C.
Brussels • Mexico City • Tokyo • Toronto

This book is available at a special
discount when ordered in bulk quantities.
For information, contact Special Sales Department,
AMACOM, a division of American Management Association,
135 West 50th Street, New York, NY 10020.

This publication is designed to provide accurate and authoritative
information in regard to the subject matter covered. It is sold with
the understanding that the publisher is not engaged in rendering
legal, accounting, or other professional service. If legal advice or
other expert assistance is required, the services of a competent
professional person should be sought.

Library of Congress Cataloging-in-Publication Data

Adair, Charlene B.
    Breakthrough process redesign : new pathways to customer value /
Charlene B. Adair, Bruce A. Murray.
       p.   cm.
    Includes bibliographical references and index.
    ISBN 0-8144-5150-0
    1. Total quality management. 2. Benchmarking (Management)
I. Murray, Bruce A. II. Title.
HD62.15.A33   1994
658.5'62--dc20   93-36844
                                                               CIP

Printing number

10 9 8 7 6 5 4 3 2 1

This book is one step on the path to the future we envision; we
dedicate it to a successful journey

Contents

Preface

Breakthrough Process Improvement

Astute managers at all levels—in all industries—realize that the success of their organizations in today's world depends upon flexibility and responsiveness in meeting customer needs, achieving ever-higher quality levels, a high degree of internal efficiency, and cost-effectiveness. The key to success is to maximize value to the customer and successfully implement the changes that make maximum customer value a reality for any organization in any industry.

This book will show you how to answer the question of what constitutes maximum value to your customer and how to implement changes successfully to achieve that elusive goal. It shows for the first time how the customer can effectively be brought into the process of business strategy development and how to use customer feedback to identify the few areas for improvement that will have a dramatic impact on the success of the organization.

A flexible but logical step-by-step process is presented to guide you through successful cross-functional activities to achieve break-through improvements of 50 to 90 percent in time, quality, cost, and other measures of any business process. The tools for analysis of processes are described in detail, along with when to use them. A new method of analyzing processes is presented—based upon what happens to the work going through the process rather than what people are doing. Examples are liberally used to clarify the steps in the process analysis and improvement model.

And, for the first time, process redesign activities are discussed in terms of their impact and demands upon middle managers. Competencies of successful managers are identified along with the key skills required to be successful in the continuously improving organization of the future. You will learn how to reduce or eliminate organizational impediments to successfully focus business activities on the customer. A method of assessing the readiness of your organization for dramatic change is provided.

This book draws upon our own experiences as senior managers and leaders of successful change, plus our research into the requirements for success as leaders and managers of companies likely to thrive in the future. Our experience in industry and as consultants helping clients achieve breakthrough results in a wide variety of industries and sizes of companies has contributed to the development of the process redesign model, upon which this book is based. The book describes how we apply this model in a flexible, nonprescriptive way that allows for the inherent variations in processes and companies while still recognizing and capitalizing upon those characteristics of both that are commonly found. We show you how to enter the improvement/redesign process at different stages, based upon the specific needs of your own organization.

Through the use of the model we have developed, the roles of the organization leader, the senior functional management, middle management, and others in achieving dramatic change and increasing competitive strength will become clear. You will see how using the steps we describe in the model process will draw the entire organization into the effort.

Our goal is to create a process redesign model that brings together the elements of organizational strategy and action through focus on the customer that has relevance in any organization—manufacturing, service, retail, distribution, health care—and for any functional interest within those organizations. We provide a methodology that will help you achieve measurable, quantifiable breakthrough results in a few months without investing in extensive systems technology, adding costs, disrupting your organizational functions, or hurting your customer. By using our model you will have a methodology and the tools to drive a winning experience with breakthrough improvement: reduced cycle times, greater flexibility, faster response to customers and market changes, reduced cost, less work waiting to be done, improved quality of work, and a better work climate.

Our own experience in using these methodologies and tools in literally hundreds of situations has demonstrated that the mode and approach are valid and that exciting results can be achieved in any organization. We hope that you will use the things you learn from this book to create an environment in your organization that fosters deliberate and continuous focus on customer-driven competitiveness that allows you to thrive in your industry.

C. B. A.
B. A. M.

Acknowledgments

We would like to express our gratitude to those who directly and indirectly contributed to and stimulated our thinking in the development of this book, especially:

John Guaspari and Steve Crom, whose pioneering work on providing and measuring value to the customer has contributed so much to business focus.

Jim Nickoll, whose ability to find creative ways to measure and dissect complex processes is a continuous source of amazement.

Wendy Schultz, who found ways to turn our rough sketches into meaningful graphics on tight time schedules.

Dave Knight and Peggy McMahon, who cheerfully and effectively conducted the middle management research interviews amidst very busy schedules. And, those managers who so graciously gave their time for the interviews.

Our colleagues at Rath & Strong, past and present, who have helped and continue to help clients focus the business on the right things, redesign the right processes to get meaningful results, and create organizational climates that promote creativity, responsiveness, flexibility, and an atmosphere of constant improvement.

Our editor at AMACOM, Tony Vlamis, who made the sometimes annoying and time-consuming mechanics of producing a book easy for us.

xiii

Jon Zonderman, who critiqued our early efforts and helped us focus our thoughts.

Our many consulting clients, who have been willing to listen and learn with us, try our ideas, and freely share their thoughts, data, and results with us.

BREAK-THROUGH PROCESS REDESIGN

1

Competing by Redesigning Business Processes

Joe was pressed for time. That hot order for ten widgets he had worked so hard to land was late. When he asked Tom, the widget manager, about the delay, Tom replied, "You don't understand. The process just takes time." Joe asked Tom how much time was spent actually making the widgets. To his surprise, Joe found that it took only three hours to make a widget. He wondered why the order was late. It had been in process two weeks!

That same evening, Joe, who is the general manager, was reviewing the cash balances for the company. He noticed that the ABC Customer Company was always late paying its invoices. "They could save a lot of money if they paid within ten days," Joe said to himself; Joe's company offered a 10 percent discount. "I'll have to call Sally at ABC in the morning and inquire."

On the way home, Joe stopped by the development where his new house was being built. As he walked up to the front door, the painter was on the way out. Joe stopped to ask, "Why are there empty paint cans in a pile in the front yard?" The painter exclaimed, "Hey, I'm hired to paint your house, mister, not to clean up the mess." As he walked into the house, Joe noticed that the painter had tracked mud in on the newly installed carpet.

Joe began to think about the whole process of building the house: "First, there was the sales contract. Boy, was that an ordeal! The salesperson, Jim, filled out the contract (which had five copies) and sent it to the main office of the developer. It took three days for the office to check the contract and return it for corrections. Then, I had to go back over to the sales office to make the corrections. Next, the

1

main office said it would take two weeks to process the contract. How could one contract take so long?"

Finally, the contract was complete, and it was time to apply for the mortgage loan. Joe arrived at the bank on time for the appointment. The loan officer, Mr. Adams, took Joe's application and advised him to check back in about two weeks. Joe exclaimed, "Two weeks! The FBI could do a full investigation on me in less time!" The officer replied, "You don't understand. The process just takes time."

Joe wondered how long someone actually spent processing the application. Finally, after several unplanned phone calls to see if the approval was complete and one visit to the bank, the application had been approved and the builder had begun to build the house. After all of this, Joe had paint cans in his front yard and building personnel who didn't seem to care about him—the customer.

When Joe finally arrived home that evening, he was exhausted. He worried about his own soon-to-be-unhappy widget customer and how he would explain that the widget process "just takes time." Joe didn't sleep most of the night.

Early the next morning, he called the ABC Customer Company to ask about the unpaid invoices. He asked for accounts payable and was put on hold. Next, a person answered the phone, "Customer service, may I help you?" Joe explained that he was holding for accounts payable and immediately was put on hold again. Finally, Sally answered. Joe wondered how ABC's customers must feel when they called and, worse yet, if this ever happened when his widget customers called his own company!

Sally explained why the invoices were never paid within ten days. "Well, you see, this process just takes time. After all, we have to match the receiver document to the invoice, double-check the numbers, verify with quality, contact credit, check with finance, and submit a request for the check with copies to all those departments. Checks are produced every Friday, so I get the check back the following Monday to send to you. There's just no way to do all this in ten days!"

Joe asked why checks were produced only on Friday and got a not-so-surprising reply: "Oh, that's the way we've always done it. Our manager designed this process years ago. Besides, we can't suggest changes. Wow, 10 percent would add up over a year, wouldn't it?"

Joe hung up the phone and shook his head. Just as he was about to make the dreaded phone call to the customer waiting for his widgets, the phone rang. It was his daughter's teacher. "Mr. Jones,

Susie has fallen. I think her arm may be broken. Can you come right away?" Just what Joe needed: another emergency. He was really pressed for time.

Joe and Susie arrived at the emergency door of the hospital to find a nurse at the reception desk. She said, "Sir, please fill out this five-part form." In the meantime, Susie was screaming. Joe asked if they could just take care of his daughter. After all, she was in a lot of pain. Of course, the nurse's answer was, "You don't understand. This process takes time."

After filling out the five-part form, going to another desk to get an identification number, and yet a third desk to get a card and identification bracelet, they were finally ushered into a waiting area to see a doctor. After the initial examination, they were sent upstairs to X ray. Much to Joe's surprise, another five-part form, identification number, and bracelet were issued. Everyone was very busy; there was no time for chitchat with patients. Susie was still screaming. Each stage involved more forms, more busy people, and more waiting. Joe wondered why the process couldn't be simplified. No one working there had time to think about it, he guessed.

At 4:00 P.M., Joe and Susie left the hospital. They had spent a total of twelve minutes with the doctor, four minutes in X ray, and ten minutes getting the cast on—and hours waiting. What a day!

As he tried to relax that evening, it occurred to Joe that his widget customers could feel the same way he had felt as the customer. Now *that* was a disturbing thought! He began to think more about what he valued as a customer: care, respect, empathy, quality, the right price, flexibility, responsiveness, and timeliness.* After all, Joe usually felt pressed for time! Joe decided that first thing in the morning he would look into the widget process at work and try to find out why there were always unexpected problems and why it took so long.

Early the next morning, Joe went to talk again with Tom, the widget manager, about the last customer order. Tom began to explain all the problems associated with the order: "Well, first, there were

---

*Value as the customer sees it is "what the customer GOT divided by what it COST the customer," in the words of our colleague John Guaspari.[1] The customer not only expects to get the goods or services contracted for but also intangibles, such as confidence plus the good feelings of being serviced well and of being an important part of the supplier's business. These attributes are examples of what is called Total Quality. Cost includes not only the dollars spent but also the frustration, anxiety, and time that it took to do business. As a customer, Joe was missing many of the attributes that he valued, particularly respect, empathy, and *timeliness*.

problems with the widget prints. Those engineering drawings require a Ph.D. just to read them! Then, we realized that the customer order had some problems: Customer service transposed some numbers in the part number, and purchasing ordered the wrong raw material. By the time we got that straight, the scheduler had no way to prioritize this order above the other late orders. Do you realize that we now have three categories for late orders? Anyway, we finally got ready to run the order on the widget machine when maintenance insisted it was time for some work on the machine, so we were shut down for two days! We'll do everything possible to get the order out next week. You know, it's clearly not our fault that the order is late. After all, I just sent you the latest report outlining the improvements that we've made setting up the widget machine; we can now do it in 25 percent of the time previously required."

Joe's head was spinning. He thanked Tom and went back to his office, closed the door, and forwarded his phone calls.

How could this be? He thought about other improvement reports: 25 percent more calls answered in customer service than ever before, three new highly technical engineers hired and a state-of-the-art CAD system in engineering to produce the drawings in half the time, and a preventive maintenance process implemented to ensure that equipment was in good working order—even the copy machines. So why were there so many problems getting this order out? Then it struck him. Managers were trying hard to improve the things within their own departments, but the activities were disconnected from each other and, obviously, from the customer! Joe wondered, "What if we stopped focusing on each department and instead paid attention to the entire customer order and order-fulfillment business processes?" He would have to think about that some more.

Joe wondered why Tom had not coordinated the maintenance with Hank, the manager of maintenance. There must have been a big uproar when the mechanic showed up to do the work! It occurred to Joe that the best people to solve this problem would be the mechanic and the widget machine operator. So why didn't that happen?

Joe became excited at the prospect of having his employees just solve their own problems in order to take better care of customers. It would sure mean fewer unpleasant phone calls to customers like the one he was about to make. He decided to go talk with the widget machine operator. When he asked him why maintenance had interrupted production at such a critical time, the operator's reply was, "We don't have any control over that. Managers determine the schedules. It didn't make sense to me, but what could I do?"

Process Redesign

The foundation of maximizing customer value is a focus on the business processes that drive the business along with creating a climate that values innovation. There are various degrees of process redesign to evaluate as the gap between customer value and present performance level is identified (see Figure 1-1). The range of redesign is from 0 percent (no change) to 100 percent (eliminate the process or create a new process). The focus of this book is on radical redesign— the type of redesign that creates improvement in processes of 60 percent or more.

As the degree of redesign increases, so does the associated risk, as shown in Figure 1-2. No matter how complete the planning and analysis is for a change, the results are not certain until the new ideas are tried out. As the amount of change increases, so does the risk. Although changes are not expected to work perfectly the first time, it is expected that people learn from each experience and continue to adjust the change until the desired results are realized. When innovation is valued, willingness to take risks increases, and breakthrough results eventually occur.

In this book, we provide step-by-step methodologies and tools to ensure your success as you identify and redesign processes. But much of your success will depend on how well your organizational climate supports innovation and, therefore, employee involvement. Throughout the book, we provide guidelines for management as empowerment increases.

The Redefinition of Quality Through the Years

In the 1970s, great product quality with the right price and products was enough to make almost any company competitive. The focus was on a useful product/service that worked. Strategy could afford to be relatively static. Competitiveness was based more on clearly de-

Figure 1-1. Degrees of process redesign.

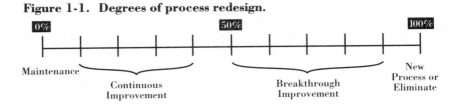

Figure 1-2. Risk associated with process redesign.

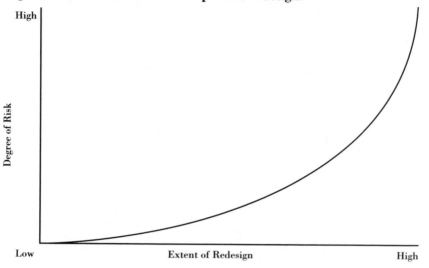

fined market segments. Gradually, as more companies were able to provide quality products and services, the customer wanted more. As the 1980s began, changes in the basis of competition included the proliferation and fragmentation of markets; accelerated product life cycles; and globalization, which began breaking down barriers between national and regional markets.

The definition of quality evolved into what is now commonly known as Total Quality: quality of the entire transaction with priorities and activities better aligned with the customer. Time became a key competitive factor. As markets became more dynamic, a key competitive attribute became that of responding fast to changing customer needs.

The 1990s have brought a focus on delivering customer value in everything a company does. The way to create this customer value is not just through products and markets but through business processes: the integration of functions, departments, and even suppliers, customers, and competitors into a company's strategy.

These growing marketplace demands for the ever-expanding notion of quality have been met by a host of improvement efforts, from quality tools and statistical process control (SPC) in the 1970s, to Just-in-Time (JIT), employee involvement, and visionary leadership in the 1980s, to innovative process redesign and true middle management leadership, focusing on new and expanded roles for middle managers, in the 1990s. Quality has been redefined (see Figure 1-3).

The Maximization of Customer Value

The foundation of maximizing customer value is a focus on business processes that begin and/or end with the customer. The organization structure, as well as the people/climate/leadership, support these business processes in order to maximize customer value. The company vision, business imperatives, and strategy operationalize the process of providing maximum value to the customer, as shown in Figure 1-4.

According to John Guaspari and Steven Crom, at any given time for any given market, there is a minimum level of value required to be competitive. The level of Minimum Acceptable Value by the customer is a function of three things:

1. The customer's experience base has an impact on what he or she accepts. Before cars were built defect-free, buyers accepted an average of seven defects per car. Today, that would be an outrage.
2. What the competition is doing has an impact on expectations. Until Marriott implemented the automatic check-in process with no waiting, people were perfectly willing to stand in line to check in at a hotel. Now, this inconvenience seems unnecessary.
3. The desired level of value is affected by technology. Some ideas are simply not possible today because of technological limitations.[2]

Figure 1-3. The redefinition of quality.

Figure 1-4. The maximization of value to the customer.

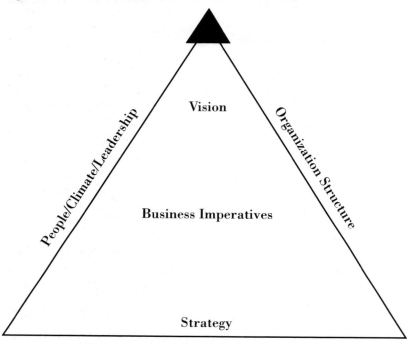

Business Processes

Therefore, the customer's idea of value is a moving target. Anticipation of customer needs, alertness to market changes, and constant deliberate innovation are required to maintain competitiveness. In fact, in thinking about the attributes that best describe a company maximizing customer value, we have concluded that there are really only two:

1. The business processes, organization structure, and people/climate/leadership are all aligned and focused on delivering maximum value to the customer.
2. Innovation is highly valued throughout the organization.

Let's take a more detailed look at the gap between a company described by these two all-important attributes and a company that is not. Let's look at the first attribute: that the business processes, organization structure, and people/climate/leadership be aligned and focused on delivering maximum value to the customer.

The customer and market is well understood and confirmed through constant data gathering.

vs.

Internal assumptions about what the customer (and possibly the market) wants are followed. Customer surveys are done only every year or two.

The focus is on proactive leadership of the customer (providing value that the customer has yet to articulate as desired).

vs.

The focus is on keeping up with the competition and staying in the market.

The entire organization structure is like a giant feedback loop that begins and ends with the customer.[3] Cross-functional business processes and integration with suppliers, customers, and competitors drive the organization structure.

vs.

The organization structure focuses on functional departments, and the way to get ahead is to grow these departments.

The company vision for the future (three to five years) is clear and well understood by all employees. This includes what the business is (the mission) as well as how it will realize the vision.

vs.

No time has been invested by the company's leadership in developing the vision. The leadership feels that having a mission and goals is sufficient. Everyone is too busy meeting short-term goals.

Business imperatives (those things that must be done for success) are clear and well understood. Goals and objectives are aligned to focus efforts on meeting these business imperatives.

vs.

Disparity exists within the company on what the primary business imperatives are. Focus is lacking, and goals and objectives are departmental.

The company strategy focuses on both the climate of the organization and business processes that align with providing value to the customer, and success is measured in terms of how well value is provided. Employees have input and involvement in strategy development, and all employees not only understand it but also know their role in achieving the strategy. Planning is emphasized and execution is efficient.

vs.

The company strategy is focused on short-term profitability and traditional measurements of margin and utilization of resources. The strategy is developed from the top of the organization, and very little of it is understood by employees. An emphasis on quick execution results in high rework.

Measurement is deliberate, visible, and always tied to customer value. What the customer values is translated within the organization so that each employee is compelled to drive the organization to satisfy the customer better.

vs.

Measurement is tied to short-term goals and is understood and visible to only a few managers. Individuals are not informed on a regular basis about the performance of the company.

The company utilizes employee involvement as a process to maximize value to the customer. Teamwork is the norm at all levels within the organization.

vs.

Employee involvement was begun with no clear objectives in mind, and teamwork is only talked about.

The environment encourages and supports employees learning from customers and the market.

vs.

Only sales and marketing have access to the customers and the market. Many employees may not understand how their products and/or services are used by the customer.

Core business processes, such as order fulfillment and product design, are aligned with providing customer value and are identified and well understood, since those core business processes involve many functions. Cross-functional teamwork is the norm, as these processes are constantly improved. Breakthrough (50 to 90 percent) improvement is expected and accomplished on a regular basis, generating energy for continued improvement.

vs.

The focus is on improving efficiency within functional departments, with a goal of continuous (10 to 40 percent) improvement at best. Work is not thought of as cross-functional processes.

Now let's look at the second attribute: that innovation is highly valued throughout the organization.

Many new ideas from all levels of the organization thrive and are celebrated.

vs.

Fewer ideas are offered, and those that survive are usually offered by management.

Innovation is managed. Systems are in place to encourage new ideas and winnow them with the customer in mind.[4]

vs.

Most ideas are lost in the shuffle.

Risk taking is valued and encouraged. After all, to try a new idea is to take a risk; there are usually no guarantees that a new idea will work the first time as intended. Managers know how to drive the creative process.[5]

vs.

Risk aversion exists. The stakes are simply too high.

Employees at all levels exhibit courage and initiative, affirming their power to affect change.

vs.

Employees fear retribution and failure. They tend to keep a low profile to play it safe.

Ideas that don't work are celebrated and valued as learning opportunities.

vs.

Ideas that don't work are considered failures.

Employees utilize most of their strength in proactive, innovative activity. They have the knowledge, skills, and tools required to succeed.

vs.

Employees utilize 90 percent of their strength in protecting themselves and only 10 percent in proactive, innovative activity.

Learning and growing are promoted throughout the organization. Even leaders and managers openly share their personal growth goals.

vs.

Learning and growing are considered "extras," often only considered when a short-term payback can be confirmed. Leaders and managers are supposed to know it all.

Training and education are directly tied to development that will enable the organization to serve the customer better. Employees are able to apply learnings immediately and are provided training and education when needed. Concrete learning experiences are the norm—in other words, learning by doing.

vs.

Mass training and education are provided as deemed necessary by top management. Employees are expected to apply learnings on their own.

Employees accept and welcome responsibility to increase the quality of their work experience—for themselves, for their work group and its members, and for the organization.

vs.

Employees have a "victim" attitude: They do not consider it *their* responsibility to make improvements. The focus is on what is being done *to* them rather than what they can do. They wait for someone else (usually management) to "do something."

Employees affirm their power to affect change. They feel enabled to realize their full potential in creativity, productivity, and personal fulfillment.

vs.

Employees do not feel able to make changes.

The Challenge for Middle Management

Top management is excited and energized when presented with ideas to maximize customer value through innovative process improvement. Employees within the organization are easily energized to get more involved and implement the ideas that they have probably had for years. But middle managers get caught in between. They often feel threatened by the idea of employee involvement. After all, they have always been the decision makers and directors of how work gets done.

This dilemma reminds us of a story about a circus high-wire act, which is sometimes done with no net below to compensate for mistakes. In any case, imagine one trapeze artist swinging on one of those swings up in the rafters; another artist is swinging on another swing. The idea is that they synchronize themselves, and eventually the first artist lets go of her swing, flips, and grabs the hands of the second artist. But before the first artist is willing to let go, she needs to be clear about what she will grab and have a high confidence level for success!

Now, let's imagine that the first artist is blindfolded and the entire audience is yelling, "Let go!" The fear in the artist's mind of going "splat" is great. In fact, she holds on for dear life. However, if the blindfold is removed and the artist clearly understands the moves necessary to reach the second artist's hands, and if she has had a chance to develop the skills necessary to do the trick (with a net!), she is willing to let go and make the move.

More often than not, companies ask their middle managers to "let go" with no vision of their future role and no skills development to ensure a successful transition. The "splat" for them is failure in their job, so they hold on for dear life, resisting change. But contrary to what many say, there is a role for middle managers in the process-driven, innovative, risk-taking company. It is an exciting and dynamic role, and one that is crucial to organizational success. This book paints the vision for middle managers of their new role, how to be successful in it, and how to develop the behaviors and skills that will be required.

Notes

1. John Guaspari, *The Customer Connection* (New York: AMACOM, 1988).
2. John Guaspari and Steven Crom, "Ultimately, There Is Just One Issue: Value," *Rath & Strong Leadership Report* (Winter 1993).
3. George Stalk, Philip Evans, and Lawrence E. Shulman, "Competing on Capabilities: The New Rules of Corporate Strategy," *Harvard Business Review* (March–April 1992).
4. Brian Dumaine, "Closing the Innovation Gap," *Fortune* (December 2, 1991).
5. Ibid.

2

Understanding Business Processes

Joe arrived at work early. He needed some time to think: "Why is it that it takes two weeks to fulfill a widget order when people only work on one for three hours? Why is it that Sally over at the ABC Customer Company can't produce a check in ten days? Why is it that it took all day with Susie at the hospital to get a grand total of twenty-six minutes of service? And the house—can you believe two weeks to process my agreement to buy the house and another two weeks for the mortgage application? All this time being wasted, and no one seems to be very concerned about the customer!"

The phone rang. It was Sally from the ABC Customer Company. "Joe, I've been thinking about your question," she said. "You know, the one about taking so long to process those checks that we send to you. I added up the savings that we would have if we could pay the invoices within ten days and decided that I would look into it a bit more. When I went out into accounts payable, everyone seemed really busy, and I guess they all work overtime at the end of every month. There are piles of paper waiting to be processed, and the manager of the department tells me that all they need is more help."

Sally continued, "When I began to ask questions about what happens to produce these checks, I got some very interesting answers. Everyone talked about what the people do. Apparently, we didn't always have all these steps to go through. The double-check, verify, and contact credit steps were added over the last two years because of problems we were having at the time. For instance, we added the step to contact credit back when our new computer system was being implemented and we lost our link with credit. Even though we now have an automatic check in the computer, we still send the paperwork to credit to be checked!"

Joe was intrigued. "Sally, you could be talking about making widgets instead of checks. I seem to find the same things happening out in the widget department. Everyone is too busy, there's lots of work waiting to be completed, and the deliveries are late to the customer, just like your checks are late getting to me. Do you suppose that the check that you are producing is a product just like my widgets? Boy, we sure do complicate our lives a lot, don't we? There must be an easier way."

Sally responded, "You know, Joe, you may be onto something. I think I'll look into this a little more. Maybe there are some books that would help me think about this whole mess in a clearer way. If I could only sort out what's going on here, we could probably solve some of the problems that take so much time. I'll go to the bookstore this week and let you know what I find, but right now, it's back to work."

In order to be successful in maximizing customer value by innovative redesign of business processes you may have to overcome some paradigms in the way you think about those processes. The purpose of this chapter is to help you gain a clearer understanding of what constitutes a process, how processes evolve over time, how processes interrelate in a business, and characteristics of processes that work well versus those that do not work well. Hopefully, this will help clear away those paradigms and open the door to break-through redesign opportunities. Methods of analyzing processes, effective ways of implementing process changes, the basics of break-through redesign techniques, and the keys to providing true customer value will be more easily grasped.

Discussing processes can be confusing because different people have different perceptions of what a "process" is. To some, a process is a secretary typing a letter, an assembler installing wheels on a machine coming off the assembly line, or a clerk putting invoices in envelopes and sealing them for the afternoon mail. To others, a process might be all of the tasks performed by a hospital admitting clerk, a shipping clerk, or a scheduler. Or to some, a process might be all of the steps in the manufacture of an automobile, the preparation of a corporate annual report, or the development of an employee benefits program.

In most of these examples the focus is clearly on the tasks or activities that people are doing, which is how we tend to think of work. Often, the focus is on what is done by the personnel of one functional department such as hospital admitting, shipping, financial reporting, or purchasing.

But you need to think of processes in a different way in order to analyze them effectively and introduce breakthrough improvements. The methods and tools of breakthrough process improvement work best when a process is well defined, with a clear starting point and ending point; is measurable in one or more ways; and can be analyzed step by step.

Identifying a Process

How can we solve this dilemma of describing the right process to concentrate on for our breakthrough improvement? It should be helpful to begin with an easily understood definition of a process, then build on that definition to discuss processes in the context of improvement opportunities. For our purposes, a process is a series of tasks or steps that receive inputs (materials, information, people, machines, methods) and produce an output (physical product, information, a service) designed to be used for specific purposes by the recipient for whom the output is produced.

Processes are likely to cross functional boundary lines. And individuals may well be involved in more than one process in the performance of their day-to-day duties. For example, a manufacturing assembler is involved in several different processes as part of producing different products. An accountant is involved in several different processes in order to produce outputs consisting of sales reports, income statements, expense checks, and payroll checks. A bank customer service representative is involved in different processes for loan application and processing, new account service, and investment services.

The Four Core Business Processes

Virtually all companies are built around four key core processes upon which the ultimate success of the company depends in providing significant customer value leading to survival and growth: (1) the product-development process, (2) the order-generation process, (3) the order-fulfillment process, and (4) the customer-service process.

These four processes may look different from industry to industry, and even from company to company within an industry. In fact, you may question where these processes are in some industries. But they are, in fact, present in one guise or another, and they are the processes upon which a company focuses the most attention. All other processes, such as financial processes, human resources processes, and legal processes, exist to support and measure the success of these four core processes. Figure 2-1 describes how the core processes relate to each other and how other processes support them. Figure 2-2 identifies more specifically how the four key core processes would appear in a number of diverse industries.

Using our definition of a process, you can see that all processes share certain common characteristics:

- They consist of multiple steps, tasks, operations, or functions performed in sequence, or sometimes of sets of tasks, operations, or functions performed concurrently and in sequence.
- They produce some identifiable output or product, which might be a physical product, a report, written or electronic or verbal information/data, a service, or any other identifiable end result of a series of steps.
- There is an identifiable recipient of the output/product who defines its purpose, characteristics, and value, whether that recipient is an external customer or an internal client. (We prefer to call internal customers "clients" to differentiate them from the true customer.)

The latter point may be a bit subtle at first glance. But isn't it true that every output, as we are using the term here, is of value only if it

Figure 2-1. The interrelationship of company processes.

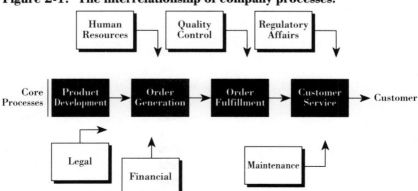

Figure 2-2. Core processes in different industries.

Industry	Product Development	Order Generation	Order Fulfillment	Customer Service
Manufacturing	Design/ Engineering	Advertising/ Sales	Order Entry/ Manufacture/ Shipping	Warranty/ Repair
Banking	New Loan/ Savings/ Checking Plans	Advertising/ Promotion	Processing Applications/ Transactions	Service Clerks/ Personal Banker
Home Building	Architecture/ Design	Advertising/ Sales	Construction/ Option Selection	Warranty Service
Publishing	Reporting/Edit- ing/ Creative Development	Advertising/ Sales	Printing/ Delivery	Subscription Service
Hospitals	New Commun- ity Service/ Insurance Plans	Education/ Advertising/ Prepaid Contracts	Medical Services	Home Care Follow-Up
Airlines	Route Selection/ Pricing Development/ Vacation Packages	Advertising/ Visual Image in Airports	Flying Routes/ Handling Baggage	Customer Service on Delays/Lost Baggage /Frequent Flyer Programs

meets the needs of the recipient? Does it not then follow that the recipient is the ultimate judge of the value of that output, and the one responsible for specifying its characteristics?

Separating Processes From Tasks

Our definition of process specifically rules out individual tasks and operations from being considered processes, such as the secretary typing a letter, the accounting clerk putting invoices in the envelopes, or the assembler installing wheels. These individuals are performing tasks within processes. The definition also rules out functional activities such as the family of duties performed by one individual in the hospital admitting office, the shipping department, or the finance department. There are some single functional processes, such as all of the tasks done by the hospital admitting department to admit a patient. If all of those steps are performed by one person, that person performs a process; this, however, is rare, and that process usually does not include all of the tasks he or she performs.

The key to the definition is that a process is defined not by the *things people do* but instead by the sequence of *things done to, or tasks performed to produce, the output.* In other words, every process consists of a series of steps that somehow changes the output or product as it moves through the sequence of tasks or functions. (Figure 2-3 may help clarify this point.) This is a very important concept. It defines how we will analyze processes in detail. And it helps us expand our

Figure 2-3. Processes vs. tasks or functions.

We typically think of work in terms of *tasks* or functions:

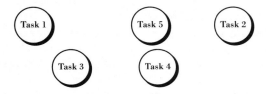

A *process* is a series of tasks or functions that occur in sequence to produce an output product or service:

The focus is not on what people do:

| Process Receiving Documents | — | Process Invoices | — | Pay Invoices | = | Check to Supplier |

Instead, the focus is on what happens to the material or work as it moves through the process:

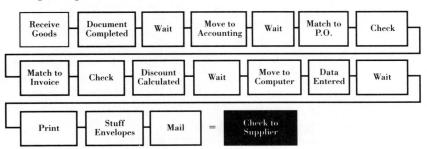

understanding of processes to add an additional common characteristic: A process accepts inputs/supplies, and then changes, adds to, or combines them to produce the desired output.

This definition of the starting and ending points of any process—receipt of inputs/supplies to delivery of the output—will be important later as we discuss chartering redesign projects and setting manageable boundaries on the improvement efforts.

Another characteristic common to all processes that will be key to our analysis and redesign efforts as described in later chapters is: The individual steps and tasks in a process sequence are typically separated by waiting times, involve movement of the output/product from place to place, and require transfer from one responsible individual to another throughout the sequence.

You almost always find this to be true, even in administrative processes where the process is moving information electronically. Unless processes have already been the subject of innovative redesign efforts, very few are so closely linked from step to step that this characteristic is not present. Exceptions might be a process wholly performed by a single individual in one continuous work task or a continuous flow manufacturing process in an industry such as chemicals or paper manufacture.

The common characteristics found in all processes should begin to help you clarify the important distinction between tasks or functions performed by individuals and true processes that meet the criteria of the definition. Figure 2-4 compares some typical processes with tasks or functions found in those processes and may help to further clarify this point.

You may find that the distinction is fuzzy in some cases where the task produces an apparent output, such as the secretary typing a letter. But these tasks fail the test of the definition because they do not consist of a series of steps that change the output and they do not produce an independent output for use by an identified unaffiliated recipient. For example, although typing a letter is a task, there is a process somewhat like the following, of which that task is a part:

Production of a Letter

1. Author dictates letter.
2. Secretary types letter.
3. Secretary proofs letter.
4. Author edits and changes letter.
5. Secretary retypes letter.

Figure 2-4. A comparison of processes with tasks and functions.

Processes	Tasks
Producing Monthly P&L Statement	Summarizing Sales, Recording Inventory Changes, Summarizing Expenses, Entering Adjustments, Printing Reports
Order Entry Process	Accepting Phone Calls, Opening Mail, Entering in Computer, Assigning Number, Printing Order, Transferring to Production
Producing Reproduction Artwork	Drawing Art, Checking Art, Making Proofs, Obtaining Customer Approval
Producing a Pill	Mixing, Grinding, Pelletizing, Drying, Coating
Loan Approval Process	Obtaining Application, Requesting Credit Report, Reviewing Application, Reviewing Credit Report, Determining Qualification Against Guidelines, Recommending to Committee
Manufacturing a Key Ring	Stamping, Bending, Polishing, Imprinting, Testing

6. Author reviews and signs letter.
7. Secretary copies letter.
8. Secretary mails letter.

Note in this example that a sequence of steps occurs, an output is produced, the steps are most likely separated by waiting time, and there are several transfers of responsibility between individuals, all consistent with characteristics commonly found in all processes.

Accepting Similarities of Processes

If is often suggested that "a process is a process is a process," regardless of functional area, industry, company size, or other differences. The identification and recognition of common characteristics of processes would seem to support this contention. But in truth, processes vary significantly in design and the way they operate from function to function, company to company, and even from manager to manager within the same company over time.

Administrative processes frequently cut across more organizational boundaries than production processes. The bottlenecks and imbalances in financial and service processes may be more difficult to identify than in production processes, where they appear as piles of product (work-in-process inventory) in clear view on the manufacturing floor. Files and transaction records may be hidden but are nevertheless present in those financial, administrative, and service processes.

Despite their common characteristics, processes also vary significantly in how they work depending upon their stage of evolution, their interrelationships with other processes, and the specific nature of their outputs. The value of recognizing the common characteristics is that it provides a rational basis for applying common analytical tools and proven remedies for common problems. We do not have to start over on every process as if it were all new to us. A real methodology for process improvement can be identified and employed with a high degree of confidence in its success across a wide variety of processes, companies, and industries. It is not necessary to force all processes into a generic mold to make this possible so long as the common characteristics are readily identified.

Recognizing Levels of Processes

In considering the processes identified for different industries in Figure 2-2, you can see how the definition encompasses a range of processes, from a few steps producing a minor output product used by an internal client as an input to another process up to a long, complex process of many steps producing a major product output for the customer. In fact, the entire operation of the company could be viewed as meeting the definition of a process in an all-encompassing set of steps. But that, of course, would represent a process too complicated to analyze. Therefore, you want to break down the "family tree" of processes in the company to manageable process scopes for analysis.

The first step is to move to the level of the four core processes and the supporting processes. You quickly realize that this, too, represents a level of process that is too all-encompassing and complex to be analyzed readily, and you need to move to further simplification. You generally find that at the third or fourth level of the process family tree, you have finally reached a level of processes that is discrete enough to be manageable in achieving a breakthrough improvement. At this level the processes are generally, but not always, producing outputs for internal clients.

A typical family tree of processes in a business is shown in Figure 2-5. Each level on the family tree is defined by where you establish the beginning and ending points of the process. The number of steps in the selected process decreases as you move lower in the family tree to more discrete segment processes of more specific scope.

The process of loading circuit boards is more easily understood, for example, than the entire manufacturing process for a computer or the entire process of ordering components, manufacturing, testing, and delivering the computer. Similarly, the process of closing the accounting books monthly is more readily dealt with than the entire financial record-keeping process plus the closing process.

As you will see later, we typically choose processes at the lower levels of the process family tree on which to focus redesign efforts both in order to make the task more manageable within a reasonable period of time and to make breakthrough goal setting more credible to the process redesign team. The selection of the right processes is discussed further in Chapter 3.

It is often useful to think of one long, complex process as a series of shorter, more specific processes that can be analyzed concurrently or sequentially over a longer period of time until the entire complex process has been redesigned. Care in selecting the process segments makes this practical without having to redo work already done on certain portions of the process.

Understanding Process Evolution

A basic assumption underlying our discussion of maximizing customer value in Chapter 1 and this discussion of business processes is that business processes are almost always in need of improvement or redesign. You may ask why we make this assumption or why we believe it to be true. The answer, based on our experiences with hundreds of processes in a wide variety of industries over the past ten years, is that we very rarely see a process that cannot be improved by 75 percent or more when redesigned with an effective methodology and tools and with an open mind free of paradigms about how the process "has to be." Almost any process is a viable candidate for improvement. Most are glaringly obvious with no more than a cursory evaluation.

The reason for this is really quite simple. Processes evolve over

Figure 2-5. Family tree of processes.
The entire company can be considered as one very complex process:

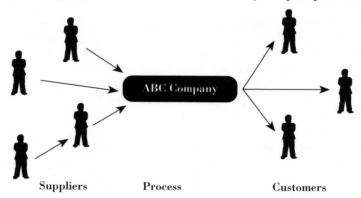

Or, major processes within the company could be identified:

Or, a finite manageable process could be studied:

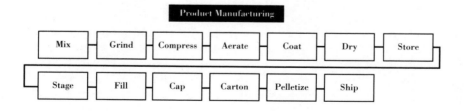

their lifetimes. When initially created to produce a specific desired output required by a customer or internal client, they are usually quite simple and straightforward. When they are installed and first used, they are usually quite efficient. They may undergo some initial refinement and adaptation as experience is gained in order to make them work effectively in the specific organization climate in which they are found. These changes are usually minor and constructive.

But as time goes by, the initial process design evolves further in response to customer/client needs, individual variances introduced by those working within the process, organizational growth and changes, and changes in process interrelationships, as well as to solve problems as they arise. These changes become more complex and more serious the longer the process remains in place. They result in the process achieving some degree of institutionalization and maturity. But at the same time, they begin to erode the effectiveness of the process. These changes can also mark the beginning of the steps that eventually lead to process overcontrol and breakdown.

At maturity, the process is still working. It is not as effective as it once was, but the output product still meets the customer/client needs and can be delivered in a timely and flexible way as needed. But the process has begun to acquire extra steps, usually designed to find and correct errors, to divide responsibility along organizational lines, and to create specialists in certain functions. There begins to be ambiguity in responsibility and authority. Redundancy of steps is common. Once steps are added to a process to correct a situation, even a temporary one, they tend to become permanent. They now "belong to someone," are that person's job and reason for being, and are zealously protected against attack.

If this evolution is recognized by a knowledgeable and skilled manager soon enough, he or she may step in and redesign the process to restore it to its original effectiveness. But too often the manager finds that he or she does not have sufficient scope of authority to do so effectively. The process crosses too many organizational boundaries, is defined by too many standard operating procedures and protocols, and has, in effect, taken on a life of its own. The result is that the process continues to evolve in unproductive ways, adding more and more steps, increasing redundancy, and creating queues of output product at each step waiting to be completed. The length of time necessary to get through the process is extended, and there is an increase in handoffs between people, approval requirements, checks, double checks, and rework. More and more time and energy are spent working the process rather than

Figure 2-6. Life cycle of a process.

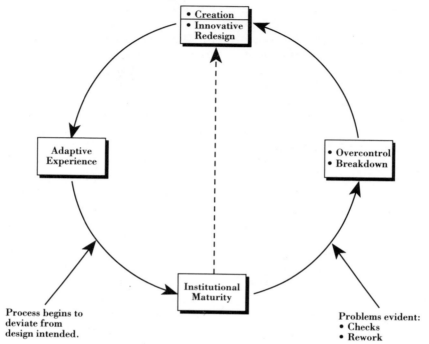

doing the work for which the process was originally designed. Break-down has occurred. Value to the customer is compromised. The picture is pretty ugly. Redesign for breakthrough improvement is essential. Figure 2-6 illustrates the life cycle of a process in graphic form.

As you begin to consider processes in your company you will realize that most require redesign. The task may appear overwhelming. But Chapters 3 and 4 introduce you to techniques for narrowing down the choices to those that are most essential to the success of your company in maximizing value for your customers. And you will begin to learn how you can become effective as a manager in preventing the processes you work with from reaching the overcontrolled/breakdown stage and begin to redesign those that are headed in that direction.

3

Refocusing the Business for Process Redesign

The following Tuesday, Joe received a package from Sally that contained copies of a couple of chapters from a book with a note that said, "Read this, and give me a call. I think it's a different way to think about our businesses."

Joe looked over the material that evening instead of reading the newspaper. He was feeling desperate. Something had to give! He had gotten a second call at work from the customer who was so unhappy about not getting his widgets on time. As he read the material that Sally had sent, Joe tried to think about the widget process and what would happen to him if he were a widget rather than think about the process in terms of what the people involved do.

Early the next morning, he called Sally. She was excited. "Joe, this idea of thinking of your business as a series of processes really works!" she exclaimed. "I spent all day yesterday pretending that I was the bit of information that comes in on your invoice that eventually becomes part of the check payable to you. Following the inputs of the process all the way through the steps until I became a check being stuffed into an envelope was exhausting. You wouldn't believe the amount of time that I spent buried in some in-basket and being passed from person to person. Maybe this is a new way to sort out what needs to be done to produce checks in ten days and get our discount."

Joe was intrigued by what Sally said. He had always thought of widget making as departments with certain specialties. His worst fear was always that the resources—machines and people—would not be fully utilized. He never thought of what happens to the work as it goes through the process. He thanked Sally for the information and said that he would get back to her soon.

Then he remembered the late order. "No one took responsibility for the order being late," he thought. "It was passed around like a hot potato. And what about those improvements that are supposedly being made within the departments. The reports keep landing on my desk, but we still have late deliveries. How can I get all those departments to understand just how important it is to the customer to have the widgets on time? And to further complicate my life, the customer keeps asking for faster deliveries and better quality."

When it was time for lunch, Joe decided to go to his favorite restaurant. As always, the hostess greeted him by name as he entered and ushered him to his favorite table right away. He thought, "It's a relief to be here. Everyone who works here seems focused on me as the customer. They each know the role they play and almost seem to have a picture of what they want the whole business to be like and what their part is in getting there. I remember this place two years ago when it was risky coming here. Sometimes it was good and other times it was terrible. I wonder what they did to change all that."

The waitress came over to take Joe's order, and he decided to ask about the change. "I've noticed a lot of changes here—you all seem so happy now and I feel special as a customer. How do you do it?" Janey, the waitress, answered with a smile, "Well, it was about a year ago. Our new owner, Liz, came from a large, successful company that was constantly innovating to stay ahead of the competition. When Liz decided to buy this restaurant, she thought some of the same ideas that had made the large company successful could work for us."

Janey continued, "Liz invited us all to what she called a visioning session. Frankly, we all thought she was crazy! After all, what does visioning have to do with running a restaurant? Of course, she is the owner, so we all went. Much to our surprise, it was very exciting. We imagined what we would like our restaurant to be like: how the customers would feel, what it would take to keep people coming back, even what the place would look like. We actually created some images that we shared with each other of how the business would operate. Then we went to work on how to make it happen. It's really a lot of fun to be so involved in becoming our vision. Oh, I have to go now. Another customer needs me. I'll be back with your order in a few minutes."

Joe was dumbfounded! He wondered how he could generate that kind of excitement in his organization.

We all recognize that competitive success in today's markets—whether local, regional, national, or global—requires that companies change the way they do business and that they relate more closely to their customers. Traditional methods of operation are no longer adequate or acceptable in any industry. This is probably one of the factors motivating you to read this book.

The evolution in competitiveness factors depicted in Figure 1-3 was first evident in manufacturing industries and has been a factor in separating successful from unsuccessful companies for twenty years. Although slow to recognize the need to reshape their priorities, other industries are now following the lead of manufacturing and reshaping how they do business in ways similar to manufacturing. We can find successful and dramatic evolution in such diverse industries as financial services, retail stores, hospitals, community development, law enforcement, education, transportation, construction, lodging, tourism, and a host of others in addition to manufacturing.

Figure 3-1 shows the process redesign model and describes the methods by which organizations of all kinds are reshaping how they function. The top loop of the figure describes how these organizations develop the focus to successfully drive innovative process redesign efforts. The lower loop describes how this new focus is translated into definitive action to make change and to redesign individual processes in order to reshape the organization.

Expanding Your Thinking and Actions

It is fairly easy to see top management's responsibilities for the activities in the top loop. It is equally evident that middle management and first-line supervisors, as well as individual workers, play a key role in the implementation steps in the lower loop. What may be less clear is that everyone in the organization must be touched by every element of *both* loops if the organization is to succeed in reshaping itself and achieving breakthrough process redesign results.

It is no longer enough for a manager to wear only the hat of his or her functional area. Or an employee, for that matter. What is required is people who can hold two guiding thoughts in their heads at the same time: (1) the needs of the company as a whole as dictated by customer needs, and (2) the needs of their individual department. Only by giving these two requirements parallel attention can managers and employees begin to think cross-functionally about processes and how those processes affect the customer. Only then can they

Figure 3-1. The process redesign model.

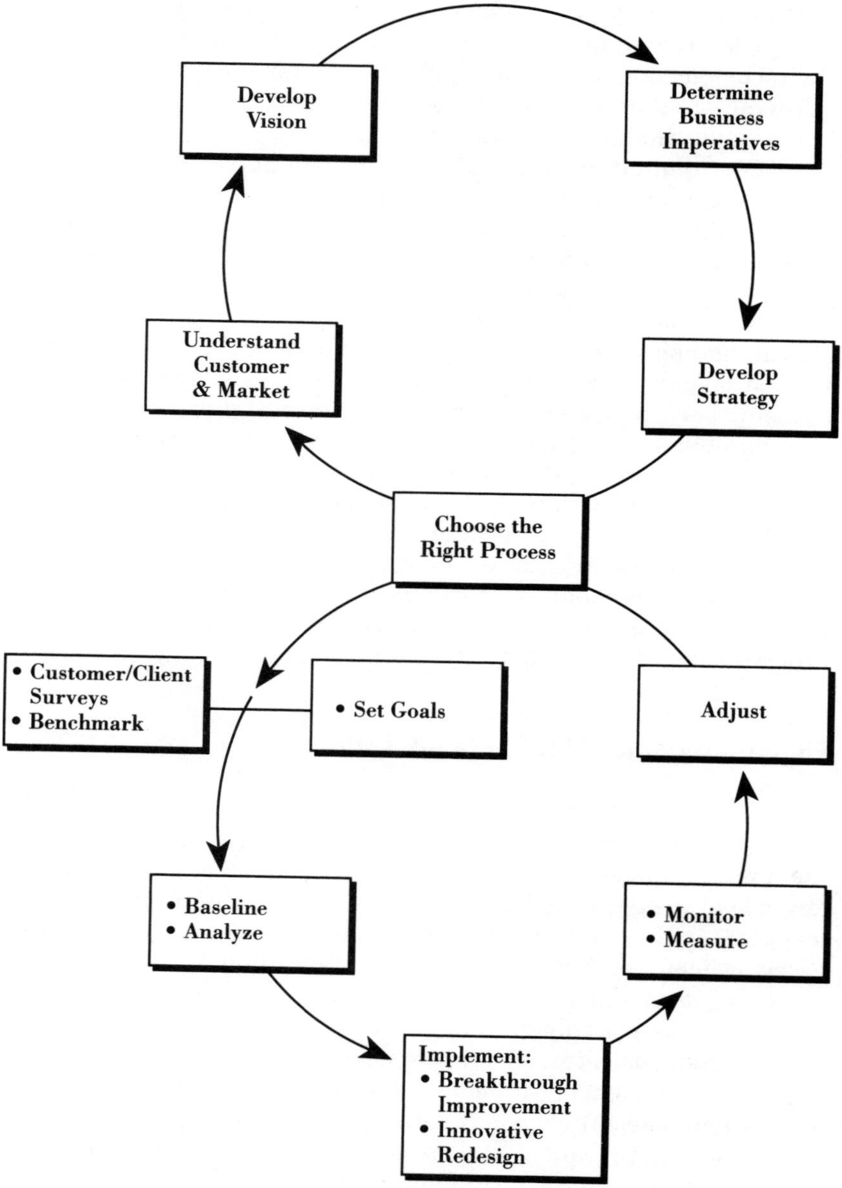

work effectively to maximize value to the customer in everything the organization does.

Sounds simple enough. It may not even be revolutionary. Lots of people have been talking about focusing on the customer. But how do you do it? Talk is not enough. How do you get it to happen in your organization now, today? It is not an easy task, but it is being done in all industries, and it can be done in your industry, in your company. Let's see how to begin.

Understanding the Customer

As shown in Figure 3-1, the process ideally begins with gaining an understanding of the customer and the market. Later, we will talk about exceptions to this ideal. Think back to the discussion of maximizing customer value in Chapter 1. Customers know what they want in your product or service and in their transaction with your company, although they may not be able to articulate it well. In addition, there are dynamic forces at work in the market. All markets are fluid to some degree, and these dynamic forces and shifting customer values cause change in what your business needs to do to prosper. Skill is required in monitoring these changes, identifying their impact, and deciding on appropriate actions.

Most organizations believe they understand their market and their customers pretty well. Many are wrong in that belief. Their "understanding" is based upon perceptions built up over years, often manipulated to satisfy ingrown company paradigms or to fit the limitations of the organization's capabilities. For example:

- A manufacturer of high-technology surgical products believed so strongly in its technology that it continued to reject available competing technologies in which it was not competent. Eventually, shifting market shares forced the company to make radical changes in thinking and adopt new technologies.
- A company whose processes required nine to twelve days between receipt of an order and shipment refused to believe that customers valued fast delivery, even though 25 percent of orders received requested shipment in 48 to 72 hours and 20 percent of new customers did not place repeat orders.
- Building industry paradigms about what customers value in selecting a community to consider are so well established that the management of one home builder initially rejected the

results of their own surveys as invalid. Eventually, they realized their error and responded to what their customers were telling them. Sales and profitability improved.
- A manufacturer of products for the agricultural market believed so strongly in its perceptions of the customer and what he/she valued that service efforts were focused almost exclusively on low-value items—until a sound value survey identified the key items and drove a redesign of strategies.

Finding Out What the Customer Values

The key is that only the customer knows the right answer to the value question, and you will find the right answer only if you ask him or her.

There are many ways to gain an understanding of your market and your customers. We believe the Customer Value Survey and Customer Value Profile developed by Guaspari and Crom to be one of the best.[1] The process is described in more detail in Chapter 4. There are other ways to obtain information, such as benchmarking; relying on industry data, independent data, and various forms of market research; and using informal customer contacts on a daily basis.

The interpretation of these data to develop Customer Value Profiles is difficult. But whatever the source of the data, if the facts are valid, they can be analyzed and reduced to four to six key indicators of what motivates customer behaviors and buying decisions. An objective assessment of how your organization is performing against the customer's Minimum Acceptable Value level identifies gaps in your performance. Assessment of how competitors are doing against the same criteria helps identify competitive gaps and provide insight into when the Minimum Acceptable Value level may be moving up because of expectations created by competitors or by your own efforts.

With a sound understanding of customer values, market dynamics, and gaps to be closed, management can begin to develop a vision of what the company might be like in the future to better meet customers' Minimum Acceptable Values. This is the key to the future: Those who consistently *exceed* Minimum Acceptable Values will *thrive*; those who only *meet* Minimum Acceptable Values may *survive*; those who *fall short* of Minimum Acceptable Values over the long term will inevitably *fail*.

Developing a Vision

The vision that we would encourage management to develop is not a mission statement or list of objectives, goals, or strategies. It is an imaginative, hypothetical, broad description of what the organization would look like in three to five years if all the right things were done to reshape it to focus on maximizing customer value through encouraging innovation and through development of its leadership and people.

The concept of a vision can be fuzzy to management. The vision differs from the mission statement in several respects. A mission statement is usually written in terms of what the company is striving to accomplish as its goals—its control of the market or technology, the way it treats employees, its community position, etc. It may include some declarations related to the values of the company. The vision, on the other hand, tends to describe what the company will look like in the future—how it functions, what people are doing, how they interact, what customers say about the company, what the relationship is with suppliers, etc.

The vision may initially form in the mind of the leader. We often see leaders who have a vision for their company but are unable to convey that vision to the organization effectively and create the fire and energy to drive the whole organization toward that vision. The problem is that the vision is the leader's, not the organization's. That vision has to become a common, shared vision that all identify with, or it will not drive the organization.

The process of instilling the vision in the organization begins with developing a common management vision. Managers together must develop a shared vision that encompasses all of the elements that they collectively see as important in describing the company they want to become in three, four, or five years.

Describing the Vision

Members of a management group working together on a common vision can describe it in different ways. Some describe physical images of what they see in the future: buildings, machinery, technology. Others describe images of personal interactions: work force makeup, teamwork, leadership styles, how decisions are made. Still others describe external forces: suppliers, customers, regulators, competition. Here are some actual examples of how a few executives have described their specific visions:

- A sales vice-president describes a vision of customers applying in the company lobby for the right to buy from the company just like new job applicants because the company is in such demand it can choose only the best customers.
- A manufacturing executive describes a factory in which all equipment is levitating so that he can quickly reconfigure the factory to respond to changing demands.
- A financial executive describes a paperless company with all transactions—purchasing, billing, collections, payments, etc.—done electronically.
- A regulatory executive describes a vision of his company as so advanced that regulatory agencies send their personnel to the business to be trained.
- A human resources executive describes a company with its own "college" to develop employees.
- An executive describes a company in which it is impossible to tell the management from the employees because there is so little need for management intervention and the organization is so flat in structure and informal, yet professional, in its activity.

An interesting sidelight to these particular examples is that when they were presented by these executives, we were able to tell them that we could show each of them a company in which his/her vision was already a reality or nearly so.

Bringing Individual Visions Together

By working together on the vision, company leadership develops a broader, more comprehensive and, above all, commonly held and understood vision embracing elements of all areas. And they are able to mold the sometimes functional visions into a meaningful whole that is focused on the customer and maximizing customer value in the future.

A brief example of a vision might be something like this:

The organization functions smoothly and professionally. Employees talk to each other across functional boundaries and solve problems together on their own initiative to satisfy customer needs. There is an appreciation for helping each other in these endeavors, and there are thank you notes from salespeople to office and production people posted on the walls. Employees are continually coming up with new ideas and improvements and implementing them spontaneously in response to customer inputs. The organization is known in its market as very flexible and responsive to customer requests. Equipment can be converted quickly to do different things in response to customer needs. Programs are ready for market changes ahead of time. Customers share their future ideas with the organization to help make that possible. Products are developed faster than anywhere else in the industry and are right when delivered to the market. There is an air of confidence and success. Results reported to the board of directors are outstanding.

The vision is often difficult for managers to describe concisely after they develop it together. Often, someone in the group sums up the vision in a graphic image. This is valuable because it creates a concise focus that is sometimes missing in the narrative descriptions, and the image often helps in transmitting the vision to the entire organization. Figure 3-2 describes some companies and the images that emerged during their vision sessions. Notice how you can almost

Figure 3-2. Some companies' visionary images.

Image	Organization Description
A lobster, shedding its shell annually as it grows	A consulting organization constantly shedding old ways and learning new while growing annually
A forest fire parching the area, followed by strong new growth	A turnaround company tearing down the old organization and building a new, vibrant company to emerge and grow
A wall of pictures of the company through its history, with the section for the current decade having only empty frames	A company in a market undergoing dramatic change affecting how they sell, manufacture, and develop products
A bridge under construction over a turbulent river with planking being laid from both ends by large crowds of workers	Two companies with two complementary technologies attempting to merge over a major obstacle, although both will benefit

fill in the complete visions from the image and the little we tell you about the company.

Integrating the Organization Through the Vision

The value of developing a common vision of the future for the organization, based upon the market and customer value descriptors, is that it allows the customer to drive the integration of the organization:

- When the entire company is focused on maximizing customer value, functional silos become irrelevant.
- When you are focused on maximizing customer value, the cross-functionality of key processes becomes obvious.
- When you are focused on maximizing value to the customer, internal paradigms must be rejected.

On the other hand, if you try to force the same integration of the organization without a driving, energizing motivator recognized as important by all levels of the organization, one of two things will probably happen:

1. In a noninnovative, unempowered organization, functional defensiveness arises, and little, if any, progress is made.
2. In an innovative, empowered organization, acrimony develops. Without the common vision as a focuser and an energizer, innovative and empowered people go their own ways, creating more and stronger functional barriers and setting their own goals. The result is disharmony, increasing conflict, and eventual loss of effectiveness of the management and the organization.

The vision—driven by customer values, mutually developed, commonly shared, and communicated throughout the organization— is the necessary integrating force to generate energy to drive constructive refocusing of the business.

Developing System Pullers

A system puller is an affirmative statement in the present tense describing the vision as if it existed today. If the vision is clear, management is able to develop four to six statements that present the vision as a current reality. Developing these and communicating them to employees is a powerful affirmation of belief and a strong drive to make the statements reality. It has been said that "if you can't visualize it, you can't accomplish (design) it." That is what a system puller is all about—it helps everyone visualize today what tomorrow would look like, and it pulls everyone to the realization of the vision.

Some examples of system pullers might be helpful:

- We are empowered to take responsible risks and grow with our mistakes.
- Each of us understands our customers, and we focus our activities on meeting their needs and exceeding their expectations.
- Hospitals buy our product because they know it will prevent patients from being injured in the operating room.
- Artists come to our company first.
- We retain 100 percent of our profitable customers.
- Everyone masters a new skill every six months.

All of these statements describe in an affirmative way—as if it existed now—something that the company knows would be the case if the vision was realized.

Identifying Business Imperatives

System pullers help identify business imperatives. By describing what the vision is in a present affirmative tense, gaps are uncovered between what the organization should be and what it is. Gaps between Minimum Acceptable Value and what is provided today are clarified, and the vision of the organization needed to correct them becomes clearer. Actions necessary to close the gaps—that is, the business imperatives—begin to emerge.

Business imperatives are those few things—usually only three to five—that *must* happen if the vision is to be realized or approached and the gaps closed. Those few things become the overriding focus of strategy and tactic development from the present to the vision horizon. They are the benchmark against which plans and projects are measured. (For instance, you might ask whether planned projects will help support and accomplish the imperatives. If not, why invest resources in doing them?) The future success of the organization

rests on accomplishing the imperatives, closing the gaps, and pursuing the vision. Figure 3-3 shows a decision matrix depicting the
relationship among business imperatives, their supporting strategies,
and actions under consideration. The matrix shows which business
imperatives are supported by each strategic plan. A similar matrix
analysis might be used in ranking alternative processes for selection,
along with other data discussed in this chapter.

Although business imperatives may sometimes include needs or
actions wholly new to the business, they often revolve around doing
things currently done, but in better ways: faster, more flexibly, more
responsively, with better quality, at lower cost. Strategic actions and
tactical needs develop easily from the business imperatives. Major
processes that must be innovatively improved and redesigned begin
to emerge. Tentative goals for redesign of these processes begin to
develop. Initial targets for innovative process improvement efforts

Figure 3-3. Evaluating strategies against business imperatives.

	Imperative 1	Imperative 2	Imperative 3	Imperative 4	Imperative 5
Strategic Plan A		X			
Strategic Plan B		X		X	X
Strategic Plan C	X				
Strategic Plan D	X			X	
Strategic Plan E		X			
Strategic Plan F					
Strategic Plan G	X				
Strategic Plan H		X			
Strategic Plan I				X	

Notes: • Strategic Plan F does not support any imperative. It may
          be abandoned, or will be very low priority.
        • Imperative 3 is not supported by any strategic plan,
          suggesting a need for additional strategy development.
        • Strategic Plan B supports three imperatives. It would
          likely have a high priority.

begin to become clearer, although choices still have to be made based upon further analysis.

Figure 3-4 shows a somewhat different view of the relationships from the recognition of customer values to identification of processes for improvement than is shown in Figure 3-1. Figure 3-4 shows how as the organization moves around the top loop of Figure 3-1, the organization is reshaped and becomes integrated through the focus on the customer values. The extent to which the organization is driven by the focus on customer values is clear.

Communicating the Vision

If the vision is to be effective in integrating and focusing the organization and in reshaping its character and how it functions, it must be effectively communicated to the entire organization in ways that excite response and achieve buy-in. There are several ways to do this.

We have found it very effective to begin by sharing the vision with the organization's middle management in a dynamic way. We ask the top management group to sit together in the center of a circle of middle managers—in the "fishbowl," so to speak—and informally share their individual visions and images and how they fit together. The system pullers are presented, describing the organization today as it would be if the vision were realized. Middle management has an opportunity to question and respond to the vision. The goal is for middle management to begin reflecting on the vision, see the system pullers as reality, and understand the impact their activities have on the realization of the vision.

Business imperatives are shared with middle management at the same time. The vision, system pullers, and resulting business imperatives are ultimately shared with the entire organization.

Imperatives are stated in a positive way focused on the customer values, often with some strategies attached to them if development has proceeded that far. Considerable thought needs to be given to the statement of the imperatives and their translation into strategies if they are to be exciting to the organization as a whole. It can be a difficult task and should be undertaken jointly by top and middle management in a workshop for that purpose.

Two simple examples might help clarify the evolution of the process:

COMPANY: A high-technology medical products company.

VISION: Includes customer recognition of the company's inno-

Figure 3-4. Reshaping the business to a customer focus.

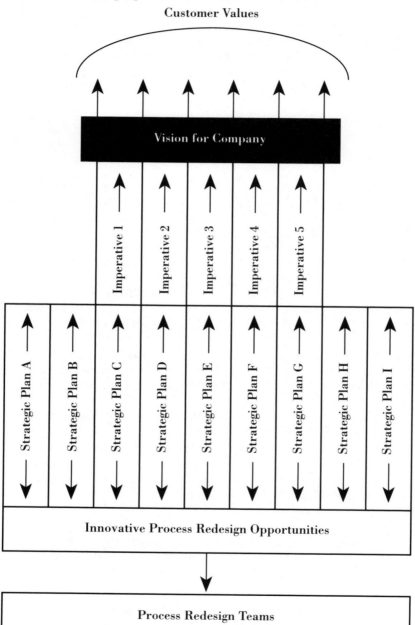

vative technology, which has brought safety to a hospital product that has caused serious injury to hundreds of patients annually for over forty years.

SYSTEM PULLER: Surgeons and nurses insist on purchasing our equipment for their operating rooms to the exclusion of our competitor's equipment because they recognize that use of our product will prevent the patient injuries they have seen.

BUSINESS IMPERATIVE: Product safety in this class of equipment must be established as a key customer value driving buying decisions, and the company must set the Minimum Acceptable Value in safe technology.

STRATEGY: Educate nurses (who make the buying decision) on hazards and prevention of patient injury through use of the company's safety systems.

TACTICS:

- Create a noncommercial course earning continuing education credit for nurses that focuses on this technology and its safety.
- Shift advertising from institutional orientation to safety features.
- Collect accident statistics and obtain third-party articles reinforcing the safety concept.

PROCESS OPPORTUNITIES:

- Develop a training program.
- Speed the advertising development process for quick reaction to industry data.
- Design a process for obtaining third-party endorsement articles from physicians.

This company was founded on the development of a new technology for its type of equipment that essentially rendered obsolete a technology that was over forty years old and caused hundreds of hospital patient injuries annually. It was very easy to energize the company around this vision and the associated imperatives and strategies. The company was successful in its effort and now dominates its industry segment. The former dominant company is now an insignificant factor.

COMPANY: A community development/home-building company.

VISION: Includes the capability of responding to customer desires to customize their home choice, while maintaining a volume building schedule and having the capability of going from contract to move in within ninety days or less.

SYSTEM PULLER: We allow our buyers to customize their homes, and we still complete construction within the time period of their mortgage commitment, usually ninety days.

BUSINESS IMPERATIVE: Develop a methodology for providing "mass customization" in home building that provides maximum flexibility in response to customers.

STRATEGY: Develop a capability to respond to customer design change requests as the buying decision is being made and the purchase negotiated.

TACTICS:

- Develop basic designs affording flexibility in change and expansion.
- Utilize computer-aided design systems for fast customization.
- Develop sales personnel into design consultants.

PROCESS OPPORTUNITIES:

- Develop sales training program.
- Shorten cycle time of contracting process.
- Shorten cycle time of design process.
- Shorten cycle time of production of site-specific plans.
- Shorten cycle time of construction.

This organization prides itself on its award-winning community designs. It was easy to energize the entire organization around providing customers with a unique capability that would enhance the salability of their communities and provide professional development for sales, design, and construction personnel.

Choosing Where to Enter the Model

Referring again to Figure 3-1, note that the process redesign model presumes that the effort is a continuous one. Because the modeled process is continuous, it is practical and reasonable to enter the circle at any point for which the organization is prepared. Although it is typically "ideal," it is not necessary to enter the loop at the point of assessment of market and customer values if that is not appropriate for the particular business.

It may be that the urgency for improvement is so great and the imperatives so clear that process improvement should begin immediately, and Customer Value Analysis and development of a common vision should be part of the overall process of reshaping the company after the immediate crisis or urgent need is past. A turnaround situation is a good example. Those things that must be done for immediate short-term survival take precedence over visioning and customer analysis except to the extent they are necessary to maintain immediate viability. Later, the organization can focus on the steps that ensure long-term growth and avoidance of a similar crisis. No two businesses are exactly alike, and the plan for improvement must take that into account.

Often, the first stage of a breakthrough improvement or process redesign effort is a quick preliminary determination of some key imperatives and an assessment of opportunities afforded by processes supporting those imperatives. Then, the development of a common vision based upon customer values brings direction to the expanded business redesign effort over time, or refines the selection of processes to be studied. This allows the company to begin work in areas that are readily identifiable as important without delaying benefits until all key opportunities are fully identified. For example:

• A printing company recognized the need to shorten lead times from receipt of order to shipping. Key processes affecting lead times were order entry, graphic arts, and production. Graphic arts had an impact on only first-time orders, about 15 percent of the total. Production included coating, slitting, and printing operations. It was possible to choose order entry, slitting, and printing as the three processes for initial work without significant customer value research and identification. Customers were telling the company they had a delivery time problem, and it was obvious delivery time was significantly impacted by these processes.

• A home builder was receiving low ratings on subcontractor quality in its surveys of customers thirty days after move-in. It was clear that a key customer value was not being met and a problem-solving team could be formed to address the issue, although other key customer values were unknown at that time.

• A manufacturer of animal feed products noted that there was a continuing upward trend in the number of orders for custom formulations, which had to be handled through the research department and by special manufacturing activities that disrupted regular operations. Custom formulations were expected to be an increasingly important part of the business. Shipping times for these special orders did not meet customer expectations. An effort could be launched to make the custom-order process more effective.

• A hospital recognized that by taking over thirty days to produce bills for patients after discharge, it was losing a very significant cash-flow opportunity. The key processes were development of charges, coding, and production of the statement to the patient.

Innovative Process Redesign Beginning With Middle Management

If the process redesign effort can be begun at any point, does this imply that any middle manager can jump in and undertake innovative process redesign in his or her functional area? The answer, unfortunately, is a qualified maybe. The likelihood of such a manager's success depends upon the functional area he/she represents, his/her level in the organization, the extent of his/her informal influence, the breadth of his/her responsibility over the process he/she chooses to address, and the attitude of management above him/her.

It is clearly a responsibility of middle managers to improve the processes for which they are directly responsible. They are quite capable of making process improvements in their own sphere of authority and should feel empowered to do so. But such improvements are usually more in the realm of continuous improvement results, 10 to 20 percent, rather than breakthrough improvements. Breakthrough results are usually obtained only when cross-functional involvement can be established. So unless top management establishes a climate in which innovation is encouraged, where middle managers are allowed to team up across functions and where solid leadership is provided, the opportunities for middle managers to strike out on their own for breakthrough results are quite limited.

A self-administered organizational readiness assessment is included in the Appendix to this book. It provides some insights into the climate of your own organization and the obstacles that you might face if you were to attempt cross-functional improvement activity using the tools you learn in this book.

There is a risk raised when a middle manager attempts to strike out on his or her own, especially if the organization is considering undertaking an overall business redesign effort. The selection and successful completion of pilot team efforts at the beginning of an improvement effort are critical to the successful launch and ultimate success of the improvement effort. The opportunity to undertake and successfully complete initial quick-win breakthrough pilot projects should not be compromised by a middle manager striking out on his/her own with the limitations inherent in his/her sphere of influence. Rather, the interested manager should enlist the support of his or her peers in influencing top management to consider a properly structured and led business process redesign effort.

Selecting the Right Processes

Selecting the right processes for focus of innovative process redesign efforts is a critical transition in reshaping the business and how it operates. This is the step that moves from the macro vision to the micro implementation in order to ensure reaching the vision. The selection of pilot projects in a new business process redesign effort is a particularly critical step. As seen in Figure 3-1, this is the linkage between the application of process redesign methodologies and the focus on the customer that develops in the business as a whole. This is the stage at which you begin striving for effective application of redesign tools to critical core processes that will close the gaps between Minimum Acceptable Values of the customer and what you are now providing.

Regardless of the point at which you enter the upper loop of Figure 3-1, the candidates for process redesign that emerge from an analysis of business imperatives are linked to closing those gaps. So, on the surface, all are equally important.

Some processes offer greater opportunities than others. It is particularly important that the first processes chosen for application of improvement tools be carefully selected. The success of those first efforts sets the expectations of the entire organization for any future redesign activity. You want those results to set an expectation of breakthrough results that are important to the success of the organization and that are achievable by empowered employees.

Criteria for selection of the first few processes should include consideration of a number of factors, such as the following:

- The link to business imperatives is clear to all.
- The process chosen is highly visible in the organization.
- Breakthrough results are possible (50 to 90 percent).

- Achievement of goals is highly probable.
- Goals can be achieved in a maximum of sixteen to twenty weeks.
- The process requires multifunctional participation to achieve goals.
- Goals and results can be objectively measured.

Piloting Innovative Process Redesign

The initial objective should be to select three to four processes that offer the potential for quick, visible, recognizably important and measurable breakthrough results. These are the pilot projects for the embryonic innovative process improvement effort. These pilot projects are where the organization begins to learn how to conduct the improvement process, tests its skills and capabilities, develops future internal trainers and guides, and proves that "it can be done here." Success then creates energy and drive in the organization, and people volunteer to serve on process redesign teams and to have teams deployed in their areas. The business redesign effort will be solidly launched and self-perpetuating because of the visible results and the energy created.

Processes that meet most of the criteria given above and that tend to make good pilot projects because of their high visibility, relative ease of accomplishing goals, and close ties to business imperatives include:

- Order-entry processes
- Production processes (especially in custom or make-to-order businesses)
- Product-development processes
- Processing of customer documents (e.g., insurance claims, applications, and payments)

Future efforts may include some processes that, although important to business imperatives, do not offer such visible and dramatic results. This becomes more and more acceptable as the redesign process becomes more mature and permeates the organization. Once the redesign philosophy is ingrained in the organization, the skeptical scrutiny of employees will be gone, and they will welcome even those efforts that do not seem so dramatic in the beginning. Examples are regulatory submissions, financial closings, and service processes.

Even with well-designed selection criteria in mind, choosing three or four pilot projects from an extensive list of options can sometimes be difficult. Data and analysis are required to sort through the options and make the best choices. Much of the available data may be somewhat cursory, since the first step for the process redesign team is usually to establish a detailed data baseline for the process being studied, and this is not yet available. Enough meaningful data can usually be acquired to allow well-informed choices to be made. But it is entirely appropriate to employ some of the tools taught later in this book to analyze processes for the purpose of clarifying the opportunities and validating the choices being made. Normally, processes selected to follow the pilot projects are chosen from a more detailed data baseline, often developed as a part of the study of the processes from initial efforts.

Avoiding a Focus on Cost Reduction

A common mistake in choosing among the project options available is to focus on cost savings. Remember that the business imperatives and the requirements to close gaps between customer's Minimum Acceptable Value and what is currently provided is most often driven by the need for improvement in time, flexibility, responsiveness, and quality instead of or in addition to cost. Cost is rarely the sole driving force. And reducing cost is rarely a strong motivator for employees because they hear that demand constantly in connection with budgeting processes, purchasing decisions, etc. Worse, they equate cost cutting with staff reductions and can hardly be expected to be enthusiastic about a project to do that! Cost alone is often more of a demotivator than a motivator.

But reduced cost is a common outcome of improvement in time, flexibility, responsiveness, and quality. Thus, it is an appropriate consideration in the choice of projects if evaluated from the standpoint of payback of investment in the improvement effort and business opportunities opened by reduction of cost. It should not be the single overriding determinant in project selection.

Acquiring Preliminary Data

If the data focus is on those things more immediately important to satisfying business imperatives and ultimately customers, the key areas in which data are desired are:

• *Time.* How long does it take an item (which could be a person in a hospital, a bank, or a similar process) entering the beginning of the process to reach the end? For what percentage of this time is actual productive work being done? How many changes of responsibility (handoffs between people) are involved? How many storage areas or buffers are there?

• *Flexibility.* How quickly and easily can change be made from one activity to another, whether that involves changeover of equipment or completion of one run of work before another can begin? What is required to accomplish that changeover? Who has authority to make the changeover? Are specialists required to assist in the changeover? How large are work batch sizes?

• *Responsiveness.* How responsive is the process to customer requests related to the output? Who controls what the process is doing—the company or the customer? Is the process and its associated forms, outputs, input needs, etc. designed for the company's convenience or the customer's?

• *Quality.* What is the error, rework, or reject rate at each operation? What is the cumulative error rate through the entire process, i.e., the first-pass yield or likelihood that something will enter the process, pass through all steps, and come out of the process without an error? How extensive are inspections, checks, rechecks, verifications, etc? Who is responsible for process quality?

• *Business importance.* What are the revenues from the product in the process? What is the volume of data or material handled? How many people are involved? Who in the organization manages the process? How does the process connect to the customer?

In walking through a process, a person experienced in process redesign observes a number of characteristics of the process. For example:

• Piles of material, whether paper on desks or manufacturing parts in bins, represent unnecessary work-in-process inventory. Old work mixed with new is a "red flag."
• Tags indicating special handling requirements, such as "HOT" tags, indicate quality or process-flow problems.
• Customers waiting in line indicate a lack of responsiveness.
• Personnel working constantly against deadlines, frantic or noisy activity levels, and a high degree of supervisory intervention usually indicate a process that is not working well.
• Long, convoluted work movement routes, crisscrossing work

paths, and other indications of chaotic processes usually lead to uncovering long "wait" times and rework loops.

Figure 3-5 is an opportunity assessment matrix that includes a worksheet that can be used for preliminary data gathering of this type. The worksheet has been found to develop enough information about target opportunities to allow sound project selection.

From these nondetailed and fairly surface-level and easily obtainable data, choices among potential processes can be made. The use of data to make the decision, regardless of the depth of the data, helps avoid the problem of private agendas and emotion in selection. Throughout our discussion of innovative process redesign techniques, we continually encourage the use of data in decision making and problem solving to ensure maximum validity in what is undertaken.

Choosing a Steering Committee

The process of choosing the pilot projects is usually most effectively done by a top management group that is familiar with the driving business imperatives, the desired outcomes of the improvement effort, the functions involved in the process, and the resources that are available to be brought to bear on the effort. This is the Steering Committee for the entire process improvement effort throughout the organization.

The Steering Committee may consist of the business leader and all of his or her direct reports, or it may consist of selected top management personnel. It should be comprised of people who understand the vision, recognize its connection to the customer, are themselves innovative and open to change, have good coaching skills, and represent areas in the company from which projects will be selected. Usually, we encourage management in the visioning process to assign responsibility for each key imperative to one top-level executive. The Steering Committee should include those individuals.

The Steering Committee remains in place throughout the effort as the body responsible for project selection and resource allocation, leadership vision transmission, and monitoring of progress toward the goal as team results begin to emerge. In selecting the process improvement efforts, the Steering Committee develops Team Charters setting out specific goals, a process described in detail in Chapter 5.

(Text continues on page 53)

Figure 3-5. Opportunity assessment matrix.

The opportunity assessment matrix is a data collection device for quickly assessing a process for possible redesign. It is deliberately general. It is intended to be a guide, not a prescription, and can, with a bit of liberal interpretation, be used on almost any process.

The following definitions may help.

1. *Sample Period Dates:* Data should be collected for a representative period of time, which might be a few days or a few weeks. If seasonal variations are significant, select samples from various times in the cycle.

2. *Unit Volume:* The number of items processed, whether products, documents, entries, etc.

3. *Dollars per Period:* The dollar value of units from (2), if meaningful.

4. *Batch Size/Number of Batches:* The number of parts, documents, units, etc. moved in a typical batch. The number of batches in which to do the work in this period.

5. *Percentage Completed on Time:* The percentage of units processed that went to the customer or internal client on or before his/her first request date. (Not a negotiated date.)

6. *Percentage Complaints:* A measure of returns or complaints on the final output of the process. Older time periods can be used, but note dates.

7. *Cycle Time:* The length of time it takes one typical product, document, person, or transaction to move from the start of the process to the end.

8. *Theoretical/Standard Time:* The estimated actual active work time to complete the process or manufacturing standard time.

9. *Lead Times:* The length of time necessary to obtain inputs to the process after first request.

10. *Dollar/Quantity Work in Process:* The dollar value or number of units within the process at one or more times in the sample period. Do not include items that have not moved to the first step.

11. *Dollar/Quantity Raw Materials:* The dollar value or number of units in the company's possession that have not moved to the first process step.

12. *Scrap/Reject Units:* The number of units discarded cumulative for all steps of the process, including those partially completed.

13. *Scrap/Reject Dollars:* The dollar value of units discarded.

14. *Quantity Reworked:* The number of units found to have errors or defects that were corrected or reworked and returned to the process.

15. *Quantity Rechecked:* The number of units rechecked, retested, and reinspected at any point in the process.

16. *Cumulative Yield:* The percent of units at each step that are acceptable the first time multiplied together ($.80 \times .60 \times .90 \times .90 \times 1.00 = 39\%$ yield).

17. *Number of Handoffs:* The number of times a typical unit is passed from person to person while moving through the process, excluding rework.

18. *Number of Queues:* The number of places in the process that batches of units are found waiting.

19. *Approximate Travel Distance:* The approximate distance a typical unit travels in moving from the beginning of the process to the end.

20. *Number of People Involved:* The total number of people involved in work on this process from all departments.

21. *Major Process Problems:* Problems noted in the time period.

(continues)

Figure 3-5 *(continued).*

Process: _____

Process Description:_____

1. Sample Period Dates (day, week, month)							
2. Unit Volume/Period							
3. Dollars/Period							
4. Batch Size/Number of Batches							
5. Percentage Completed on Time							
6. Percentage Customer/Client Returns/Complaints							
7. Cycle Time (actual hours)							
8. Theoretical/Standard Time							
9. Lead Times							
10. Dollar Quantity (units)/ Work in Process							
11. Dollar/Quantity Raw Material or Waiting to Start							
12. Scrap or Reject Units							
13. Scrap or Reject Dollars							
14. Quantity Reworked							
15. Quantity Rechecked							
16. Cumulative Yield							
17. Number of Handoffs							
18. Number of Queues							
19. Approximate Travel Distance							
10. Number of People Involved							
21. Major Problems Seen							

The selection of process redesign targets, the establishment of goals, and the selection of teams to pursue those goals in both the end point of the upper loop of the redesign model in Figure 3-1 and the beginning point of the bottom loop. Referring to Figures 3-1 and 3-4, we have completed the cycle from customer value input through vision development, identification of business imperatives, development of strategies, selection of processes upon which to focus, and formation of customer-focused process redesign teams.

Continuing the Process

This process continues almost endlessly, evolving through the two loops of the redesign model to revisit the customer inputs and revisit the process selection steps to continue achieving breakthrough improvements until the entire character and business level of the organization is transformed. In most large organizations, opportunities for new breakthrough efforts continue to emerge for eighteen to thirty-six months, depending upon the breadth of involvement, as the methodologies are established in the company. The cycle may continue indefinitely in an organization in a fast-moving market or industry, or it may evolve into a climate of continuous improvement through all activities as breakthrough results over time elevate the internal quality of the organization.

As processes are selected for focus, it is time to apply the methodologies and tools of innovative process redesign to the target processes following the road map of the lower loop in Figure 3-1. As the detailed baseline data for the process are being developed, further customer input or competitive benchmarking may be necesary to analyze the gaps and refine goals. Measures of the target process being analyzed are established for the process as it exists. The process is analyzed to develop improvement ideas using well-tested tools. Redesign improvement ideas are analyzed, tested, and implemented. Improvements are measured against the baseline established. The process is monitored over time to prevent deterioration and to allow necessary adjustments to be made within the context of the ideal process design.

How these steps are accomplished through the use of process redesign tools and methodologies is described in the balance of this book. You will learn both the technical skills required for successful innovative process redesign and the organizational and human factors critical to their effective use. Both are equally important. We have found that technical skills alone will not produce dramatic and long-lasting results. Human skills alone cannot produce successful results. But combined, they become a powerful force to bring real change to organizations, resulting in innovative new ways to do business in today's competitive markets.

Note

1. John Guaspari and Steven Crom, "Ultimately, There Is Just One Issue: Value, *Rath & Strong Leadership Report* (Winter 1993).

4

Determining Customer and Client Values

Joe woke up early. He was scheduled to take his daughter, Susie, for her first physical therapy appointment at the hospital. As he was getting dressed, he thought, "The last thing that I have time for today is all that waiting and all those forms."

Joe and Susie arrived at the hospital on time. They stopped at the front desk and were told to go directly to the physical therapy department; they were part of a new pilot program, and there was no paperwork necessary at the front desk. Arriving at the physical therapy department, Joe immediately noticed something different from their previous visit to the hospital. Now, in the waiting room, there were headphones for those who wanted to watch television. Magazines were current, and coffee and juice were available. Chairs were varied, some with stools for propping up injured legs, some with extra arm support. Wow! They had thought of everything for the patients and those waiting for them.

Joe and Susie were greeted at the counter with a smile. The receptionist said, "I'd just like to quickly verify your address and phone number. We have just implemented a new system so our patients don't have to fill out that awful paperwork anymore." Joe was amazed and thought, "Maybe this won't be so bad after all."

After Susie was called in for her treatment, Joe couldn't resist saying to the receptionist, "This department is like a different world. Are you sure you're part of the same hospital?" She laughed and said, "Oh, yes, sir. We had the opportunity here to form a team to determine what our customers value most. All of us took part in interviewing customers. Much to our surprise, about half of them hated having the television on. We thought we were doing them a favor by providing something for them to do! So we arranged to have headphones. That idea came from one of our interns—can you believe that? After we compiled all of the data, one of our team members remarked that the straight chairs must be awfully uncomfortable. After all, our patients are here for physical therapy. Someone else on the team had the idea of having a variety of chairs for the most common injuries that we treat. Our patients hadn't even thought to ask for new chairs. We redesigned our entire check-in system to eliminate all that paperwork, and we're piloting it in our department. Eventually, the entire hospital will use the system." There was a lot of pride in her voice as she told Joe about the team's accomplishments.

As Joe returned to the office, he was confident that his company could develop a vision and do a better job of determining what the customer really cares about. It should be possible to choose a process to focus on, just as the hospital had chosen the check-in process. He would suggest that they get going right away to determine what the customer values and to develop their own vision for the company.

If you are going to establish and maintain an ongoing process redesign effort focused on customers, it is critical for success to determine what is of value to those customers. To be of maximum benefit to the company, the improvement efforts must increase value to the customer. Sometimes this is very direct, as in a process that interfaces directly with the customer. Sometimes the connection is a little more vague, as in an internal process where the output goes to another internal process. In the latter case, your internal client becomes your customer. But internal clients have values and needs just like customers, even though they may be sitting right across the hall from you. And you need to treat them like customers.

Remember, we define customer value from the concept developed by Guaspari and Crom[1] as

$$\text{Customer Value} = \frac{\text{What the customer GOT}}{\text{What it COST the customer}}$$

We said that GOT includes all aspects of the transaction from the physical product or service through the intangibles of convenience, ease of doing business, and feelings of pride, confidence, satisfaction, etc. COST includes both the monetary cost and the intangible costs of frustration, anxiety, aggravation, time lost, inconvenience, etc.

Sounds simple enough! We need to know these things to focus

our efforts properly. We can get the information from the customers. The question is, *how*?

> *How can you measure what the customer thinks he/she GOT?*
> *How can you measure what the customer thinks it COST?*
> *How can you identify the key customer values we need to address?*
> *How can you know when we are satisfying those key values?*

Maybe it isn't so simple after all. In fact, it looks like a pretty tough challenge. But you have to meet this challenge if you are going to be winners in the competitive battle through process redesign efforts.

One way to answer some of these questions and assess customer value is through the Customer Value Analysis developed by Guaspari and Crom. The Customer Value Analysis focuses on the fact that, ultimately, the person who delivers the most value to the customer will emerge as the winner. Those who fall below the minimum standards of customer value for his/her industry, product, or service are ultimately destined to fail. Customers will go to the provider of the most value—in the full sense of the word—when they have a choice. And today, they almost always have choices.

Understanding Minimum Acceptable Value

A key concept in the Customer Value Analysis is that of Minimum Acceptable Value. As we have said, if you exceed the Minimum Acceptable Value of customers, you will thrive; if you simply meet that level, you may survive; if you fall below the Minimum Acceptable Value, you can expect to fail. The goal should be to exceed the Minimum Acceptable Value. Figure 4-1 depicts this concept graphically.

The Minimum Acceptable Value is set by several factors:

- The customer's experience base with an industry, product, or service
- The customer's general experience base for goods and services
- What the competition in an industry, product, or service group is doing
- What effect technological limitations have on setting the upper limit

It might be helpful to look at some examples of how these factors work to set the Minimum Acceptable Value:

Figure 4-1. Minimum Acceptable Value.

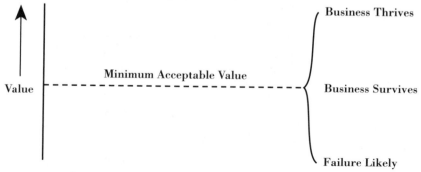

• *Customer's experience base with an industry, product, or service.* Some of us remember signs in automobile dealerships suggesting that if an automobile were 99 and $^{44}/_{100}$ths percent pure (from the Ivory Soap ads of the day), it would still contain seventeen defects. The idea was that you should accept that level of defects in a newly delivered vehicle. And people did! But not today! Customers today want zero defects or, at most, probably accept about one defect, the Minimum Acceptable Value of the industry today. The Minimum Acceptable Value has been raised by our experiences in the industry as competition produced products with fewer and fewer defects on delivery.

• *Customer's general experience base for goods and services.* Survey data developed by teams at a home-building company presented an interesting contradiction in results. Surveys overwhelmingly reported that the customers would recommend this company to friends and relatives without reservation. At the same time, they reported barely satisfactory ratings for the company for many key elements of the process. Further probing disclosed that the customers, based upon their general experiences in business and their expectations for service raised by those experiences, had relatively high levels of Minimum Acceptable Values for many factors. But their expectations, based upon experiences with the home-building industry, were much lower. Consequently, they were rating the company very high as compared to Minimum Acceptable Values for that industry and recommending it, but they were disappointed in many things based upon their general experiences. What an opportunity for a company to focus on a few things and raise the Minimum Acceptable Value for its industry and geographic area and gain a real competitive advantage!

• *What the competition is doing in an industry, product, or service group.* Your local savings and loan organization was once a great place to maintain your Christmas Club account, savings account, and home mortgage. Then, suddenly, the new savings and loan across the street started offering checking privileges, automatic tellers, automatic account transfers, investment services, and monthly discount buying offers at local stores. Plus, they said they would not sell your mortgage to an out-of-town mortgage buyer just when your own savings and loan did just that with your home mortgage. Suddenly your friendly banker didn't look so friendly any more. You began to feel you weren't getting everything you should be getting. What you GOT went down. What it COST may have gone up. The competition across the street had substantially raised the Minimum Acceptable Value, and you moved your accounts. They won!

• *What effect technological limitations have on setting the upper limit.* Following World War II, people began to think more globally. There was a huge rebuilding effort going on in Europe and Asia, and the need for faster and better transportation was clearly evident. Aircraft that could travel 600 miles per hour and fly from San Francisco to Hong Kong nonstop would clearly have raised the Minimum Acceptable Value in air transportation. Everyone in the industry recognized that, and aircraft companies worked diligently toward that goal. But it was not yet attainable. Technological limitations were going to prevent that breakthrough for a few years, but it was coming. We take it for granted today. When technology caught up, a key customer value was better met, and the Minimum Acceptable Value for aircraft and air transportation was substantially raised.

Keeping Up With Minimum Acceptable Value

An interesting phenomenon occurs when someone raises the Minimum Acceptable Value. It is evident in the examples regarding the automotive, banking, and aviation industries. When someone raises the Minimum Acceptable Value, the competition quickly catches up. It has to, or it will be at a serious disadvantage and risk losing the market or even going out of business. Regardless of where the Minimum Acceptable Value stabilizes temporarily, two things happen:

1. All viable competitors soon cluster around that level.
2. One of those competitors in the cluster does something to raise the level, and the race begins again.

Over time, the Minimum Acceptable Value always trends upward. It may go in fits and spurts of considerable magnitude (e.g., long-range jet aircraft), or it may move in a gradual and continuous way. The challenge is to be the one who constantly raises the level for your industry, product, or service. The only other viable alternative is to be a follower, constantly playing catch-up, struggling to maintain your share of the market.

Gaining the Advantage

Today, the advantage in most industries is flexibility, responsiveness, doing things faster, and recognizing the values of the customer that these things have an impact on. Gaining that advantage is what this book is all about.

If meeting or exceeding Minimum Acceptable Values is the competitive advantage desired, then you need to have ways to identify, define, and measure those values. That is the *how* dilemma with which this discussion started.

Profiling Customers Values

The Customer Value Profile developed by Guaspari and Crom[2] is an ideal tool for that purpose. It creates a one-page graphic presentation of how the marketplace—including those in the market who are not yet your customers and may be buying from competitors—defines *value* for that market and how these customers evaluate a company's performance against those values. The use of such a profile allows true focus on those things that are of most value to the customer, helps make strategic choices as to where to apply resources for the most benefit in providing Minimum Acceptable Value, and focuses on improving those processes most critical to maximizing customer value.

Figure 4-2 shows what a Customer Value Profile chart might look like. The value index is simply a measure of the value established by the market against which you can compare minimum acceptable levels and your own performance against those levels. In the actual case example, Company A had failed to recognize Assessment Ability

Figure 4-2. Customer Value Profile.

General case:

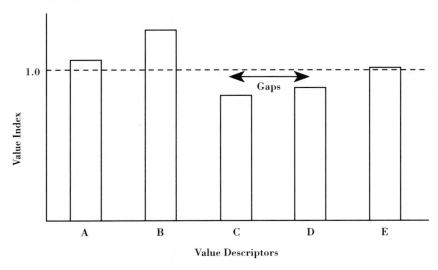

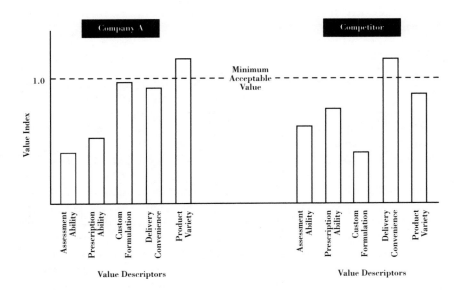

and Prescription Ability as key Customer Values, or had not focused on them, allowing a competitor to score higher on these values. The competitor was raising the Minimal Acceptable Value in delivery convenience, but was significantly behind on the Custom Formulation Score. The Minimum Acceptable Value is arbitrarily assigned a value of 1. The value descriptors are concise statements, if possible written in the customer's own words, that describe those things the customer values most. Typically, only four to six value descriptors are necessary to profile a market.

Creating the Customer Value Profile

Creating and maintaining a Customer Value Profile is a cross-functional effort involving direct contact with customers. It is closely tied to the business imperatives and involves a cross section of the company.

The Customer Value Profile will be tied to the strategic business plan, so that future attention is focused on those markets and customers most important to the company. From Figure 3-1 you can see that the Customer Value Profile, as the key element in understanding your customers and market, plays a part in developing the vision and influences the identification of imperatives. It is, therefore, most often driven by top management or the improvement process Steering Committee.

Monitoring Value Provided

Ideally, one wants to monitor and measure performance against the Customer Value Profile continuously. As a practical matter, though, this is impossible. Fortunately, it is almost always possible to measure the value descriptors through internal parameters that are more readily monitored.

For example, the new savings and loan organization across the street from yours (remember them?) installed automatic teller machines to allow twenty-four-hour cash availability. Obviously, they must have perceived ready availability of cash as a key customer value. The process of dispensing the cash through the automatic teller machine is a key process in satisfying that value, including all the steps from filling the machine with money through repairing it if it malfunctions. The key measure is how reliable the availability of cash is through the machine. So, the internal parameter that measures our success in satisfying the value descriptor is the daily downtime of the automatic teller machine. By measuring that, if the original perception of the key value is correct, we are measuring success in meeting Minimum Acceptable Values.

If you communicate the Customer Value Profile throughout the organization, tie it to the company's business imperatives, and communicate the internal parameter measurements with which to monitor success, it can change the way the organization thinks about customers, processes, and how they work. There will be compelling focus on process improvement for the customer's benefit, and the realization of the system pullers will begin.

As we have stated, development of the Customer Value Profile is a cross-functional activity that should involve, in addition to the top management drivers, representatives from all areas having a stake in key customer-related processes. Certainly sales, marketing, and customer service functions should be represented, as well as other areas with key customer-related processes.

Gathering the Data

The heart of the customer value profiling process is to obtain the data from which to define the Value Descriptors. It is necessary to determine:

- What is most important to customers
- How the company is doing compared to competitors

There are two key methods of developing these data:

1. The Customer Value Survey
2. Competitive benchmarking

The Customer Value Survey provides information on both what is of value to customers and how you are doing. Competitive benchmarking is more likely to disclose how you compare with competition, but it may also provide insights into what customers value as perceived by competitors and how competitors may be raising the level of the Minimum Acceptable Value.

The Customer Value Survey

Understanding the Customer Value Survey

The Customer Value Survey is not a customer satisfaction survey such as is commonly used by industry to test how well customers think a company is doing. The Customer Value Survey differs in several respects:

- It does not focus on existing customers only.
- It asks for comparisons of your performance with competitors.
- It asks not only what is important to customers but also how important each item is.
- It affords customers open-ended opportunities to discuss their expectations and needs at both a macro and micro level.
- Its purpose is to develop specific actionable opportunities.

In any marketplace there are customers who perceive the value they receive differently. Some feel it is exceptional, others feel it is acceptable, and some feel it is unacceptable. Their assessment of value received depends upon a number of factors: the specific goods and services they receive; their geographic location; the particular sales representative, service agent, or branch of the company they deal with; the demographics of their group; and many others. The Customer Value Survey must take into account those differences as it is structured.

Conducting a Customer Value Survey

A Customer Value Survey is best conducted by a cross-functional team of employees. These employees may normally be in contact with customers, or that might be a new role for them. It really doesn't matter.

There are distinct benefits in using a team rather than individuals to conduct the Customer Value Survey. Results often reflect upon how specific processes serve the customer and how well the customer thinks they do so. Although people are involved in those processes, the survey, in effect, evaluates how these people are doing, at least in their minds. People may be defensive and reject the data. Some may have paradigms that make it difficult to evaluate condensed data in an unbiased way. But if employees have direct contact with the customer during the study, the impact of what the customer is saying is usually so great that it cannot easily be rejected. It is more valid. The team members heard it themselves, so team members are willing to accept it and use it to guide improvement efforts.

It is sometimes helpful to begin with a preliminary assessment of what the organization perceives as key customer values. These should not be edited down or debated. The purpose of identifying them is to form a basis for the future questions to ask the customer and to identify those who should be involved on the team conducting the analysis.

Representation on the team should include the core functions of the business that most affect what are perceived as key customer values. Typically, this includes sales, marketing, engineering, manufacturing, quality, and customer service. In addition, key stakeholders—those who may feel they have a vested interest in the customer—should be interviewed to enroll them in the process and hear their perceptions of how to improve customer value.

A preliminary profile of the customer base should be developed, keeping in mind that the interest is in both present customers and those who could be customers, i.e., those who currently go to competing companies or competing technologies for solutions to their needs. Categorize them by size, location, business type, product or service, etc. For each segment, develop hypotheses about their value perceptions:

- What are their macro expectations?
- What are their micro expectations?
- What are the steps they go through in doing business with us?
- What GOTS are they likely to perceive?
- What COSTS are they likely to perceive?
- How do we think we could increase value?

Figure 4-3 depicts how expectations influence the customer perceptions of a transaction and how the results of the transaction have an impact on future expectations. These hypotheses provide a basis for developing the Customer Value Analysis methodology and questions. The value analysis survey tests the hypotheses for validity and provides more open-ended solicitation of customer input.

Figure 4-4 describes a number of ways in which Customer Value Surveys (and client surveys) might be conducted. Figure 4-5 shows how these methods might be selected based upon the size of the population to be surveyed and the degree of structure believed to be necessary in the survey to obtain valid results. And Figure 4-6 shows the relative value of the Customer Value Survey at different points in the improvement process. The key is that regardless of when the Customer Value Analysis is done—i.e., where you first enter the top loop of Figure 3-1—the process can provide valuable insights to the direction of process redesign efforts. More detail about the techniques of conducting Customer Value Surveys is included in the discussion

Figure 4-3. A model of customer value.

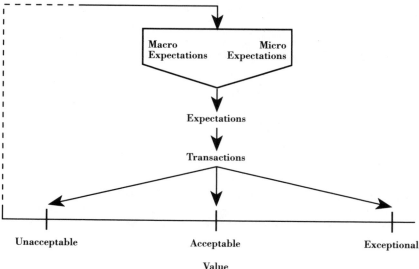

of internal client surveys later in this chapter. (Summaries of some of the principles appear in Figures 4-8, 4-9, and 4-10, which appear with our discussion of survey methods for internal client surveys.)

Benchmarking

The second method of acquiring input to the Customer Value Profile is benchmarking, which may or may not be confined to competitive benchmarking. Benchmarking offers three opportunities in connection with Customer Value Profiles:

1. It allows a more in-depth comparison with competition than the Customer Value Survey alone.
2. It allows assessment of key customer values against best-in-class companies inside or outside the industry, which might lead to raising the level of Minimum Acceptable Value for the industry and market.
3. By observing where competitors are focusing their attention, you can predict what you believe to be key customer values and where they are likely next to raise the level of Minimum Acceptable Value.

Figure 4-4. Methods for customer/client surveys.

Method	Description	Comments
Direct Observation	Watch people use products/services.	See why/how product or service is used. Effective for well-defined product/service in limited geographic area with limited survey population.
Focus Groups	Facilitate small groups as members discuss values of importance to them.	Effective for fairly specific purposes and issues where a small sample of a large population is considered adequate. But there is some diversity of needs, perceptions.
Face-to-Face Interviews	Guided face-to-face conversations.	Effective for detailed probing when a limited sample is acceptable or considerable time is available.
Telephone Interviews	Scheduled, structured interviews by phone.	Effective for probing in depth when a large sample is necessary and the time is short or access is limited.
Written Surveys	Structured written questions.	Effective for volume response on well-defined issues. Useful for continuous monitoring, geographic diversity.
User-Groups	Facilitated discussions of values by select users (or nonusers) at periodic intervals over a long time span.	Effective for probing in depth, building relationships to increase candor in feedback, and continuous monitoring.

In previous discussions of factors affecting where the Minimum Acceptable Value is set, we examined both the effect of competition and the impact of experiences that customers have outside the industry on customer perceptions. Benchmarking allows assessment of both. Benchmarking competitive performance discloses the impact of competitive activity on the Minimum Acceptable Value in the industry and how customers believe the company performs against competitors. Benchmarking against best-of-class companies—those recognized as being the absolute best at performing the process that is

Figure 4-5. Selection of survey methods.

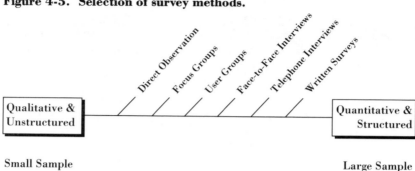

being evaluated, regardless of industry—discloses what customers may see as the Minimum Acceptable Value in their total experience. This may highlight opportunities to raise the standard in your own industry to competitive advantage.

Reasons for Benchmarking

Benchmarking is a proactive step in assessing what competition and best-in-class companies outside the industry are and will be doing. The alternative is to see what they have done after the fact and reacting to it.

The primary reason for benchmarking is to help set performance goals above the Minimum Acceptable Value by taking advantage of the knowledge gained both to choose areas of concentration for improvement efforts and set specific goals to be achieved. The objective is to target those areas of most importance and set goals that will not only help catch up with competition but also raise the level of Minimum Acceptable Value above the competition's level of performance.

Another value of benchmarking in setting process redesign goals is that it gives credibility to the goals and objectives. The notion is that "if others are doing it, we certainly should be able to do it in our company." The "not invented here" obstacles that often crop up around new ideas can be avoided. Ingrown patterns of behavior and paradigms built up around perceptions of what is possible and what should be attempted can be broken. If, in addition, insight can be gained into where competitors might be heading in the future, effective goal setting can lead to a leadership role rather than a catch-up role.

Figure 4-6. Customer Value Survey at different stages of the improvement process.

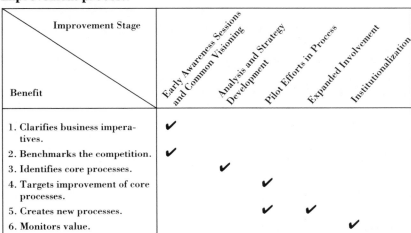

Improvement Stage / Benefit	Early Awareness Sessions and Common Visioning	Analysis and Strategy Development	Pilot Efforts in Process	Expanded Involvement	Institutionalization
1. Clarifies business imperatives.	✔				
2. Benchmarks the competition.	✔				
3. Identifies core processes.		✔			
4. Targets improvement of core processes.			✔		
5. Creates new processes.			✔	✔	
6. Monitors value.					✔

A key value of benchmarking is that it helps determine true measures and solve real problems in real time, often with proven solutions readily available. True measures come from really seeing what is going on in competitive and best-of-class companies rather than reviewing your own history. Best-in-class benchmarks allow measures and goals of the future without regard to the historical starting point baseline. A 60 percent improvement over your present baseline may or may not be enough. Knowing what others are accomplishing helps determine that, whereas historical data are often limiting in goal setting. When the goal is to try to assess opportunities for improvement in order to raise Minimum Acceptable Value levels, you want the most progressive assessment you can get of where key values will be in the future.

A clear competitive advantage should be gained if, in setting goals for an improvement effort, best-in-class performance levels can be achieved in some key customer value areas and at least Minimum Acceptable Values can be achieved in all others. The overall value rating, measured by the formula of what the customer gets divided by what it costs him/her, should be high relative to competition.

Undertaking a Benchmarking Effort

The process of benchmarking is relatively straightforward. Undertaken as a first step in an improvement process, it helps develop the vision and establish business imperatives. Undertaken later in the process, it begins with a review of the business imperatives and their objectives. The existing processes affecting those imperatives are baselined to obtain key data. This is done using some of the techniques on analyzing processes set out in later chapters of this book.

But an assessment satisfactory for initial benchmarking can be done using the more simple evaluation techniques described for initial pilot project selection in Chapter 3. This is often supplemented by internal interviews, evaluation and analysis of the data available, and site surveys to observe the processes.

All of this work is typically done by the benchmarking team assigned to study a particular process. Such a team, not unlike the Customer Value Survey team, is typically made up of those who are closest to and best understand the details of the process to be benchmarked.

Determining Benchmarking Targets

The team then determines the companies or organizations against which they want to benchmark. Benchmarking targets generally fall into one of the following classes:

- Competitors
- Leaders in the same industry who are not competitors
- Best-in-class companies for the process being studied

In the real world, the difficulty of identifying candidate benchmarking companies increases in the order listed, and the difficulty of obtaining cooperation decreases in the same order. Rarely is one able to benchmark against a competitor by direct contact with that competitor. Rather, it becomes a task of obtaining information about competitors from customers, industry sources, and publicly available data. Leaders in the same industry who are not competitors are generally more agreeable to benchmarking discussions, provided the companies do not see you as a potential competitor trying to set up for entry into one of their markets.

It is wise to choose a company with a fairly identifiably different strategic thrust or technology, but that still is perceived as a leader by many of the same customers that are in your market. Best-in-class companies outside your own industry are usually the most approachable as they see no competitive threat from sharing information with you and are often proud of what they do. They look forward to the opportunity to "strut their stuff" in a socially acceptable way, in response to your request that they do so. The exception is a very few companies that have been singled out so often for excellence in particular areas that benchmarking visits have become an intrusion and an interruption of their business activity.

Conducting the Benchmarking Visit

Benchmarking visits to other companies are a sharing event. You should be prepared to give as much as you get. Meetings should be set up by people at high levels in both companies to demonstrate sincerity and willingness to be open, even though the visit may be made by teams of workers. Willingness to share should be stated up front. Ask what the company you plan to visit might like to hear about from you. Perhaps you have another process that is of interest to them from a benchmarking standpoint, and you can be of value to them in exchange for what you are learning.

Benchmarking Without a Target Company

Benchmarking can be done without involving other companies directly. If time is a problem or suitable benchmarking candidates cannot be found, it is still possible to develop benchmark data. The following are some techniques that can be used:

• *Internal focus groups.* Most companies harbor a wealth of information within their own walls about best practices and competitive activity. They just don't know it is there or where to find it. The information resides with employees who have recently been hired from competitors or other companies in the industry, with those who attend trade shows and technical meetings and talk to peers, within the sales force, etc. One way to extract this information and synthesize it for maximum value is to conduct internal focus groups where people who might have pieces of information come together and develop a more complete picture. This can be a particularly effective way of developing competitive benchmark data in high-technology industries.

• *Literature searches.* There is a wealth of information about competitive companies and best-of-class processes in industry trade journals (even those outside one's own industry), industry association publications, regulatory filings, company annual reports, SEC financial filings, product and help wanted advertisements, etc. Sometimes, if carefully analyzed by a knowledgeable team, the collation of data from a variety of sources such as these discloses new technology thrusts, key customer value perceptions, and strategies. Admittedly, there is some conjecture in the conclusions that might be drawn, but it is better than no data at all.

• *Suppliers.* Interviews with suppliers to your industry, whether you currently use them or not, often discloses a wealth of information about competitive and industry activity that can shed light on both current and future key customer values. Suppliers are often able to provide insights as to how you measure up against key customer values as well, based upon what they hear from competitors and, in many industries, from the customers to whom they also sell directly.

• *Customers.* Interviews with customers, or with those who buy from your competitors, returns you to a Customer Value Survey activity. But it is a recognized technique in benchmarking as well. The focus may be different, and the specifics of the interviews are almost always quite different because benchmarking is more tightly focused and designed to gain rather specific data. For example, a benchmarking survey would ask:

—How does the size of our delivery truck compared with our competitor's affect you?
—Can you describe the best system you have encountered for telling you where to locate your checked luggage when you get off the plane?

A Customer Value Survey would ask:

—Tell me about your last delivery. What stands out in your mind about the transaction?
—Tell me about the experience of claiming your luggage when you get off the plane. What would make it more pleasant for you?

In both cases there is further probing. Benchmarking tries to get at what is being done. Customer Value Surveys try to get at how the customer feels about it and the value put on what is or is not done.

There are a number of widely accepted benchmarking systems. All contain the same basic steps and approaches, although they may present them in slightly different ways. The Xerox process is widely accepted as excellent. This process is described in detail in Robert C.

Camp's book *Benchmarking: The Search for Industry Best Practices That Lead to Superior Performance.*[3] Figure 4-7 is based upon steps in the Xerox process tied to what we are teaching here.

Analyzing the Gaps

The development of the Customer Value Profile, using inputs from the Customer Value Survey and benchmarking activity, generally results in identification of key customer values that the organization does not meet well or as well as competitors. The challenge is to develop actions around those gaps between what the organization provides and the customer's Minimum Acceptable Value. Such gaps fall into several categories:

- Gaps that result from different value perceptions in different customer groups
- Gaps between what the organization provides and what the customer has established as a minimum performance level
- Gaps between what the organization provides and what competitors provide
- Gaps between what the organization perceives as Minimum Acceptable Values and what the customer says are Minimum Acceptable Values

Another gap, that between what the organization perceives as key customer values and how it perceives itself as satisfying those key values, is an important one to analyze in the early stages of an improvement process. A good technique is to conduct a Customer Value Survey of the organization, asking key company personnel to complete the survey the way they believe customers will answer it. These responses are then tabulated and available before the answers from the customers are disclosed to the organization.

When the customer values and assessment of how the organization is satisfying them are released, the perceptual gap is clearly identified by the differences in the answers. When the organization realizes how it has failed to recognize some key customer values or has undervalued their importance, it generally creates a high degree of energy to get started on the process to improve. This can often be a key factor in instilling the improvement ethic in the organization. It is hard to argue with the fact that you missed identifying what your customer values most. And it is sometimes a shock.

Figure 4-7. Benchmarking process steps.

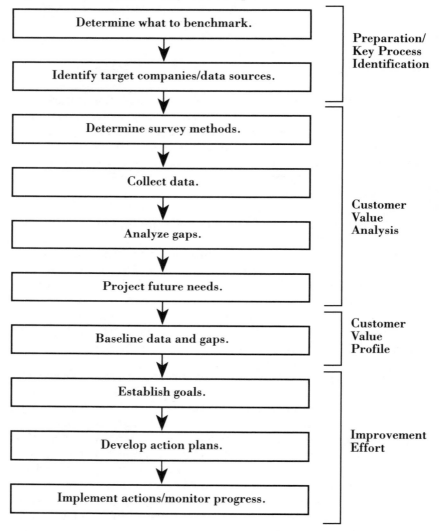

It is from the analysis of the gaps that action items are developed, targets for improvement are identified, and goals are set. If the Customer Value Profile is established early in the improvement process, it is often a key driver in establishing priorities and selecting processes for improvement. Even later in the process or on revisiting the profile in the future, imperatives may be modified and the key processes adjusted with new priorities established.

Internal Client Surveys

The final step in determining customer/client needs is an internal one often driven by the outcome of the Customer Value Profile and the actions resulting from it. This is the internal client survey. Just as the Customer Value Survey and benchmarking are designed to determine what needs to be done to meet Minimum Acceptable Values of the customer, the internal client survey is designed to determine what is necessary to meet the internal needs of those who receive process outputs in the chain of processes leading to the customer.

The internal client survey is an important weapon for a company engaged in a process improvement effort. Since a part of any improvement effort must be a relevant customer-focused effort throughout the organization, it is important to examine the work output of each department or business unit that has an impact on a key process interfacing with the customer, whether that department or unit has direct customer contact or not. The goal is to ensure relevant customer focus and value throughout all stages of the processes ultimately leading to the customer interface.

At another level, the internal client survey can be a tactical tool in improvement efforts by identifying redundant work outputs or work outputs of low priority throughout the organization as a whole. Outputs can then be continued, simplified, combined, or eliminated to reduce workload. Once outputs have been eliminated, combined, or simplified, the remaining processes producing outputs can be better analyzed for improvement using problem-solving and process analysis tools.

Why Survey Internal Clients?

A well-conducted internal client survey is a major contribution to defining the business activity of any business unit. It identifies those activities and outputs that have real relevance to internal clients and ultimately to customers. The organizational unit performing the survey can readily test its perceptions and understanding of internal client needs against the clients' stated needs and values. Hypotheses about what, how, and why activity is performed and what outputs are produced can be tested. Gaps can be identified and analyzed. A baseline is created for benchmarking the unit's activities against others. Strategic imperatives for work focus can be clarified. Improvement plans can be developed and implemented, driving actions and intervention for greater efficiency.

Key outcomes of action plans arising from a well-conducted internal client survey will be quantified, real, relevant needs of internal clients; improvement of outputs to clients; reduction of unnecessary work providing outputs of little or no value; and a stronger, more efficient, higher quality organizational link with internal clients.

Conducting Internal Client Surveys

Internal client surveys can be effectively conducted regardless of the size, breadth, or functional specialization of the organizational unit involved. But the method used may vary depending upon such variables as the issues involved, the purpose of the survey, the organizational climate and history, and the nature and number of participants and internal client representatives. Figure 4-4, which described methods of conducting surveys, applies equally well to customer surveys and internal client surveys. So does Figure 4-5, describing the appropriateness of these methods depending upon the size of the survey population and the amount of structure necessary.

Internal client surveys can be conducted on a onetime-only basis or, like Customer Value Surveys, on a periodic basis, such as annually. They may even be conducted on a continuous basis. The right frequency depends upon the purpose and issues involved. A continuous or frequent internal client survey can assess levels of internal client satisfaction as a measure of success of the process, monitor results of improvements being introduced, provide for minor adjustments from time to time, etc. A onetime-only survey might be more appropriate if the purpose is to determine relative value to clients of a set of reports issued by an organizational unit as a means of identifying and eliminating those of lesser importance as a work reduction effort.

In conducting an internal client survey, the only clear rule is that there is no single right way to conduct it. Each survey process must reflect the needs of the specific organization involved, taking into account the uniqueness of structure and the individual organizational dynamics. However, there is an effective framework in which to develop and implement an internal client survey process.

Defining the Purpose

A fairly specific and manageable purpose for the internal client survey should be established. Consider what the organization needs to learn and what actions need to be taken as a result of what is learned. What is the objective? Process improvement goal setting? Work simplification? Client needs identification? Establishing internal baselines for benchmarking? Defining the purpose begins to establish guidelines for the methodology, questions, etc.

Determining the Scope

Are internal client surveys to be conducted by only one or two organizational units, or are all units within the company to be involved in a massive effort? How many potential clients are involved? How fast must the survey be done? Answers to these questions help determine methodologies and lead to identification of potential obstacles to success.

Considering the Organizational Dynamics

In an internal client survey the inquiries of the team often involve a form of peer review in the broadest sense. Are we doing the right things? Are we doing things we don't need to do? Coming to the conclusion that something someone is doing is no longer necessary is a very threatening situation for him/her. These human factors have to be considered in determining who should be conducting the survey and how the results are evaluated and communicated.

Obtaining accurate, useful results may depend upon the candor between two parties within the same organization. There are inevitable pressures. Consideration must be given to effectiveness of communication in the organization, employee confidence and influence (particularly relative to each other between surveyor and client), and other organizational climate issues. These influence the methods used and the speed at which the survey proceeds and may influence initial scope and breadth.

Identifying Gaps and Issues

With the intended purpose and scope in mind, establish in as much detail as possible the perceived gaps and issues to be studied. This may be done by studying available information and data, holding a brainstorming session with survey team members, or other means. Categorize these data and develop a short list of key information to pursue that will have an impact on how the process works for the customer's benefit. This final list of what to survey should represent a breadth of activity that is manageable by a team in an essentially self-conducted survey. If the gaps and issues are too broad, revisit the purpose and intended focus with more critical scrutiny.

Determining Who Should be Surveyed

In determining whom to survey, consider questions such as: Who are the internal clients of the organizational unit conducting the survey? What are the process outputs? Who uses them? How many use them? Do they use them for the same purpose?

It is important to identify the true internal clients. This may not be the first recipient. For example, the client may be an executive, not the secretary to whom the output is directed, or a sales representative, not the manager to whom the output goes for distribution.

Determining the Survey Method and Developing the Instrument

When all of the outlined factors have been considered, the survey method can be effectively chosen from among those listed in Figure 4-4, based upon the relative advantages and disadvantages. And the final list of those to be surveyed can be established.

Regardless of the survey method, some form of survey instrument or guide must be developed. For personal or telephone interviews and focus groups, that might be an interview guide with one or more levels of questions to help the interviewers probe. For a written survey, it involves development of specific questions and response classifications.

Development of questions for interviews or written surveys follows similar steps, usually something like this:

1. Preliminary questions by gap or issue category
2. Consolidation of possible questions with common themes
3. Trimming down the questions to manageable scope
4. Refining the questions to final form
5. Preparing the final instrument

As is the case with all survey instruments, including the Customer Value Survey, questions may be developed in a hierarchy from tightly focused to more free-form. That structure is something like this:

Closed-Ended Questions

1. With ratings
2. Forced ranking
3. Selective choice
4. Specific answer

Open-Ended Questions

1. Adjective or descriptor response
2. One- or two-word answers
3. Narrative answer
4. Free invitation to subject

Questions may be phrased to determine "what" or "how important" or both.

Figure 4-8. Guidelines for written customer/client surveys.

The following are some things to keep in mind in developing written survey instruments:

1. Questions should be focused on the purpose and meaningful. Avoid vague generalities. Open-ended questions should be pointedly specific and answerable in a few words.

2. The questionnaire should be brief and able to be completed in ten to twenty minutes. A longer questionnaire will begin to affect the results as busy people will begin to shorten answers or rush to finish rather than give meaningful responses.

3. The format should be easy to follow. Questions should be clear and use terms familiar to the customer/client.

4. The process should be introduced with courtesy and consideration. The head of the surveying organizational unit should send out a letter setting up the process with customers/clients (why, importance, seek cooperation). Follow-up calls should be made to answer questions.

5. The survey should be administered when and as promised.

6. Feedback to participants should be provided as soon as possible.

The development of survey questions and interview guides and training of interviewers is a skill requiring some training and experience. Few survey teams are able to accomplish these tasks without help from trained personnel either within the organization or from outside. In addition, the unbiased input of an outside unaffiliated party in the development of questions may well result in a more unbiased and objective survey.

Figures 4-8, 4-9, and 4-10 summarize some of the considerations in preparing for and conducting customer and client surveys, interviews, and focus groups. Figure 4-11 shows an internal client survey

Figure 4-9. Guidelines for customer/client survey interviews.

Interviews are a more difficult task for survey teams with little or no experience, but with proper preparation they can be successfully conducted. They are usually more revealing to interviewers than data from written surveys. The following are some steps to keep in mind in conducting interviews:

1. Guideline questions should be developed for the interviewer almost as for a written survey. Second-level and, perhaps, third-level questions anticipating possible answers to the primary question could be developed to help the inexperienced interviewer probe.

2. The interview should be modeled in a role play during training with potential interviewers. Talk the interview team through the process, and instruct in principles of good interviewing.

3. Interviewers should train through one or more role plays and, where possible, an actual interview with a "friendly" subject. The goal should be to make the interviewer comfortable with the process and practice listening skills and development of follow-up questions.

4. If possible, observe one or more interviews and provide feedback.

5. Since interview data are much harder to analyze than data from written surveys, written reports should be prepared as quickly as practical after the interview to ensure data are not lost.

6. It may be helpful to have interviewers work in pairs, with one person asking a question and the other taking notes. Tape recording can be helpful but usually inhibits interviewees.

7. Feedback to participants should be provided quickly.

Figure 4-10. Guidelines for customer/client survey focus groups.

Focus groups are a more difficult methodology than either written surveys or interviews. They require more coordination to set up and conduct. Skilled facilitation is essential and probably has to be done by a trained person because appropriate skills are unlikely to be available on the survey team. The following are some points to consider in conducting focus groups:

1. Guideline questions should be developed for use by the facilitator, including follow-up questions.

2. Focus groups should be limited to eight to twelve people and should not run more than ninety to 120 minutes.

3. Some data are much harder to analyze than those from written surveys or interviews and should be written up as soon as possible after the session to avoid losing key information.

4. Notes should be taken by one or two observers. If a true focus group room is used with a viewing area, the survey team should be encouraged to observe as time permits, and observers should be completely out of the interview room. Tape recording is usually more acceptable to participants than in one-on-one interviews but may still be inhibiting.

5. Feedback should be provided quickly.

guide and data summary report used by one company. It may help sum up some of the steps in the process in more detail.

Notes

1. John Guaspari and Steven Crom, "Ultimately, There Is Just One Issue: Value," *Rath & Strong Leadership Report* (Winter 1993).
2. Ibid.
3. Robert C. Camp, *Benchmarking: The Search for Industry Best Practices That Lead to Superior Performance* (Milwaukee: ASQC Press, 1989).

Figure 4-11. Sample internal client survey guide.

Objectives

1. To identify redundant reports, tasks, and outputs that can be eliminated.

2. To establish levels of importance for work outputs so that low-priority work can be considered for elimination.

Organizing the Effort

One person needs to be designated as the responsible leader of this effort. This might be one of the three people attending the process improvement workshop, or it might be a senior manager. Duties of this individual will include seeing that each department does its initial analysis, helping with interdepartmental interviews, compiling a matrix of departments and outputs, and evaluating for redundancy.

Process Steps

1. Each department should meet in its entirety or as a group of four to six key individuals who know the activities of the department. One person can prepare some basic information ahead of time by simply completing a form with the necessary information. During this meeting, the department should list each key process in the department and the specific output of that process. The output could be data, information, or a physical product. It could be a report, a check, a permit, etc. It could be a final end product or an input to a subsequent process that produces a new output. We want the output identified at the individual department's level, but not the individual task level. For example, we want the process of preparing a file folder that contains data XYZ that is delivered to department ABC, not the preparation of the file folder itself for use in the department. The information we want, which can be summarized on charts similar to the example attached, includes:
   • Process name
   • Process output, by name
   • Output description (content, brief headlines)
   • Whom the output goes to: primary and secondary
   • Frequency (hourly, x times/day, weekly, annually, as requested, etc.)
   • Work hours to prepare output (rough estimate)

- Elapsed time to prepare output, including waits, etc. (rough estimate)
- Other sources of the same or similar output known now

2. With the above data documented on forms similar to that attached, the information should be compiled into a single summary for review by the project coordinator and/or management. Participants should also receive feedback.

   The coordinator, or a small team of two to three led by the coordinator, should review the report looking for obvious redundancies, including both those directly identified by participants as well as those identifiable by comparing department outputs. Look especially at financial analysis reports, salers reports, customer interface reports, and construction and progress reports. Obvious redundancies should be highlighted for careful examination.

3. The creators of each output should then meet with the identified users of the output. They should point out any other sources of the same or similar output to see if simplification and/or elimination of duplication can occur. The user should be asked to identify any portions of the subject output that are of little or no value and any critical part of the output that may be missing. The user should be asked to rate the importance of the particular output to him or her (for example, on a 1 to 5 scale with 1 = low, 5 = critical).

4. The individual departments should now take the information they have developed and analyze each of their outputs to see if it can be eliminated, simplified, combined with other outputs, retained as is, or improved by additions. This analysis should be reviewed by the coordinator.

5. A compilation of recommendations from all departments should be reviewed by management, if desired, before action is taken.

6. Approved recommendations should be implemented immediately.

Next Steps

1. All documents and other information retention systems and repositories from file cabinets to computer databases should be reviewed and nonessential materials disposed of to avoid costs and labor for storage, movement, updates, etc.

(continues)

Figure 4-11 *(continued).*

2. Now that essential outputs have been identified and simplified as much as possible, the processes that produce those outputs should be analyzed for elimination of nonvalue-added steps.

Comments

1. We expect to be able to identify and analyze outputs and make recommendations in thirty to forty-five days.

2. It should be possible to simplify those outputs that are candidates for simplification within thirty days after approval, including reviews by users.

3. We expect around 5 percent of outputs to be candidates for improvement, i.e., additions or clarifications would make them more valuable. We expect 20 to 50 percent to be candidates for elimination, combination, or simplification. Assuming that people are objective in their ratings, be very careful about elimination of anything rated at 4 or 5, and carefully balance available resources against demands of outputs rated 3. Anything rated 1 or 2 should probably be eliminated or drastically reduced and combined with something more essential to the pursuit of your goals.

4. Do a test in one department before going global with this process. Finance and MISs are good test cases because they have clearly defined outputs. Finance may be pretty clean, unless there are a lot of internal analysis reports. An MIS usually has lots of stuff that can be eliminated or simplified.

Department: _____

Output	Description	Frequency	Work Hours Each	Elapsed Time Each	Primary User	Other Users	Alternate Sources	User Importance	Recommendation	APPD	Target Implementation	Completed
Step 1	Step 2	Step 1	Step 1	Step 1	Step 1	Step 1	Step 1 & Step 2	Step 3	Step 4	Step 5	Step 5 & Step 6	Step 6

Example

Department:	Finance
Process:	Financial Reporting
Output:	Monthly Financial Report with Analysis
Description:	P&L, Balance Sheet, Cost Center Reports, Sales by Product
Frequency:	Monthly
Work Hours Each:	120
Elapsed Time:	14 days
Primary User:	Joe Morgan
Other Users:	Officers, Dept. Heads, Business Managers
Alternate Sources:	Sales Report Monthly by Sales
User Importance:	Joe Morgan–5 Bank–5 Officers–4 Dept. Heads–3
Recom.:	Combine Sales Reporting, Simplify Cost Reports, Distribute Full Report to Chuck and Officers. Dept. Reports with Summary Cover Memo to Dept. Heads
APPD:	Yes
Target Implementation:	Report on 2/93

5

Developing Goals and Chartering the Team

Joe was driving to his first homeowners meeting. His family had been in their new house exactly one month, and things had actually gone pretty well—much better than expected, considering it took two weeks just to process his contract to buy the house. When he entered the room, he was surprised to see not only Jim, the sales rep, but also several of the people from the office who had helped with the contract. The meeting facilitator began by reporting. "Good evening. Thank you for coming. Tonight, we would like to report back to you, our customers, what we have learned since beginning our improvement effort three months ago. As many of you know, we are rated number one in this town among home builders. That's why many of you came to us. We thought we were pretty good, until we changed the way we get information from our customers and the market—those would-be customers that we lost. We learned a lot about what our customers really care about, and frankly, some of the data surprised us."

He continued, "For instance, the process of completing your contract was problematic. It was too cumbersome and took too long. Our focus had always been on offering the best designs for homes, not on the hassle that all of you go through to purchase that home. We have selected that process for improvement and have a team working on it. Its members have contacted the bank and gotten agreement that the mortgage loan process will be done in two days in the future. Our own process now takes three days, down from an average of two weeks in the past.

"Another surprise was that you really cared about the cleanliness of the building site while your home is being constructed. You reported having paint cans all over, mud on your new carpet, and scratches on the walls. We have formed a team of our subcontractors to address these issues. They have already developed some quality standards for keeping the building sites in good order."

Joe thought, "This is neat. Not only are they telling us how we as customers make a difference; they are also telling us what they are doing about it! In fact, they have selected processes to work on based on customer input. Now, *that's* a focus on the customer."

The next morning, Joe could hardly wait to get to the staff meeting. They had agreed that the staff would function as the Steering Committee for process redesign. They now had a much better idea of what widget customers cared about and what kind of company they wanted to create: their vision after working on both. It was time for them to begin their improvement process. Each staff member was to come to the meeting with ideas based on data collected to choose a few pilot projects. Joe thought, "This will be easy. We should be out of here by noon."

In order effectively to charter teams and conduct a process redesign effort that truly reshapes the way the company works, the effort needs to be organized to function well in the particular company structure. Organizations differ, but their improvement process structures are typically variations of that shown in Figure 5-1. The Steering Committee is the governing body, the driver/coordinator is the day-to-day manager of the process, and the teams are the working entities.

Organizing for Team Activity

One of the most important responsibilities of the Steering Committee is the chartering of the process redesign team and the establishment of specific measurable goals for the team. A poorly chartered team with vague goals is destined for frustration and failure. In the early stages of an emerging improvement effort, the failure of teams can lead to unwillingness of other employees to serve on teams, doubt about the process, and the demise of the entire effort. We encourage the Steering Committee to devote sufficient time and effort to the chartering process to ensure that the team has a fair chance to succeed if it follows the steps for successful process redesign.

Figure 5-1. Process redesign organization.

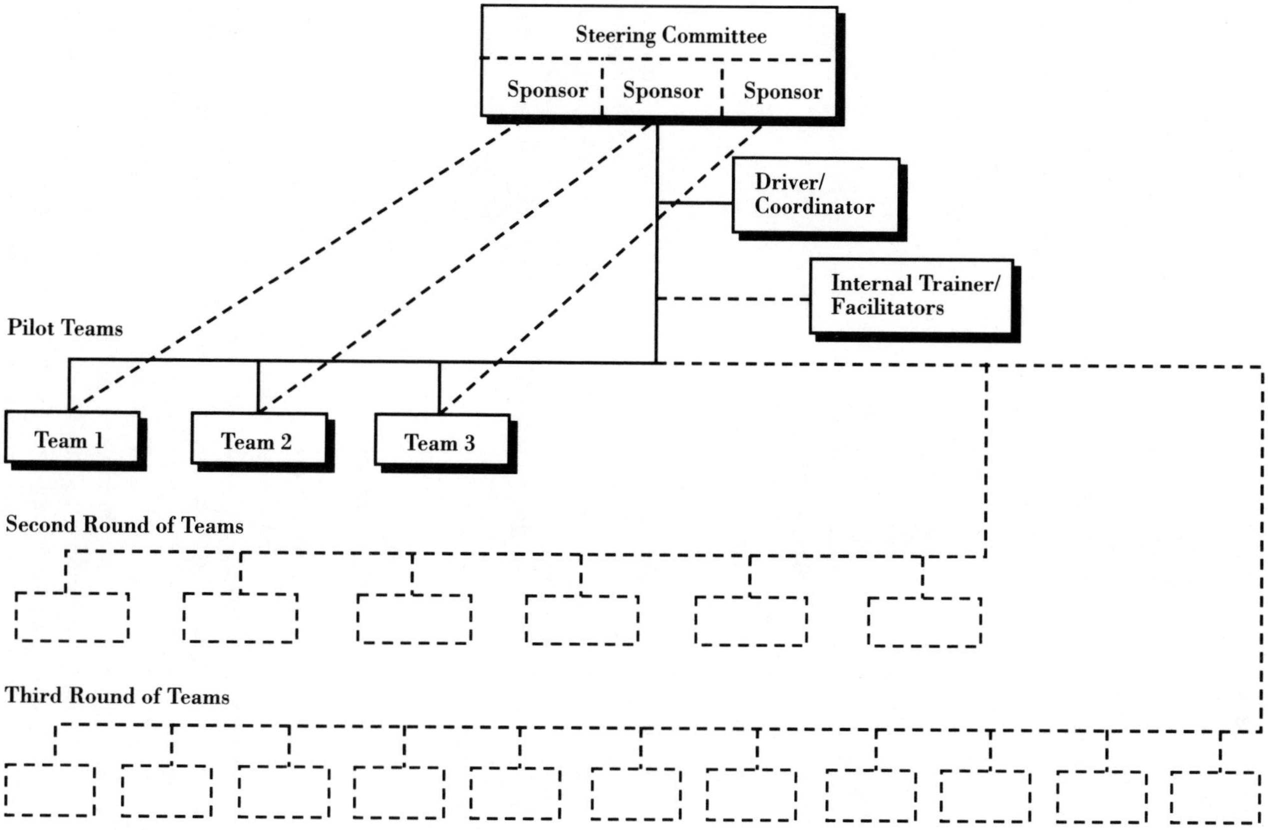

Analyzing the Opportunities

Chartering begins with the evaluation of opportunities and the preliminary selection of projects as outlined in Chapter 3. Ideally, there are several opportunities from which to choose, and the choice can be made on the basis of the extent of resources to be committed, the importance of the opportunity to accomplish the business imperatives, and selection criteria agreed to by the Steering Committee in advance.

Companies typically go through three stages in the process of identifying opportunities:

• *Stage 1.* The first time teams are chartered the opportunities are often very obvious, dramatic, and exciting. They represent the "low-hanging fruit" and are ripe, just waiting to be plucked.

• *Stage 2.* The second round of opportunities is often more difficult. The Steering Committee found it so easy the first time that members may not be prepared for the difficulty of the second choices, which are often not so obvious, dramatic, and exciting as the first set. The opportunities are good, but the decisions are harder.

• *Stage 3.* By the third round of selection, the Steering Committee is more experienced, and the potential opportunities are beginning to surface in large numbers. The prior rounds of activity have identified not only opportunities that were well hidden until now but also ways to seek out new dramatic and exciting possibilities.

The process of sorting opportunities is not an easy one. People do not like to pass up a good opportunity, even when they know they will come back and attack it later. One company president described the process as "one of the hardest set of decisions the management has ever made as a group. We want it all and we want it all now." Recognizing that the improvement effort is a long-term, permanent activity to reshape the entire company operation helps limit the effort to a manageable breadth.

Figure 5-2 shows some of the opportunities presented to one Steering Committee, the selection criteria it had agreed upon, and the projects the committee actually selected. On paper this looks like a straightforward process and a fairly easy decision. In actuality, it represented about four hours of discussion (debate might be a better word) before the decision represented a consensus of the group that all could support.

Figure 5-2. Steering Committee project selection.

Alternatives Presented

- *Order-Entry Process:* The process takes two to three days from receipt of order to release to manufacturing. Four hours seems possible. Manufacturing and shipping takes seven days. Customers want three-to-five-day delivery. The company currently quotes nine-to-thirteen-day delivery.

- *Setup Times:* Setup times on machines average four hours. A reduction to one hour seems possible. There are thirty-five setups per week.

- *Manufacturing, Packaging, and Shipping:* Manufacturing through shipping averages seven days. Actual work time is estimated at two days.

- *Scrap:* Scrap generated during the setup process costs $350,000 per year. A reduction of $250,000 seems possible.

- *Customer Proofs:* Proofs produced by the art department take thirteen days. Four days seems possible. Ten percent of orders require proofs.

- *Sales Rep Commission/Expense Payments:* It takes ten days to process sales rep expense checks after receipt of the expense report and fourteen days to process commission checks after the close of the accounting period. Sales reps are unhappy. One day turnaround of expense checks and three days on commissions seem possible.

Selection Criteria	Projects Chosen
• Tied to business imperatives	• Manufacturing, packaging, shipping
• High payback	
• Learning experience for people	• Order-entry process
• Highly visible in organization	• Setup time reduction
• Completed in six months	
• Projects in different functions	
• No more than three pilot teams	

Rationale

The greatest tie to business imperatives, the highest payback, and the greatest benefit would come from being able to respond to customer needs. Projects are in manufacturing, administration, and distribution. Great visibility comes from reducing quoted delivery time. Even sales reps will see benefit.

Interestingly, much of the discussion in this group centered around issues such as:

- Should we charter two teams in the same functional area?
- Do we really believe we can get the expected benefit?
- Can we afford to commit resources out of that department right now?
- Well, I worked on that before, and I don't think it can be better than it is!
- Are these choices going to be exciting for members of the organization?

These questions rarely surface as the members of the Steering Committee get more accustomed to their role in project selection. Early success has the same effect on them as it has on the rest of the organization: They become believers and accept on faith that they can do what has to be done and become willing to commit the resources necessary.

Setting Goals for Teams

The first question to be asked in chartering a team is: "Why does this team exist?" A team needs to understand that it has a mission, a reason for existence. The process redesign effort is not an employee involvement program for the sake of having all employees on a team and making them feel good. Hopefully they will feel good, but the team has a focused purpose related to improving how the company serves its customers. What is the business imperative this team is attempting to satisfy? What business purpose is going to be served by its success? What specific thing is it going to do to serve that business purpose? Examples of team missions might be:

- To reduce the length of time it takes from receipt of orders to release to manufacturing.
- To provide subscribers to our service faster response to their requests.
- To ensure that patients see a physician within five minutes of walking into the emergency room.
- To reduce the delay for provisioning in turnaround time of an aircraft.

• To reduce the length of time guests wait in line to register at our hotel.

As you will see in Chapters 6 and 7 on process baselining and analysis, it is only partly a coincidence that these examples all focus on time. Time is most often the compelling measure of what must be done at all levels of the improvement effort process.

Determining the Business Objective

Once agreement is reached on why a team is being formed, it is fairly easy to begin to focus in on the strategic business objective that is being targeted. This has usually been pretty well described when the opportunities to be evaluated were being identified. In a sense, this makes the process seem backward—first you look at a specific mission, and then you look at what business objective is being served. Actually, that is not the case.

The specific process has been chosen for examination in the first place because it is a part of a process or processes that support successful achievement of a business imperative. It is important not to lose sight of the fact that by this point you have worked your way down the chain of activities from understanding the customer, visioning, and setting imperatives, and you are now beginning to focus on a specific process redesign objective.

The business objective sets some broader requirements on how the mission is achieved. It would not be acceptable, for example, to reduce lead times to the customer by increasing inventory or to reduce patient waiting time by doubling the number of physicians in the emergency room. At the same time, identifying the business objective establishes the perspective in which the project is viewed from the standpoint of supporting customer-focused business imperatives and ties the project to those imperatives and the vision.

Examples of specific business objectives with which a team might be charged are:

• To increase flexibility and responsiveness to customer delivery needs while improving quality and decreasing costs.
• To increase responsiveness to subscriber needs while improving completeness and reducing costs.
• To increase ability to respond to patient care needs without increasing costs.
• To provide greater flexibility in response to aircraft reprovision-

ing needs or turnaround without eroding the quality of food and beverage service, interfering with passenger access, or increasing costs.
- To increase flexibility and responsiveness to guest needs during registration without sacrificing personal contact or increasing costs.

Establishing Measurable Quantitative Goals

Establishing measurable, challenging, and achievable goals is always a difficult task. Over time, it becomes easier for the Steering Committee as its members gain experience and confidence in what the redesign process can achieve. Breakthrough results should be improvements of 50 to 90 percent in time, quality, or other measures. If a process has not been the subject of improvement efforts and has been in place for more than a few months, such levels of improvement should be readily attainable.

Teams are usually new to the process. They often look at the kinds of goals they believe should be established for breakthrough results and think the Steering Committee has lost its collective mind. One reason people have trouble accepting the feasibility of breakthrough goals is that they think of improvement in terms of working faster or running just a bit cleaner. But achieving breakthrough results requires more than that. It requires redesign of the process to eliminate steps that add no value, to reduce delays and other wastes, and to solve problems that cause rework and scrap. This is a new way of thinking about process improvement for most people.

The ability to achieve breakthrough results at a level of 50 to 90 percent is often identified in even the preliminary data available for evaluation of project opportunities. If it takes two and one-third days from receipt of a customer phone call until delivery of an order to the manufacturing floor, while walking through the process discloses only one hour of work, it should be fairly obvious that the time is reducible by 50 to 90 percent—even if you don't know yet exactly how it will be done. Even on blind faith!

We often find ourselves pushing steering committees to set more aggressive goals. They fear that a too aggressive goal will lead to failure and be a detriment to the process redesign program. Sometimes this fear is the result of not having good quantitative data to use in setting goals. Steering committees usually have little experience to draw upon and find it difficult to set goals on faith. If benchmarking has been conducted as a part of determining customer values, as suggested in Chapter 4, quantitative data are often developed as a part of that effort and are available to use in setting goals based upon what others have found they are able to achieve. If benchmarking was not done, you may want to consider it now to help in establishing quantitative goals.

It is not unusual for such benchmarking to be a first step in team activity—part of the process of baselining the internal process the team is working on. It is entirely appropriate for the team to use the data developed by this benchmarking to test the credibility of the goal they have been assigned and even to renegotiate the goal if the data suggest that it is too aggressive or not aggressive enough.

We regularly ask teams if they would consider it a success or a failure to achieve a 65 percent improvement in a process against a goal of 75 percent. We have never had one that did not respond without hesitation, "success!" Team members understand that a goal may be aggressive. That's why they sometimes think the Steering Committee has lost its mind. But they also understand that a 50 to 90 percent improvement in something is a success in anybody's book.

The real fear, and the real risk, is to set a goal that is not quantifiable, is not measurable, or is vague and not understandable. If the team cannot understand the goal, it not only cannot achieve it, but also team members may not even know the direction in which to pursue it. If the team cannot measure it, people cannot see if they are making progress. They may well make improvements, but they won't know it or be able to demonstrate it. Where is the excitement and energy in that? Success will not be demonstrated in any way, and true failure will result.

Real care should be exercised in setting the measurables and the targets when goals are being considered. Evaluate what data are available and try to identify one to three key measures that will determine success and provide assurance that what the customer sees is a positive impact on how well you satisfy Minimum Acceptable Values.

When the measurable quantitative goal is set, you should also set a date by which the goal is expected to be achieved. Implicit in setting goals and time periods is the consideration of reasonableness, achievability, manageable breadth, and other factors mentioned in Chapter 3. Teams cannot sustain enthusiasm forever, nor do you want to wait forever for results. Typically, the goal should be achievable in sixteen to twenty weeks, sometimes less. Setting a time objective lets the team evaluate both the reasonableness of the target and the reasonableness of the time commitment and resources being made available for the effort.

Some examples of specific measurable goals might be:

- Reduce the cycle time from receipt of an order to release to manufacturing from 2.3 days to four hours within twenty weeks.
- Reduce the cycle time from receipt of a customer order to delivery of proof art from thirteen days to four days within sixteen weeks.
- Reduce the time from receipt of a research request to assignment to a qualified researcher from four hours to one hour within twelve weeks.
- Reduce the time it takes to complete the admitting process and assignment to professional care for a walk-in emergency room patient from twenty minutes to five minutes within twelve weeks.
- Reduce the number of nonvalue-added steps in the reprovisioning process of a plane by 65 percent, and reduce the number of departure delays resulting from reprovisioning delays by 60 percent within twenty weeks.
- Devise a new process for hotel check-in that reduces the time guests wait in line before contact with the front desk to ninety seconds or less. Reduce the time at the front desk for check-in to sixty seconds or less. Complete within sixteen weeks.

Note that in each case the goal is very specific and readily measurable from available data or data that can be easily obtained (except airline departure delay, which always seems to be the fault of air traffic control!) and that a time period is specified. Also, note the different ways of approaching the goals, although time is still an overriding factor.

Goal setting is so important that it is worthwhile to review other examples that do not relate to the specific processes we were using as an exercise here. Some other examples that shed light on how goal setting might be approached include:

- Reduce the amount of oil in spent beans to 0.5 percent by weight (*food processor*).
- Reduce the setup time on the slitter and presses by 75 percent (*printer*).

- Reduce the scrap created by the line start-up by 90 percent (*manufacturer*).
- Reduce the number of handoffs between people by 50 percent (*claims processing*).
- Reduce the time between completion of the service and presentation of the invoice from thirty days to three days (*hospital*).
- Reduce the error rate in the back office by 60 percent (*financial services*).
- Increase the yield on the line from 78 percent to 96 percent (*manufacturer*).

You get the idea. Although time is often the driving force, quality improvement in the form of reject and rework reduction, scrap reduction, and increased yield is often important. Taking unnecessary steps out of the process by eliminating those that do not add value is often important. Increasing flexibility and reducing response times can be key.

Selecting the Team

Once the specific process to be studied has been identified, team members can be selected. The selection of the specific process and the identification of the goals determine what functions need to be represented on the team. The Steering Committee should be able to determine the functions to be represented fairly easily, even if the Steering Committee members do not have enough detailed familiarity with people in those functions to choose the team members. If they are unable to choose team members themselves, they can do so with the help of middle management in the appropriate areas.

The most successful teams generally have between six and nine members representing the functions involved in the process being studied. Fewer than six people may work for certain problem-solving tasks, but more than nine is rarely necessary or recommended. Two or three team members usually come from the department most heavily involved in the process, with the balance spread over remaining departments having involvement. It is desirable to include representatives of departments providing inputs to the process and representatives of departments receiving work outputs of the process. Some teams even include outside suppliers or customers.

It is better to select team members from those people closest to the work, usually those directly involved in the performance of the tasks. They should be those who are most familiar with the process and the interfaces between the process and others with which it interacts.

A first-line supervisor is sometimes included if his/her presence is not expected to be intimidating to other team members or dominating in discussions. If a first-line supervisor is involved, careful consideration should be given to the inclusion of team members at the worker level from his/her department on the team. The advisability of doing so depends on the specific supervisor and employees.

Participation by higher level management is not appropriate for most teams and should be discouraged except in rare instances of all-management teams. Examples of teams made up entirely of managers might be:

- A team formed to look at the top-level flow of a process and identify all points at which scrap or rework is created to charter further study of those losses
- A team formed to review pricing policies of the company where most issues will be policy issues
- A team formed to look at the process for obtaining major capital expenditure approval in a multidivision, multisite, multinational *Fortune* 100 company

In selecting team members, consideration should be given to their work styles and personalities. The objective is to form a group that interacts effectively, allows participation by all who have something to contribute, and works toward accomplishment of the goal. A cohesive team is expected to be formed during the training and early formative stages of its efforts. Some key considerations and attributes to consider in choosing team members include:

- Demonstrated desire to achieve results
- Ability to be open-minded and think "outside the box"
- Participates well in groups of peers
- Credibility with peers
- Knowledgeable about the process
- Supportiveness of the supervisor

Choosing a Team Leader

A team leader is designated from among the team members. The Steering Committee may want to consider that fact in choosing team members. If there is no suitable candidate for the team leader position, someone originally selected for the team may have to be replaced with another person to provide a suitable candidate.

The Steering Committee normally selects a team leader at the time of team chartering. But if the team members are not very well known to the Steering Committee, the committee may want to wait until some time during the training and team formation process to make a selection after observing how people behave in the team activity. Other team positions are selected by the team members themselves during the building stages of their formation.

When the team process is well instilled in the organization and team members have experience with previous team activity and the team process, they may choose their own team leaders. By that time they are familiar with the role of the team leader and can select a qualified person. Until then, however, it would be better for the Steering Committee to make the choice after considering the people available against the required skills.

Team leaders are not intended to be the people who come up with the solutions. They are not appointed for their technical expertise but rather for their skills at managing the team process or ability to acquire those skills quickly. They may not be the team member most familiar with the process being studied. The role of the team leader is more one of making sure that the team process works. Team leaders are responsible for the mechanics of seeing that team supplies are available, that records are kept, that the team members are at the meetings, that they participate in their respective roles, etc.

Team leaders are in charge of preparing the agenda and setting times for agenda items. They may collect reports from those who are gathering data outside the meetings and distribute those facts to other team members. They should talk with individual team members who may be exhibiting behavior at meetings that suggests they are having a problem with the process or whose behavior is disruptive to the team effort. Team leaders have a conflict resolution role in that respect.

The team leader is probably the main communications contact with the Steering Committee and driver/coordinator (whose role is discussed later), although we encourage sharing that role with other team members. The leader may also be a primary communicator with middle management.

Key attributes of team leaders are very similar to those of team members. But the team leader often has more credibility with the balance of the team and with management in the early stages of team activity. As times goes on, the credibility of other team members will usually catch up.

Selecting Other Team Positions

There are two other team positions of importance, although the team members themselves should be allowed to determine whether or not they are necessary, can be combined with other positions, or should be rotated. These are the positions of team scribe and team facilitator.

The team scribe is responsible for generating minutes of the meeting in the form and on the schedule established by the team. This individual may have other duties assigned by the team for duplication of materials received at such times as between meetings.

The team leader is not necessarily the team facilitator, although the leader may sometimes fill that role. The team facilitator is responsible for calling attention to the fact that the team has digressed from the agenda, is not holding to times established and needs to decide how to deal with it, is being dominated by one person or one person is being left out, etc. Some individuals have a natural ability to perform this role, but most need special training to understand when and how to intervene in the group's activity.

Team facilitator can be a difficult role to fill. Facilitators need to be able to separate from the discussion and observe what is going on to diagnose and intervene properly. Yet they are on the team specifically because they fill a valuable role in the process analysis that is being done because of their work position, so they must also be free to participate as needed. This is one reason the team leader can seldom fill this role in addition to his/her other responsibilities. The leader is often leading the discussion, flip charting, or otherwise engaged and has a more difficult time than other team members in disengaging temporarily to observe the proceedings.

Enrolling the Team

The team approach to process redesign is a voluntary activity. Forced participation does not produce excellent results unless the team members become more motivated once work begins. This sometimes happens, but it cannot be depended upon.

Thoughtful enrollment of participants begins building the team immediately, as the members come to first activities knowing why they are there, what they are expected to accomplish, and why they are expected to accomplish it. They are prepared to take time away from their regular work for team activity and know how the regular work is being dealt with while they work on the team goals.

Enrolling team members begins with obtaining the support of their supervisors. The supervisors need to understand why someone from their department was chosen, what they will be doing, what the time commitment will be, and for how long. They need to have an opportunity to express their concerns and have them addressed. Someone from the Steering Committee who is very familiar with the Team Charter and the improvement process should meet with the potential team members' supervisors, discuss the effort with them, and obtain their endorsement of the selection.

The potential team members and team leaders should then be approached personally and shown the team goals, told who else is being invited to participate, and be given an opportunity to ask questions. If potential team members refuse to participate, someone else should be chosen to fill their spot.

Providing Team Resources

Providing Expert Support to Teams

Often a team is given a goal that requires it to explore quite specific parts of the process or to assess the impact of planned changes or improvements in technical areas for which there is no expertise on the team. They may require input from experts whose level of involvement does not justify full team membership. Examples might be cost accounting, industrial engineering, laboratory analysts, or other support functions that have data or information that would be helpful or can make contributions to specific problem solutions. A sales or marketing representative is often designated to assist a team in interpreting customer expectations.

These people are called team resources. If possible, they should go through training with the team to learn more about what the team is doing and how it is going about the task. The resources do not attend team meetings regularly but do attend when invited, usually for a specific purpose. These people may be managers whose participation on the team would be inappropriate in a conventional role. The time demands on team resource people are usually relatively low.

Sponsoring a Team

Another form of resource for the team is the team sponsor. The team sponsor is a member of the Steering Committee who is assigned responsibility for supporting one or more teams on behalf of the Steering Committee. The sponsor does not have to be the managerial representative for the functional area or areas affected by the team, but that is often helpful in resolving problems during the process and in understanding what the team needs when it is preparing to test changes or improvements. Figure 5-3 describes some guidelines for team sponsors that clarify the duties of that position.

Driving/Coordinating the Improvement Process

The position of process redesign driver or coordinator is both a team resource and a Steering Committee resource. The driver/coordinator reports to the Steering Committee and attends its meetings as an active participant and member. The coordinator/driver normally spends 25 to 100 percent of his or her time ensuring that the overall process redesign effort is progressing as expected and that results tied to customer-focused business imperatives will be achieved.

As a team resource, the driver/coordinator can make sure that meeting space is available, technical training and support are available when necessary, interpersonal conflicts are resolved, middle management is informed of what is going on, and communication with stakeholders is occurring. Driver/coordinators attend most team meetings and may provide technical expertise in analyzing processes

Figure 5-3. Guidelines for team sponsors.

- Works through team leaders, not through team meetings.
- Helps the team remove roadblocks and solve problems.
- Serves as liaison between the team and Steering Committee.
- Has a supporting rather than initiating role with the team.
- Has no decision-making role with the team.
- Can attend team meeting with advance notice.
- Should meet with the team leader weekly to discuss progress.
- Should informally stay in contact with other team members.
- Keeps Steering Committee up to date between team reports.

and solving problems to assist the teams. They can assist in the process of implementing solutions when the team is ready. They may also be the training resource for the teams and often act as a facilitator.

As a Steering Committee resource, driver/coordinators run the process redesign effort. They provide a readily available communications link between the Steering Committee and the teams, supplementing that provided by the team sponsor.

The driver/coordinator may be an upper-level manager, usually one level below the Steering Committee members, but is often a "rising star" lower in the organization. The position is an excellent one in which to test the capabilities of a person being considered for higher management responsibility. It is a highly visible position, interacting with all parts of the organization and requiring real coordination, facilitation, coaching, and management skills. Figure 5-4 outlines some attributes and duties of a good driver/coordinator.

Placing Limits on Teams

Although teams need to be given a great deal of freedom in analyzing processes and testing and implementing solutions, management does not give them unlimited authority and freedom in their efforts to

Figure 5-4. Attributes and duties of a driver/coordinator.

Attributes	Duties
• Broad organizational familiarity	• Identifies key issues needing attention.
• Knows how the company works	
• Organized, detailed	• Plays a major role in communication to organization.
• Credible with most in company	• Helps team leaders and facilitators.
• Good facilitator	• Acts as an internal process consultant.
• Achievement-oriented	
• Makes thing happen/gets results	• Attends team meetings regularly.
• Comfortable, at ease with workers	• Is a coach and cheerleader.
• Excellent communicator	• Coaches managers and supervisors.

reach the established goal. Boundaries are placed around their activity to protect the organization and the team members.

Defining the Scope

One boundary that is established is a clear definition of the scope of the process the team is charged with improving. The Steering Committee needs to ensure that the activities of the team do not encroach on areas that were not intended and that the scope is manageable for the team to reach its goals in the prescribed time. For example, a team goal of improving the process from receipt of an order until availability for release to manufacturing could be interpreted in a number of ways:

Receipt of the order might mean:

- By the sales rep in the field
- By the mail room
- By the clerk who opens the envelope
- By the person assigned to enter the order in the computer
- By the person who answers the phone

Ready for release to manufacturing might mean:

- A work order is ready to be cut.
- A work order is cut and released.
- A work order is cut and materials are staged
- A work order is cut, materials are staged, and the line is ready.

Ambiguities like these can lead to the team spending time on the wrong problems and failing to solve the real problems it was chartered to address. This is avoided by specifying starting and ending points for the project scope. The Steering Committee should specifically define the process to be analyzed by choosing those starting and stopping points and identifying them to the team.

Determining What the Team Can and Cannot Do

Further boundaries are placed on the team by defining certain key things that in the minds of the Steering Committee the team can or cannot do in the pursuit of its goal. One overriding "cannot" that should probably always be present is "The team cannot do anything in the pursuit of its goal that might hurt the customer."

Other "cans" and "cannots" that are often found include the amount of funds that might be expended without Steering Committee review (usually $500 to $5,000), the extent of physical layout changes that might be made without review, or the contacts outside the company that might be made without review. Each situation and team goal is unique with respect to the things that teams can and cannot do, and the lists ought to be tailored to those specific situations and the needs of the company at that time.

Determining the Resource Commitment

The primary resource commitment in improvement team activity is the time of the team members. The team members need to understand clearly how much time they can spend away from their regular work tasks in order to support the improvement team activity. Typically, two hours per week for a team meeting and an average of two hours per week outside the meetings for preparation, data gathering, data analysis, and other work are a minimum for breakthrough process redesign.

Some organizations double the time commitment in the first four to six weeks of team activity to accelerate the start of team efforts on process analysis and understanding the problems. Usually, adding to the time commitment to allow two team meetings per week, or more time for outside study, is not productive after the first few meetings. There are tasks in data gathering and analysis that simply require elapsed calendar time and passage of some volume of work in order to be valuable. There is no way to speed that up.

Managing the Team

The teams need to know to whom they report and to whom they are responsible for guidance and direction, if necessary. Normally, this is the Steering Committee, assisted by the driver/coordinator and the team sponsor. The Team Charter should specify who or what the governing body is.

To reinforce this relationship, and to improve communications in both directions between the team and the Steering Committee, we like to have teams meet with the Steering Committee monthly for a brief report on what they have done in the past month and what they intend to do in the next month. This is an opportunity for the team members to ask for approval of planned actions or for authority to do things they feel are necessary to reach the goal. The Steering Committee can also ask about why the team is doing certain things and provide support and encouragement.

Stakeholder Identification

As the team pursues its goal, its activities affect a number of people in the organization who are not directly involved in the team activity. These are people who have an impact on or are impacted by the work the team is doing. We call these people stakeholders. They have a "stake" in what the team is doing. They need to be identified as quickly as possible so that lines of communication can be opened with them in order that the team may keep them informed and enlist their support.

Some stakeholders are directly and significantly affected by team actions. They are usually obvious to the Steering Committee and are identified right away. Others are not so obvious. Perhaps it will not be clear that there will be any impact on them until the team begins to identify solutions to problems and recommend actions. Perhaps they have no direct real relationship with the process at all, but the team knows that they worry about some piece of the process or that they see connections that do not appear valid but are nevertheless potential issues. They are stakeholders as well. The team identifies these people as the process moves along and takes care to recognize the need for communication and reassurance.

An often overlooked group of stakeholders are the members of the departments represented by team members. These coworkers have a great interest in the team's activities and are directly affected by any changes. Often they are picking up the work of team members when they attend meetings and do team work. Sometimes, because a representative of the department is on the team, it is easy to forget that these people have concerns and expectations that may be very strong. Special effort needs to be made to communicate what the team is doing to solicit input and ideas from these peers of team members.

Failure to deal effectively with stakeholders of all types leads to resistance to changes and skepticism or suspicion about the process. Properly dealt with, stakeholders can become powerful allies of the team in implementing changes and accomplishing the goal.

Figure 5-5. Team charge/charter guide.

1. The mission of the team (why it exists) is _____

   _____ .

2. The business objective the team is working to achieve is _____

   _____ .

3. The quantitative measure of team goals are _____

   _____ .

4. The team will begin work _____ and reach its goal by _____ .

5. The team leader is _____ .

6. The team members are _____

   _____ .

7. The team sponsor is _____ .

8. The governing body to whom the team reports is _____

   _____ and reports will be given to them at _____ intervals.

9. The scope of the team responsibility begins with _____

   _____ and ends with _____ .

10. The team members are authorized to devote up to _____ hours
    per week to the effort.

11. The boundaries of the team activities are:

They can:

_____

_____

_____

_____

_____

They cannot:

_____

_____

_____

_____

12. The stakeholders the team should recognize are: _____

_____

_____

_____

_____ .

13. Other comments: _____

_____

_____

_____

Converting a Charge to a Charter

What has been referred to as a Team Charter throughout this discussion is really a "team charge" at this point. It is a product only of the Steering Committee and has received only preliminary review by team members during their enrollment, if at all. At the first team meeting, the team needs to be given an opportunity to review this charge in detail, have a preliminary discussion of what data are already available, and determine whether they can buy in to the charge as written or not. If not, they need to negotiate any differences with the Steering Committee. Typically, the areas teams ask to negotiate are centered around resources, beginning and ending points of the process, "can" and "cannot" boundaries (particularly additional "cans"), and the addition of stakeholders.

Surprisingly, teams rarely seriously disagree with the specific measurable goals. Perhaps their greater familiarity with the problems regarding the processes in the company makes them more confident that breakthrough improvement can be made, and they accept truly challenging goals without reservations. If the team does desire to negotiate the goal, the Steering Committee is usually able to show why it believes the goal can be met.

Once the team reaches a consensus decision that all can support the charge and it is willing to commit to the Steering Committee to accomplish the goal as specified, the charge becomes the team's formal charter. The team is now ready to begin forming, training, and pursuing the goal.

Documenting and Communicating the Charter

When the team has accepted its charter, it is valuable to document the charter and publicize the goals within the company. The vision, system pullers, and business imperatives have been communicated to the entire organization by now, and every effort is being made to create and sustain a customer focus. Communicating the charters of the improvement teams is the final step in showing the organization the commitment that is being made to achieving the organization's goals and realizing the vision.

Figure 5-5 is a sample charter document that has been used by many companies for preparing team charges and charters and communicating those charters to the organization.

6

Creating a Value-Added
Flow Analysis

Joe and his fellow staff members filed into the meeting room for their Steering Committee meeting. Each had a list of favorite projects tucked carefully under his or her arm. They had gathered some preliminary data to determine where the greatest opportunities for improvement might be. "This shouldn't take long," Joe thought.

The meeting began with the president saying, "First, let's review the data that we have all collected, and then we can list all the possible processes to consider for redesign." The list for consideration had ten different options. Joe, of course, suggested the widget-making process and the engineering change process. Other options were the process to create a purchase order, the process for job postings and hiring, the financial closing and reporting process, and the product-development process.

Then the debate began. The engineering manager and the quality assurance manager immediately said, "The engineering change process can't really be improved. You don't understand. The widget regulatory agency insists on having those signatures in place. All we need is more help in that area to catch up, and we'll be fine. We really think widget making is the place to begin."

The engineering manager continued, "The product-development process is different: No two products are alike, so you can't measure it. Besides, this is not a science, it's an art. Products get created when they get created. There's no way to know when they will finally work. You can't schedule creativity. If widget making could just get its act together and be able to make widgets when we need them, everything would be fine."

Joe was beginning to think about ordering lunch in. This was going to take longer than expected. The finance manager was next. "The financial closing process can't really be any quicker," he said. "We're working overtime already. We can't close the books any faster without the information, and the information just takes time to get." The information systems manager chimed in to say, "Yeah, and don't expect major systems changes. We have a one-year backlog of work already."

The human resources manager added, "I don't know how you can improve the hiring process to get better candidates more quickly. It seems to me that it just takes time." Joe thought, "Obviously, everyone agreed to beginning process redesign as long as it wasn't in his or her department."

The president had been patient long enough. He exploded, "Wait a minute. I thought that we had agreed that in order to satisfy our customer's values and remain competitive, we must improve at breakneck speed. The whole reason for process redesign is to challenge the way we've always done things and do them better in the future. We can't wait. You'll each buy some time by improving these processes."

"Hooray for the president," Joe thought. "Now we can get on with things." After carefully considering their criteria for pilot selection, the group decided on widget making, financial closing and reporting, and product development.

The group struggled with the Team Charters, constantly challenging whether breakthrough goals could be met. Finally, at 7:00 P.M., the staff filed out of the meeting room—exhausted, but ready to go.

You now have an understanding of how to select processes for innovative redesign efforts. You know how that selection ties back to the customer and the realization of the collective vision for the successful organization of the future. It is time to begin looking at specifically *how* to analyze and redesign those processes. This chapter introduces you to the important concept of value-added flow analysis. Later, we will examine other tools for baselining and analyzing processes and techniques for problem solving. You will then have a complete and flexible tool kit for innovative redesign of processes that you can successfully apply to any type of process—manufacturing, administrative, service.

Innovative process redesign requires an understanding of:

- The components of a process
- The characteristics of flow

- The value-added concept
- Process analysis tools
- Problem-solving tools

We introduced you to the components of a process—inputs, linked tasks, work outputs—in Chapter 2. As we continue, we will revisit those components in more detail and relate your understanding of processes to an understanding of the analysis tools and when and how to use them.

Understanding Process Flow

In Chapter 2 we described a process as a series of tasks or steps that receive inputs and produce work outputs. We said that the tasks or steps are linked for that purpose. Work outputs are used by specific customers or internal clients of the process. Inputs are received from external suppliers or internal providers. Figure 6-1 shows some of the things that could be considered as inputs to the process or work outputs from the process.

The inputs, tasks, and work outputs are linked by "flow." Flow is what changes the process from a static entity consisting of the work progressing through the inputs, tasks, and outputs into a dynamic

Figure 6-1. Process inputs and outputs.

Process Inputs	Process Outputs
Materials/Supplies	Materials/Supplies
Information	Information
Data	Services
Documents	Data
Measurements	Documents
People	Scrap
Methods	Effluent
Machines	By-products
Services	Reports

concept. It introduces the variables that both require and open the door to innovative redesign techniques. Flow varies from hour to hour and day to day. Flow is affected by volume, mix, problems, new customer requirements, changes in people, environment, and a host of other factors. It is affected by the inputs and must be responsive to what customers and internal clients want from the outputs. Flow is the work process in action.

Innovative process redesign is a combination of redesigning the static entity (the steps from inputs to work outputs) and the dynamic entity (the flow). The two go hand-in-hand.

Continuous Flow

The ideal flow through a process is continuous and regular, hour after hour, day after day. The process is consistent and the outputs come in a "drumbeat": regular, linear, and with even capacity utilization, while synchronized with the needs of the customer or client. Continuous and regular flow is very difficult to achieve in most processes, but we can come very close with careful process design and balance. Examples of processes that come closest to continuous flow are chemical processes, glass manufacturing, and paper making. Continuous flow does not occur in administrative or service processes or most manufacturing processes unless it is designed in. It is not inherent in those processes, even if they are running very well.

Continuous flow is like liquid running through a pipe. Most processes handling discrete items, whether they are manufacturing materials or paper or information bits, move their work in batches. The bigger the batch, the further we are from continuous flow. Reducing the size of the batches moves us closer to continuous flow. A batch size of one unit would be the ideal and would be as close to continuous flow as we could get with discrete products. Figure 6-2 shows how batches of discrete product can approach continuous flow.

The closer the process is to continuous flow, the more balanced and synchronized it is. Balance and synchronization are concepts that we will discuss further in more detail as they are important to effective redesign of the process. They are both the way of creating and the outcome of a regular drumbeat of work flow through the process. We must solve the problems and correct the conditions that are preventing balance and synchronization before we can approach continuous flow in any process.

Figure 6-2. Approaching continuous flow.
The ideal of **continuous flow** is like flow through a pipe:

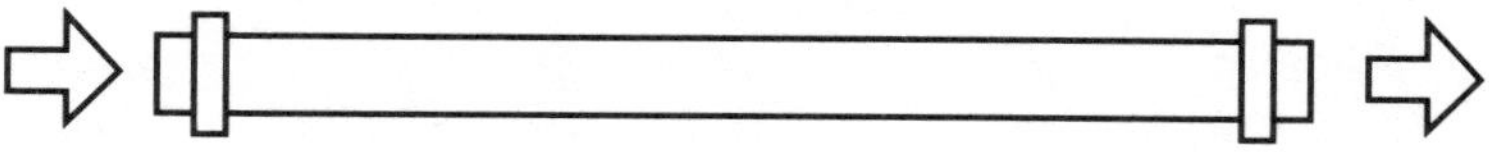

With discrete products, a **one-at-a-time** flow comes closest to this ideal:

In traditional processes, activities are often separated from one another and are run as independent operations. Work is moved between them in **batches**, resulting in **intermittent flow**:

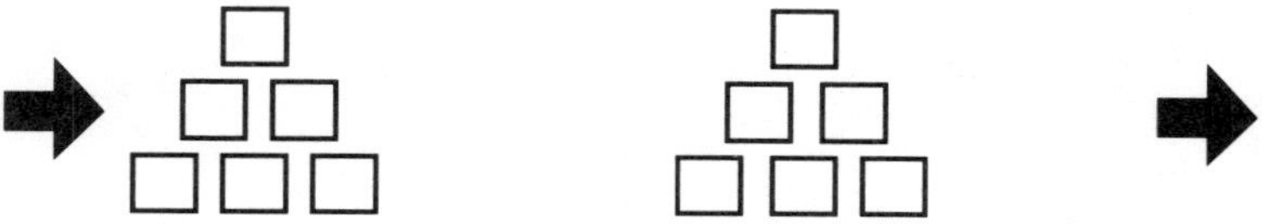

Reducing the quantity moved at any one time and increasing the frequency at which the moves are made will make the flow more continuous:

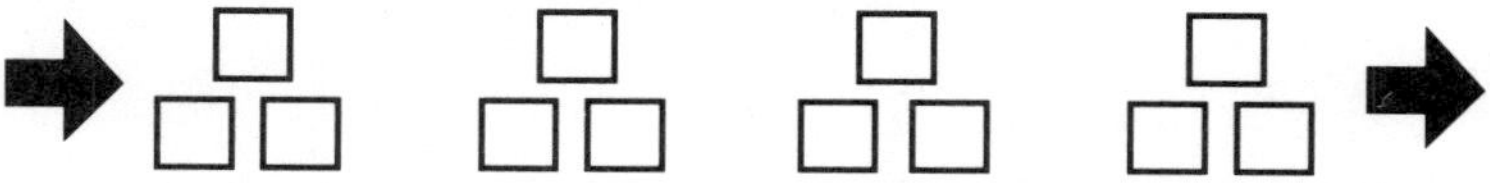

Continuing to reduce move quantity and increase move frequency will ultimately result in a **one-at-a-time** flow:

Balancing the Flow

A balanced flow is one in which all of the linked tasks or steps produce at exactly the same rate. When we achieve this there is no need for piles of work between steps and no need for waiting periods caused by those piles of work. Batches can be eliminated. Work can proceed from step to step without stopping. A perfectly balanced flow has the least work in process and the lowest cost and takes the least time. It is the most responsive and flexible in meeting changing customer requirements. Figure 6-3 shows the difference between balanced work flow and flow that is not in balance. The tank represents any pile of waiting work—manufacturing materials, paper on desks, people in lines, etc.

Synchronizing the Flow

Synchronized flow works in unison with the customer or client and the suppliers or providers to develop balance all the way through from inputs to work outputs. The process can quickly produce work outputs in response to changing customer needs. It produces what is needed when it is needed. It is flexible and responsive and readily accommodates changes while remaining in balance. It is the ideal flow and it results when:

- Flow is balanced.
- Problems are eliminated.
- Flexibility exists in the process.

Figure 6-3. Balanced and imbalanced work flow.

If all operations have different flow rates:

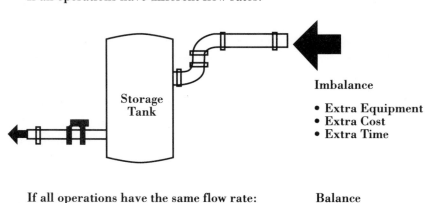

Imbalance

- Extra Equipment
- Extra Cost
- Extra Time

If all operations have the same flow rate: Balance

- Least Equipment
- Least Cost
- Least Time

Recognizing Interruptions to Flow

Unfortunately, processes are rarely designed to be balanced or synchronized. Even if they are, they don't stay that way long when you begin making changes to accommodate new requirements or the desires of individuals working within the process.

Regardless of the nature of the process—manufacturing, administrative, service—there are common conditions that cause interruptions and make work going through the process wait. Waits are when flow stops at some point. It could be work in process manufacturing inventory, or a pile of unprocessed forms on an office desk, or you standing in line at the bank. Some common conditions that cause flow interruptions and cause work to wait include:

- Tasks that are not balanced producing at different rates, causing piles of work to build up between tasks.
- Physical separation of operations, causing work to move in batches and creating piles of work between moves.
- Working in batches, causing intermittent flow. (A "typical" unit of work can be viewed as always the first one into a batch and the last one out because it waits the entire time.)
- Long setup or changeover times to convert equipment or parts of the process for a new purpose (machine setup, form changes in printers, setting up for manual collation, creating a new waiting line at peak periods), causing the process to stop and all work to wait. This often creates the perception that large batches will be better—which introduces all of the problems of batches.
- Variation in process inputs, such as out-of-specification material, errors on forms, machine breakdowns, late arrival of needed supplies, an approval supervisor not available, or people needing training.

These variations add time and cost to the process and reduce flexibility and responsiveness. They are contrary to maximizing customer value and are almost always in conflict with the needs of your business imperatives. Correcting them is key to innovative process redesign.

The interruptions to flow just described all lead to waiting time in the process. A good way to characterize many processes is continuous waiting rather than continuous flow. When you examine most of the processes in your company you find that the waiting, or idle, time for work going through the process far outweighs the time in which productive effort is actually being applied to the work. It is not uncommon to find the waiting time representing as much as 99 percent of the time the work is going through the process. What a waste!

Understanding the Value-Added Concept

The concept of value-added is one of the most important in our study of process redesign. By our definition, all processes exist to produce a work output: a physical product, information, reports or services, etc. for customers or clients. The customer describes what is of value to him/her about that work product or service.

Some internal processes feed work outputs to other processes rather than directly to the customer. But their work output must also be of value to the customer by providing needed inputs that allow internal clients to better meet customer needs. Providing value to the customer has to be the overriding reason for the process and all steps in the process.

If the work output is of value to the customer, he or she is willing to pay for it. Process steps that add value are essential to satisfying customer needs and cannot be eliminated. Most often, these steps are the ones that physically change the work and affect the work output in a way that makes it more valuable to the customer. Activities that are done at the specific request of the customer, but that do not physically change the work output, are also of value because the customer, by requesting them, is showing willingness to pay for them.

Legal and Regulatory Steps

Legal and regulatory requirements are a tricky area when it comes to determining whether or not a step is of value. Clearly, if there are regulatory requirements applicable to a process, a product, or a service, such as in the pharmaceutical industry or medical services, customers are willing to pay to have those requirements met. They cannot sell or use the product unless it is in compliance with regulations. It is of no value to them otherwise.

The difficulty arises in looking at tasks that are done individually. The regulatory requirements in most industries do not specify step-by-step activities for compliance. They specify a required outcome.

The steps to arrive at that outcome have been dictated by a company quality control or regulatory affairs department under the guise of being "required by the regulatory agency." Sometimes a financial process includes steps "required by the auditors or the taxing agencies" for the same reason. If the required outcome can be achieved without the step that the quality, regulatory affairs, or financial department has specified, that step is not adding value.

Steps Necessary to Run the Business

There are a number of processes in businesses that are essential to running the business but that do not appear to meet the requirements of adding value by physically changing the work or product or being something for which the customer is willing to pay. You might question whether the entire process is of value or should be eliminated. Sending an invoice is a good example. Do customers really care if you send them an invoice? Are they willing to pay you to do so? Surprisingly, the answer is "yes."

Think back to our family tree of processes in Chapter 2. The top-level process is the entire company receiving inputs and converting them to work outputs to the customer. That process, in its entirety, is of value to the customer if the customer pays for the product or service. It is producing the product or service that the customer values enough to pay for. Processes such as sending the invoice, managing the cash, collecting delinquencies, and managing employee benefits are of value to the customer because they allow the business to survive and prosper so that it will remain able to supply the products and services the customer values in the future. If the business fails because it never sends invoices, the customer suffers. Preventing that is of value to the customer.

These processes, like any other process, may contain individual steps that do not add value, however. Steps that do not add value are a waste; they add unnecessary time and expense while providing no value in the eyes of the customer. A key step in the innovative redesign of processes to reduce time, increase flexibility, maximize responsiveness, improve quality, and reduce cost is the elimination of these wasteful activities.

Nonvalue-Added Processes

We sometimes do find processes offering no value to the customer in their entirety. The most common examples are the process that

develops in many companies to expedite orders around the normal
order process system, the process to expedite "hot" parts to the
production floor, or the process to deal with customers "impatient"
about the normal process at the bank.

Organizations tend not to think of these as processes because
they are not specifically designed by someone to meet a need. They
grow up spontaneously, in most cases, in response to a pressing
need recognized by the people working in the intended process who
cannot get the necessary work done in that "normal" process. Often
these "invisible" processes have printed forms and documentation
and other controls, suggesting that they have a value and importance
that really does not exist. In reality, they are temporary solutions to
process problems for which the root cause needs to be determined,
and they are of no value.

Defining Value

The discussion of these concepts leads us to some definitions:

A *value-added step* is one that (1) physically changes the work
passing through the process or the work output produced to
make it more valuable to the customer, (2) is a step requested by
the customer that he/she is willing to pay for, or (3) is a legally
required mandate.

A *nonvalue-added step* is one (1) for which the customer is
unwilling to pay, and (2) that does not change the work output
in a way that makes it more valuable to the customer.

Most value-added steps in manufacturing processes are fairly
easy to identify. They physically change the product as it moves
through the process. The distinction may be less clear in administrative or personal service processes. Figure 6-4 gives some examples of
value-added and nonvalue-added activities and may help clarify some
of the distinctions.

Omitting those processes which offer no value at all, the typical
process we encounter in innovative process redesign opportunities
has 5 to 20 percent value-added steps. This suggests that 80 percent
or more of the steps in most processes could be eliminated without
adverse impact on the value offered to the customer. What an
opportunity!

The concept of value-added and nonvalue-added steps provides

Figure 6-4. Examples of value-added and nonvalue-added activities.

Value-Added Activities	Nonvalue-Added Activities
Entering Order	Waiting/Storing
Ordering Materials/Supplies	Moving
Preparing Drawing	Kitting/Staging
Assembling	Counting
Legally Mandated Testing	Inspecting
Packaging	Checking
Shipping to Customer	Recording
Processing Customer Deposit	Obtaining Approvals
Examining Patient	Testing
Filing Insurance Claim	Reviewing
Dispensing Event Tickets	Copying
Fueling Airplane	Filing
	Revising/Reworking
	Tracking Work

us with a very valuable tool for initial analysis of a process: the value-added flow analysis. Using this analysis we can:

- Identify and measure significant redesign opportunities.
- Establish a baseline of performance against which to measure improvement.
- Determine which tools are most useful in redesigning the process.

A value-added flow analysis involves several steps:

1. Defining and mapping the process to be studied step by step
2. Quantitatively measuring some key characteristics of the process
3. Identifying the ideal process flow
4. Analyzing the process using the appropriate tools to find how to approach ideal flow

The balance of this chapter is devoted to the first three steps in this process.

Mapping the Process

The process map is useful to gain an overall understanding of the process and identify major steps. A process map can be developed at several process levels, much like the family tree of processes discussed in Chapter 2. It generally avoids detail and concentrates on providing an understandable graphical description of a process that would be difficult to understand or describe in narrative form. It is likely to describe the process in terms of the operations performed. The end product is a diagram that shows how the major steps in a process link together.

The process map is particularly useful for analyzing very complex flows—those with many routes or feeder branches. These are particularly difficult flows to describe in words, but a process map makes the relationships very clear. Understanding these relationships and the complexity of the process is useful in setting starting and stopping points for the redesign effort and ensuring that the scope of the effort is both complete and manageable by a team in the specified time period.

Figure 6-5 shows some process maps at different levels. As you can see, the development of the process map also affords an opportunity to begin collecting some data about the process. Cycle time—the time necessary for one unit to pass through the process or step—is a particularly useful measure to begin adding to the map. Areas of significant buildup of piles of work, major defect-producing steps, and other data also become apparent. We will discuss additional measures further in Chapter 7 as we begin to analyze other aspects of the process in detail.

Constructing the Detailed Process Map

The value-added flow analysis begins with construction of a detailed process map at the lowest level. This is a detailed examination of the process with some unique characteristics:

- It documents the flow of work, not the things people do.
- It follows one unit of work as it passes through the process. The unit may be one item, one batch, a particular service, or

Figure 6-5. Process maps at different levels.

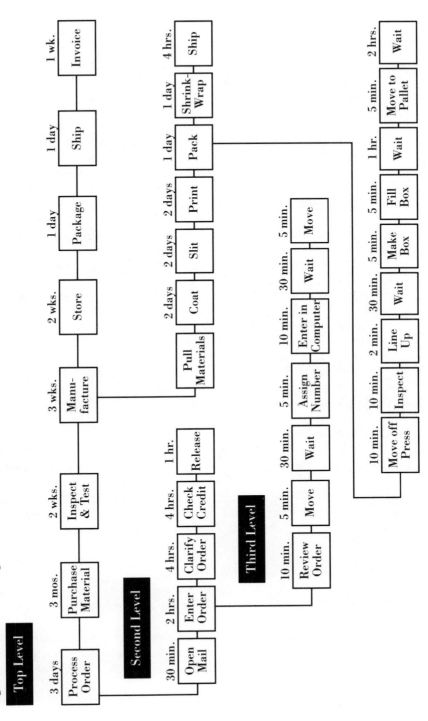

some other increment, but it is always the smallest unit possible to follow separately.

- It documents every step—moves, waits, delays, operations— not just major steps.
- It identifies what really happens to the typical unit of work, not what is supposed to happen according to documentation or what the supervisor may believe to be the process.
- It is developed with and by the employees who actually do the work on the process, not from engineering documentation or supervisory process descriptions.

Developing the detailed process map is like attaching yourself to a unit of work as it begins the process and going through the process with it. The map documents what actually happens to the work going through the process, not what the process design or instructions or routing sheets say is to happen. When complete, the detailed process map tells you everything that unit of work went through.

A detailed process map, or detailed process flow analysis, can be organized in either flow chart form or as a list of steps. The two forms have different advantages and are often used for different purposes.

The flow chart form is a convenient way to develop the detailed process map in a team setting. You can identify the steps one by one and post them on the wall with note cards or Post-it Notes. This lets everyone see the flow as it develops, and all can contribute. It also makes it easy to make changes.

There is usually debate as the team develops the flow, and steps have to be moved around or new steps inserted between steps already identified. This is one of the key values of having a team of people who actually do the work develop the value-added flow analysis. The team interaction is a key part of developing a true picture of the flow. If instead you document what the supervisor says happens or what the standard operating procedure says, you will not have a true picture of what really happens to the work the way the process runs today. You will know only how somebody thought it would run. Interviewing individual team members gets you closer, but you will still be missing the dynamic interaction that brings out the small steps that can be critical to the analysis.

When complete, the flow chart form of a detailed process map is easy to understand and easy to use for discussion purposes. Figure 6-6 shows examples of a detailed process map. Value-added steps are highlighted. Notice how few there are.

The list form of a detailed process map is more appropriately called a detailed flow analysis because it does not look like a map or flow chart. It is easily developed from the graphic flow chart form by simply documenting what the group has agreed to as the true flow for the process. The list form is convenient for adding columns to record data such as time, rejects, inventory, and distance traveled and tabulating them for analysis. As we discuss more data that you can use in analyzing a process in Chapter 7, the value of the list form in collection and analysis of data will become more apparent. Figure 6-7 presents the detailed process map charts from Figure 6-6 in list form.

Teams consisting of people who work with the process are generally surprised by the number of steps in a detailed process map or detailed flow analysis. We often ask the team to estimate the number of steps before the analysis begins. The actual number is usually three to four times their estimate.

Identifying the Value-Added Steps

Once the detailed process map is completed, the next step in the value-added flow analysis is to classify each step as value-added or nonvalue-added. On a flow chart this is easily done by marking each box with a different color keyed to whether it is value-added or nonvalue-added. On a list it can simply be indicated by a code. In Figure 6-6 the nonvalue-added steps have been designated by a line through the corner of the box. The steps are also classified on the lists in Figure 6-7.

Classification of steps may not always be as simple as it appears, and people can disagree about the classification. Controversy often develops around steps such as the regulatory control steps discussed earlier, inspection steps, counting, sorting, and checking. Some feel these are value-added and others do not. We believe that almost without exception these steps are nonvalue-added.

There are valid reasons for some disagreements of this kind. For example, one company produces a class of products consisting of about twelve models of a subassembly for a class of medical devices. The company is a certified just-in-time vendor to one customer that purchases about 75 percent of the production of this class of products from the company. That customer specifically requires, and pays for, a test on each batch produced and a certification document showing test results. The company prefers to run a standard process for all product running on this assembly line, so it performs the same test

(Text continues on page 128)

Figure 6-6. Value-added flow analysis: detailed process map in flow chart form.

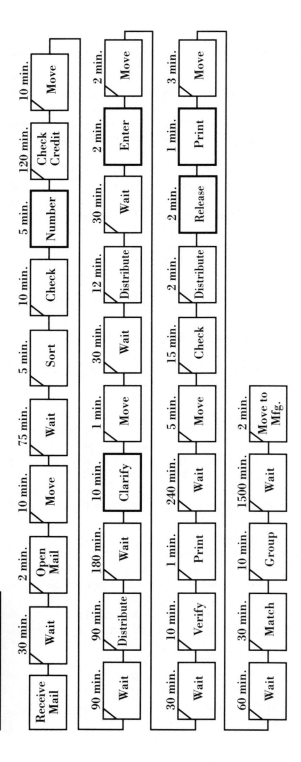

Production Process

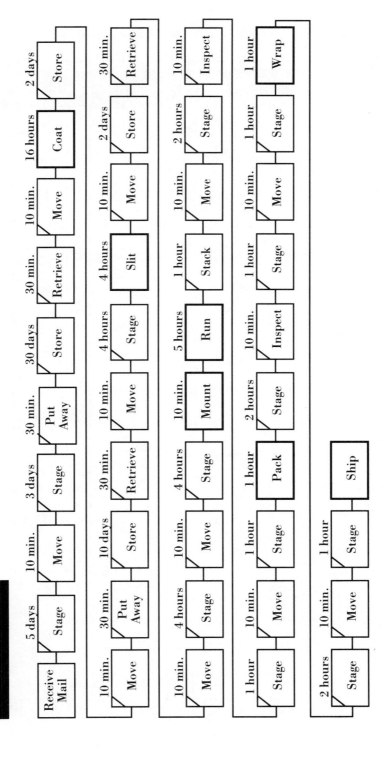

Figure 6-7. Value-added flow analysis: detailed process map in list form.

Case 1— Order Entry Activity	Time VA	Time NVA
Receive mail		
Wait		30 min.
Open mail		2 min.
Move		10 min.
Wait		75 min.
Sort		5 min.
Check		10 min.
Number	*5 min.	
Check credit		120 min.
Move		10 min.
Wait		90 min.
Distribute		90 min.
Wait		180 min.
Clarify	*10 min.	
Move		1 min.
Wait		30 min.
Distribute		12 min.
Wait		30 min.
Enter	*2 min.	
Move		2 min.
Wait		30 min.
Verify		10 min.
Print		1 min.
Wait		240 min.
Move		5 min.
Check		15 min.
Distribute		2 min.
Release	*2 min.	
Print	*1 min.	
Move		3 min.
Wait		60 min.
Match		30 min.
Group		10 min.
Wait		1500 min.
Move to Mfg.		2 min.
Total Time:	*20 min.*	*2605 min.*

Total Steps:	34
*Value-Added Steps:	5
% Value-Added Steps:	14.7%
Total Time:	2625 min.
*Value-Added Time:	20 min.
% Value-Added Time:	0.76*

* All value-added steps in this example are of value to the business only. There are no customer value-added steps.

Case 2— Production

Activity	Time	
	VA	NVA
Receive material	1 day = 8 hours (one shift operation)	
Stage		5 days
Move		10 min.
Stage		3 days
Put Away		30 min.
Store		30 days
Retrieve		30 min.
Move		10 min.
Coat	16 hrs.	
Store		2 days
Move		10 min.
Put away		30 min.
Store		10 days
Retrieve		30 min.
Move		10 min.
Stage		4 hrs.
Slit	4 hrs.	
Move		10 min.
Store		2 days
Retrieve		30 min.
Move		10 min.
Stage		4 hrs.
Move		10 min.
Stage		4 hrs.
Mount	10 min.	
Run	5 hrs.	
Stack		1 hr.
Move		10 min.
Stage		2 hrs.
Inspect		10 min.
Stage		1 hr.
Move		10 min.
Stage		1 hr.
Pack	1 hr.	
Stage		2 hrs.
Inspect		10 min.
Stage		1 hr.
Move		10 min.
Stage		1 hr.
Wrap	5 min.	
Stage		2 hrs.
Move		10 min.
Stage		1 hr.
Ship		
Total Time:	*26.25 hrs.*	*444.66 hrs.*

Total Steps:	43
Value-Added Steps:	6
% Value-Added Steps:	13.9%
Total Time:	470.9 hrs.
Value-Added Time:	26.25 hrs.
% Value-Added Time:	5.6%

on the remaining 25 percent of the products and completes a certifi-
cate even though the other customers do not require it and, in fact,
perform their own testing on receipt. The test and certification is
value-added on the products produced for the customer that requires
it, but they are nonvalue-added on the product produced for the
other customers.

Other examples where controversy or confusion may arise include:

- One count might be value-added; additional counts likely are
  not.
- Moving and storing material in a freezer when required may
  be value-added; other moves and storage may not be.
- One approval signature on a document may be value-added
  (for the company); others may not be.
- Sorting documents into classes to assign work once might be
  value-added if a particular skill is required; multiple sorts may
  not be.

The fact that questions such as these arise is one reason it is so
valuable to have the analysis done by those who work on and are
most familiar with the process. They are usually in the best position
to make the determination as to whether or not steps in these gray
areas are value-added or nonvalue-added.

Once all of the steps have been classified, the ratio of value-
added to total steps can be calculated. In our experience with many
hundreds of processes, this ratio falls between 0 and 20 percent, with
the vast majority under 15 percent. Ratios higher than 20 percent
most likely indicate that some steps are improperly classified and the
analysis should be reviewed. This is an important measure of the
specific process and helps establish goals for redesign.

Determining Value-Added Time

When the value-added flow analysis is complete and documented in
either flow chart or list form, the team can begin adding times to each
step. Figures 6-6 and 6-7 include these data as examples.

There are several ways to establish times by step in the process.
Many times are very easy to measure in a few minutes by observing
the process. Others can be determined by referring to dates on
documents or other records, including electronic records. Some can
be estimated accurately enough that the team reaches consensus on

the time used. Others may require that a simple measurement system
the time used. Others may require that a simple measurement system
be set up for one day to two weeks to gather data to determine the
time a step takes. This is usually possible by attaching a tag to the
work product and having individual operators sign and note times
received or move times.

It is important to document actual or carefully estimated actual
times as accurately as possible. Standard times in manufacturing
documentation should not be used unless they are first verified with
actual data. Supervisory estimates that "it takes about five minutes"
should be verified by observation.

None of this effort should be made excessively complex in an
effort to achieve great accuracy. The fact is that when the data are all
tabulated and the times utilized for the value-added steps are toler-
ated, they represent a ratio of between 0 and 5 percent of the entire
time the product spends moving through the process. Most are under
3 percent, and a significant number are under 1 percent. All of the
rest of the time is nonvalue-added—and wasted.

There is a very simple reason the ratio comes out the way it does.
Most value-added times are measured in minutes. Most wait time is
measured in hours or days. Most processes include a lot of waits. It
should not be surprising that the value-added time—the time really
required to process the product—is a very small percentage of the
total.

It is obvious that one of your goals in redesigning the process is
to eliminate waits. They are clearly an obstacle to making the process
flexible and responsive to customer needs. Other large amounts of
time devoted to nonvalue-added steps can also be found. These, too,
should be targeted for elimination, if possible.

Some time-consuming nonvalue-added steps are included in the
process by design. The team's goal is to challenge these steps by
determining the rationale behind including them in the process.
Challenging that rationale often leads to their elimination. This is
commonly true of quality inspections and checks or verifications of
previous steps.

Other nonvalue-added steps have grown up spontaneously and
are the creation of particular people assigned to tasks. That is how
work grows to fill time and make everybody look very busy. These
people may feel quite attached to these steps and threatened by their
removal. "You are eliminating my job" is a common reaction. What
you are actually doing is freeing these people up to do new work that
is value-added and supports the customer. Their work will be more

productive for the company, more valuable to the customer, and more meaningful to themselves.

But "waits" remain as a major target. Waits seldom result from being designed into the process and only occasionally result from how particular employees decide to do their jobs. They are usually caused by other characteristics of the process. We will look at how to analyze and correct some of those causes of waits in Chapter 7.

Designing the Ideal Process

Now that you have completed the value-added flow analysis and have added the times, you can see the ideal process. The ideal process is simply the value-added steps and the times associated with them—nothing more or less. Unfortunately, it is almost never possible actually to reach the stage of having 100 percent value-added steps. There are almost always some inevitable nonvalue-added steps that remain even after all of the problems are solved, the reasons for moves and waits are eliminated, and other nonvalue-added steps are removed.

This does not mean that the redesigned process is not close to optimal. Often, nonvalue-added steps cannot be removed. Some are important to the operation of the business. Some are required by realities of being a part of a larger corporation (although those should be challenged). Some are left in as a deliberate trade-off against an unacceptable cost of changing the process, or there may be practical limitations on physical space. Other valid reasons may also result in some nonvalue-added steps not being removed from the process.

Thus, aggressive removal of nonvalue-added steps and the resolution of problems in the process will achieve a "practical ideal process." This is your real goal. But the "theoretical ideal process" gives you a goal to shoot for. A good rule of thumb would be to remove 60 to 80 percent of the nonvalue-added steps. Another is that the total steps remaining should be no more than one and one-half to three times the value-added steps, depending somewhat on how strictly the definition was followed in categorizing the value-added steps.

Keep in mind that the time associated with the nonvalue-added steps will be 95 percent or more of the total time and you will be targeting the largest of those blocks of time for elimination. So, achieving a 60 to 80 percent reduction in nonvalue-added steps will result in an even greater breakthrough reduction in time, resulting in dramatic improvement in responsiveness and flexibility in the process.

Figure 6-8 shows some typical results of the value-added analysis of representative processes. Notice that there is variation from situation to situation but that breakthrough results are achieved in every case. These examples are quite representative of the results we have seen in hundreds of process redesign efforts.

Reviewing the Baseline

The value-added flow analysis you have completed at this point gives you a good start on establishing a baseline for the process. You have identified the total number of steps, the number of value-added steps, the ratio of value-added steps to total steps, the total cycle time, the value-added time, the ratio of value-added time to the total time, and the ideal process. You have begun to identify major non-value-added steps that will be targeted for elimination or improvement.

This baseline will not only help you target redesign goals, it will also help you identify the tools from Chapter 7 to use in making

Figure 6-8. Typical results of the value-added analysis of representative processes.

Process	Total Steps	VA Steps	% VA Steps	Cycle Time	% VA Time	Redesigned Steps	Time
Order Entry	73	4	5.4%	20 hrs.	5.0%	21	3 hrs.
Printing/Slitting	61	9	14.7%	13 days	7.7%	19	1 day
Contract Review/Approval	47	7	14.9%	8 days	3.0%	21	2 days
Custom Order Plan	71	11	15.5%	47 days	8.5%	34	15 days
Electronic Production	135	4	3.0%	37 days	5.4%	41	5 days
Ad Art Production	241	14	5.8%	13 days	11.5%	47	4 days
Plastic Product Manufacturing	68	4	5.9%	21 days	1.2%	19	1 day
Loan Application	61	4	6.6%	28 days	3.6%	14	3 days
High Technology Manufacturing	756	15	2.0%	17 days	5.9%	135	3 days

improvements. It also gives you a basis against which to compare your results when the redesign is complete and implemented.

Creating the redesigned process almost always requires that significant changes be made in how the work moves through the process, how the organizational responsibilities are assigned, how some work is done, and other considerations. Problems must be solved. Quality issues must be resolved. These issues will be addressed in Chapters 7 and 8.

7

Analyzing Processes for Breakthrough Improvement

Joe woke up anxious. Today was the first Steering Committee meeting with the three process redesign teams. It had been one month since the teams were trained, and they were going to report on their progress to the Steering Committee, which was made up of the staff members.

The meeting began with the widget-making team. The members showed a map of the process that included 189 steps! The team leader described what had happened: "We all thought there would be about thirty steps in our process. But when we all got together and started talking about what really happens out there, we were amazed. We discovered that several steps are repeated by different members of the group, and we didn't even know it! It's no wonder that most widgets take two weeks in widget making. We had lots of good ideas on how to improve the process as we developed the process map. Are you managers really going to let us fix this mess? We have three widget orders being made right now with no customer order, and we have two customer orders on back order. It doesn't make any sense, does it? If we could only make widgets fast enough to just make them when the customer needs them, it would sure save a lot of trouble. We did this value-added flow analysis and found that 11 percent of the steps add value. We're not sure what to do next."

The other team reports were similar. The financial closing and reporting team began by looking at the inputs and outputs for its process. The team members identified thirty-five reports that were distributed to seventy-two different people! Their first step was to do a client survey to determine their internal clients' real need for these reports. They reported, "We weren't sure how many of these reports were really used. We saw a lot of them piled up in managers' offices. When we asked if they really needed them, they all said that they did need them and would like more. We were supposed to make this process simpler, and it was quickly becoming more complex. Our sponsor helped us sort this out, and we tried something a little different. One morning, we printed all the reports but did not pass them out. We then logged who asked for what as the day went on. We were quickly able to identify the reports that were really used. This became our baseline. We are now mapping our process and plan to quickly eliminate those steps that were there to create these unneeded reports."

The product-development team members reported that they had baselined their cycle time by creating categories of different product-development projects and then averaging each category. The team leader reported, "It was a real struggle to average the times. Some of us are used to having every number to the third decimal. We identified eighteen different functions that are involved in the product-development process. The value-added steps are 9 percent of the total steps."

Joe was thrilled. The teams were doing well using the tools that they had been taught during their team training. It seemed that they needed more to continue.

By employing the tools of process mapping and value-added flow analysis, you identify the steps in the process that are causing costly waste. These are the nonvalue-added steps. The price you pay for leaving them in the process is loss of responsiveness, less flexibility, continued quality issues and rework, long cycle times, and higher cost. Clearly, your competitive strength lies in eliminating as many of the costly nonvalue-added steps as possible. *The key to eliminating any nonvalue-added step is to understand what causes it to exist. Then eliminate the cause.*

This chapter introduces you to a variety of tools for analysis of processes that will help you understand what causes the nonvalue-added steps to exist. You will then be prepared to eliminate them using the understanding you have gained here and/or the problem-solving tools that will be introduced in Chapter 8.

Analyzing the Process Map

As you begin creating process maps, you find that processes tend to fall into two categories with significant differences in their flow characteristics:

1. Processes consisting of a series of *sequential* steps producing the work output
2. Processes consisting of sets of sequential steps performed *concurrently* to produce the work output

The process maps for the two types of processes can be analyzed to gain insight into other process characteristics.

Analyzing Sequential Processes

Sequential processes are sometimes the easiest to analyze because the straight line of flow steps is simple to chart and understand. Examples might be an order-entry process, a hospital admitting process, a ticketing process, or a final assembly process. Figure 7-1 shows a simple process map for a sequential process. Times have been added to the process map.

Another way to look at this map would be to plot the steps in time sequence, showing what steps occur at what point in the total cycle time. Time rather than the sequence of steps then becomes the baseline for the picture of the process. This is a time-based process map. Figure 7-2 shows this method of looking at the process map.

This analysis can be carried a step further, and the detailed value-added flow analysis can be examined in the same way. With the addition of the identification of value-added steps and their associated times, you have another option for the presentation of the data. You can now analyze the sequence of steps against the time baseline and look at all of the elements of the cycle time and the value-added times. This is another time-based method of looking at the value-added flow analysis.

On this chart, you can also look at the ideal process versus the process as it is today. And you can graphically show a target "practical ideal process" that you will attempt to achieve. Taking this step forces the identification of potential target nonvalue-added activities that consume large amounts of time. You will attempt to eliminate these in your redesign effort. Figure 7-3 examines our sequential process in this detail.

(Text continues on page 139)

Figure 7-1. Sequential process map.

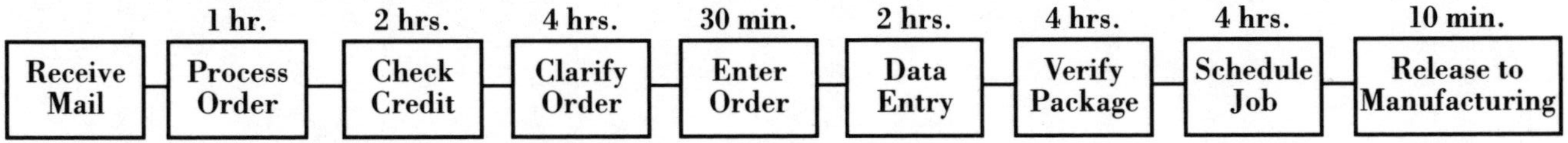

Figure 7-2. Time-based process map.

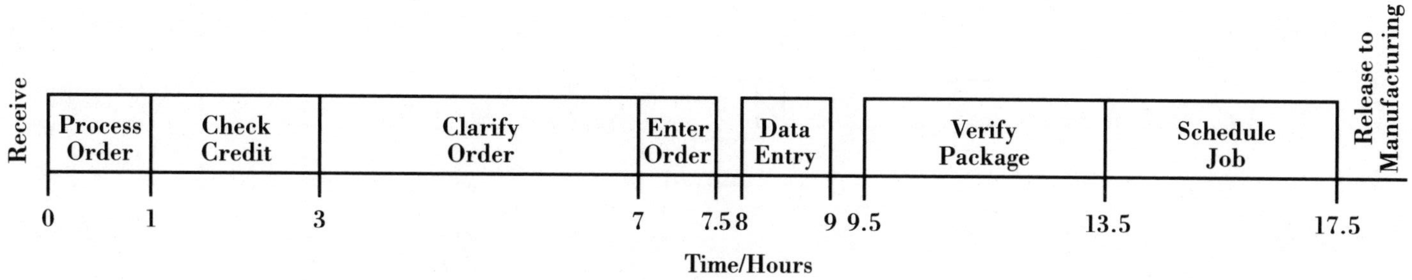

Receive							Release to Manufacturing
Process Order	Check Credit	Clarify Order	Enter Order	Data Entry	Verify Package	Schedule Job	
0	1	3	7	7.58	9 9.5	13.5	17.5

Time/Hours

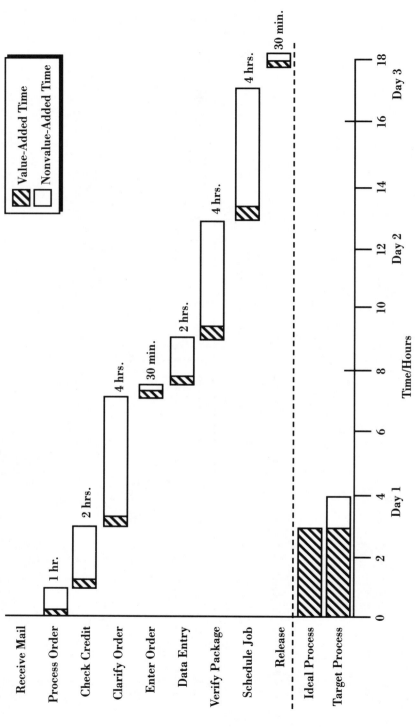

Figure 7-3. Time-based value-added flow analysis.

Analyzing Concurrent Processes

Many processes are combinations of sequential steps and concurrent activity. One sequence of steps creates a work output that becomes an input for the main sequence of steps and occurs concurrently with the main sequence. Concurrent processes, or processes that have some concurrent branches, are more difficult to visualize and understand. Their apparent complexity causes confusion and masks the fact that they can be broken down into understandable pieces. Product-development processes are examples of complex concurrent processes. A mortgage application process is an example of a primary process that has some concurrent tasks.

Figure 7-4 depicts process maps for a complex concurrent process and a primary process with concurrent branches. It is possible to analyze each of the concurrent process branches individually, as if they were independent sequential processes. The data presentations for each branch would look just like those in Figures 7-2 and 7-3. This is often done to assess the reasonableness of the work scope assigned to a project team. It may be more appropriate to address each branch as a separate project in order to ensure that the project scope is manageable within the time and resources allocated.

Unfortunately, addressing each branch separately is not always suitable for reaching the goal. If, for example, the goal is to reduce the length of time it takes to develop products and get them to the market, or to reduce the total time to process a mortgage application, the branches are too interdependent to allow reaching the goal by addressing them all individually. You need to have ways of analyzing all or most of the process as a single entity.

Figure 7-5 shows one method of mapping complex concurrent processes (with times shown) that aids in visualizing the process and helps identify target areas for redesign efforts. Note that it is in many ways similar to the simple graphical presentation for sequential processes. But the impact of complex organizational interaction is evident. The ability to see these organizational interactions clearly helps analyze the processes in other ways that we will discuss later in this chapter.

Evaluating Organizational Complexity

People are sometimes surprised that we examine the organizational structure and its impact on processes as a part of innovative process

(Text continues on page 143)

Figure 7-4. Concurrent process maps.
Product-Development Process—Numerous Concurrent Tasks

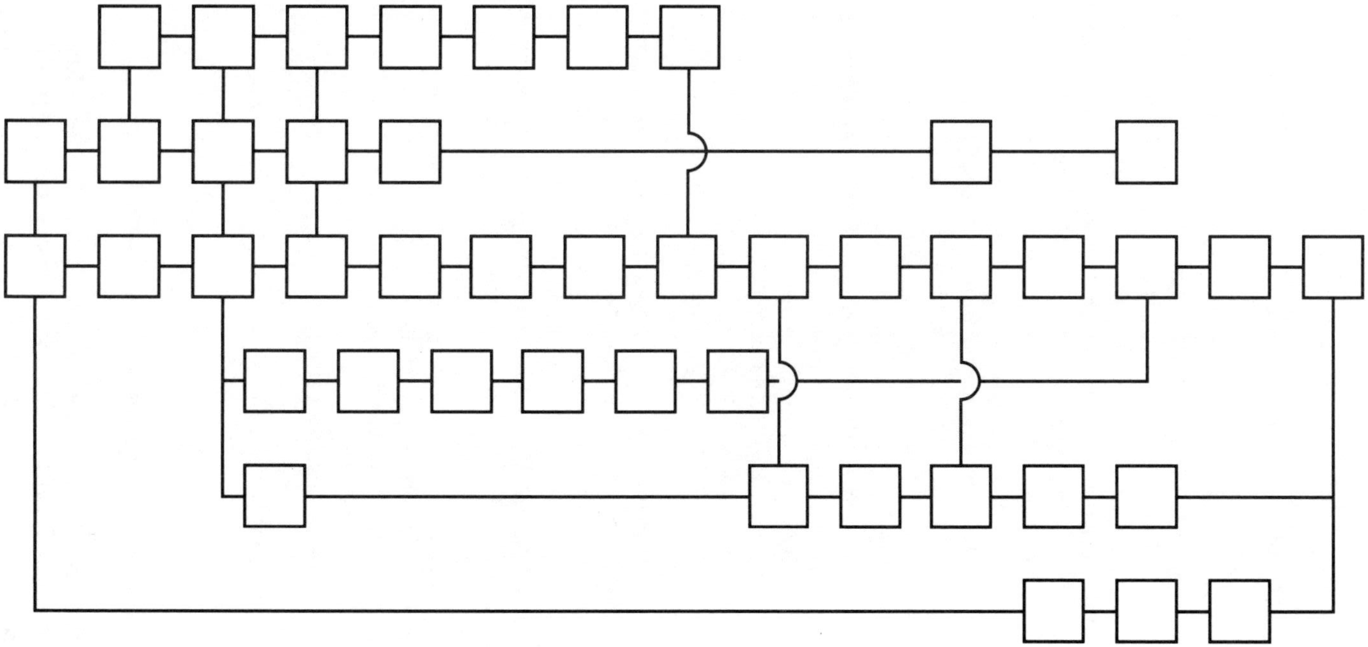

Mortgage Application—Concurrent Branches

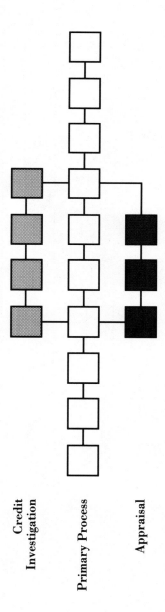

Credit Investigation

Primary Process

Appraisal

Figure 7-5. Concurrent process time-based map (product development).

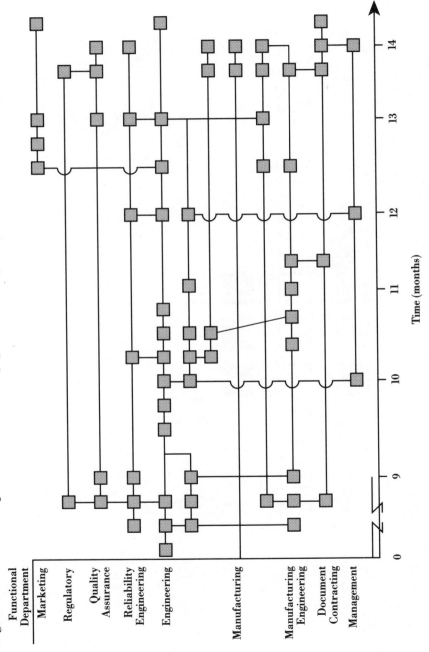

Functional
Department

Marketing

Regulatory

Quality
Assurance

Reliability
Engineering

Engineering

Manufacturing

Manufacturing
Engineering

Document
Contracting

Management

Time (months)

0   9   10   11   12   13   14

redesign. But the organizational, or functional, ownership of the pieces of the process is important in determining causes of nonvalue-added activity and in redesign to eliminate those activities.

Let's revisit the sequential process shown in Figures 7-1 and 7-2. But this time, in Figure 7-6, we have added the organizational entities responsible for each of the steps. Look at the number of departments involved and the number of corporate officers who at one time or another have responsibility for the work in the process—and the process has a cycle time of only 2.3 days. Who owns this process? Who is ultimately responsible for it? The answer probably is: nobody.

If that is the case, who is going to ensure that the process runs efficiently? Again, probably nobody. Each department or function worries about its own responsibility, and nobody worries about the whole. Each department solves problems for its own best interests, without regard for the whole. Two departments might even work at cross purposes.

In fact, that is exactly what was happening in this example. There were several departments of specialists who did their task and passed the work on to someone else in another department for the next step. No one challenged the process, which had run this way for years. In fact, when new employees did question it, older employees made it clear to them that they should not ask questions.

When the process redesign effort was completed, the cycle time had been reduced from 2.3 days to less than four hours, and the process looked something like Figure 7-7. People had been cross-trained. Work was reassigned out of one department. Two departments had been combined into one. Many nonvalue-added tasks had been eliminated. The process had truly been redesigned to eliminate the causes of many of the nonvalue-added steps.

Consider again the complex product development process depicted in Figure 7-5 and the extent of the organizational interaction that must work effectively for this process to be efficient. Do you think the organizational factors helped or hindered the process? In this case, before the analysis had proceeded very far, it was evident that the organizational issues were a major deterrent to efficiency in the process. Even though one of the key business imperatives of the company was fast product development and introduction, the people in charge of product development, manufacturing, manufacturing engineering, quality assurance, regulatory affairs, and marketing acted as if they each had their own priorities and schedules. (One

(Text continues on page 146)

Figure 7-6. Organizational considerations in a sequential process.

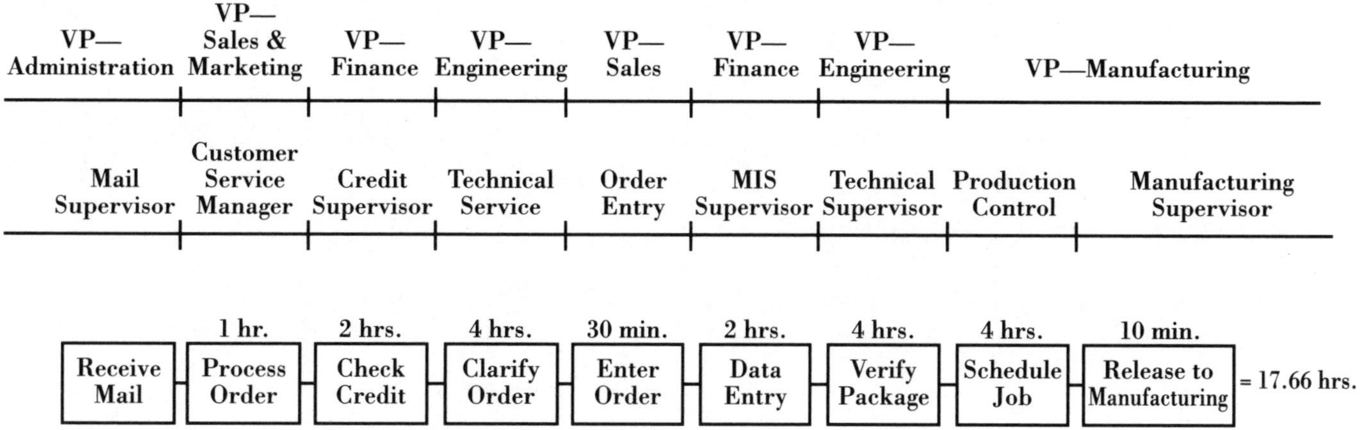

VP—Administration	VP—Sales & Marketing	VP—Finance	VP—Engineering	VP—Sales	VP—Finance	VP—Engineering	VP—Production Control	VP—Manufacturing
Mail Supervisor	Customer Service Manager	Credit Supervisor	Technical Service	Order Entry	MIS Supervisor	Technical Supervisor	Production Control	Manufacturing Supervisor

	1 hr.	2 hrs.	4 hrs.	30 min.	2 hrs.	4 hrs.	4 hrs.	10 min.
Receive Mail	Process Order	Check Credit	Clarify Order	Enter Order	Data Entry	Verify Package	Schedule Job	Release to Manufacturing

= 17.66 hrs.

Figure 7-7. Improved organization.

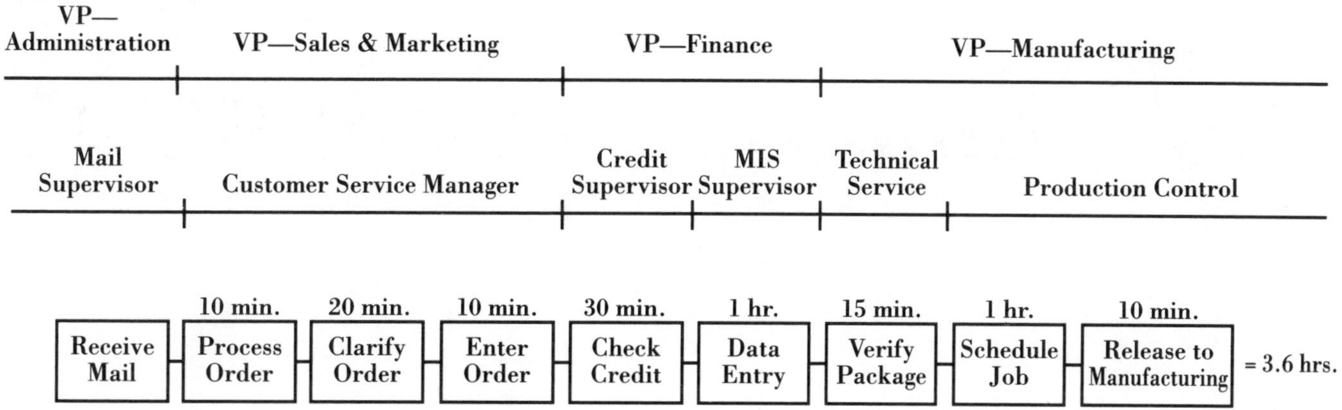

VP—Administration	VP—Sales & Marketing	VP—Finance				Technical Service	VP—Manufacturing
Mail Supervisor	Customer Service Manager	Credit Supervisor	MIS Supervisor				Production Control

Receive Mail	Process Order	Clarify Order	Enter Order	Check Credit	Data Entry	Verify Package	Schedule Job	Release to Manufacturing
	10 min.	20 min.	10 min.	30 min.	1 hr.	15 min.	1 hr.	10 min.

= 3.6 hrs.

might question the depth of communication of the vision and imperatives, but it was early in the improvement effort.)

When the process redesign effort was complete, the cycle time for product development and introduction had been reduced from thirty-six months to nine months. To consolidate responsibility and eliminate many of the causes of the nonvalue-added activities that interfered with the efficiency of this process, the organization was restructured to make one vice-president responsible for all of the technology functions: product development, manufacturing, manufacturing engineering, and quality assurance. Responsibility and authority were clear. The ownership of the process was no longer in doubt. Leadership around the vision and imperatives was strong.

It is not always necessary to restructure portions of the organization to accomplish these goals. Sometimes just opening the lines of communication has the same result. Encouraging horizontal communication rather than communication up one functional silo across the organization and down another functional silo can often do as much as changing the organization. Bringing departments into closer proximity can also help. The key is to identify how the organization might be affecting the flow of work in the process. If those impacts are negative rather than positive, they need to be corrected as a part of the redesign effort.

Determining the Number of Handoffs

Understanding the work flow through the organization gives us insight into yet another factor in analyzing the process—the number of handoffs. Adding the organizational departments to the time-based process maps discussed earlier, as we did in Figures 7-5 and 7-6, allows you to make a preliminary estimate of the number of handoffs. Handoffs occur whenever work passes from one person to another, e.g., from an order-entry person to a credit check or from a material handler to an assembler.

The true number of handoffs, however, can be determined only from the value-added flow analysis where every step in the process is documented in detail. Using the less detailed process map hides handoffs that occur between people in the same department or activity on the process map.

The significance of handoffs is that in almost all processes, there is at least one wait with every handoff, and often there are two. Unless the process is balanced and synchronized, the handoffs cause work to move in batches. Batches always mean that a wait occurs, because each work unit in the batch has to wait for all of the others to complete the step before they all move to the next step together. The result is usually a wait going into the step and a wait coming out of the step.

The total number of handoffs is not necessarily significant by itself, since processes differ in length and complexity. The most valid measurement would be the number of handoffs per value-added step, with the goal being to make that ratio as low as possible. In a balanced, synchronized operation where employees are cross-trained to do more than one operation, this ratio could be less than 1.

Calculating this ratio is really very simple. You have already counted the number of value-added steps on the value-added flow analysis. You can now count the number of handoffs shown by the steps in the value-added flow analysis and make the calculation from the formula:

$$\text{Handoff Ratio} = \frac{\text{Handoffs}}{\text{Value-Added Steps}}$$

Analyzing Work Movement

Work moves each time there is a handoff. Sometimes it moves without a handoff. This would occur any time an employee performed a task and then carried the work to another location and performed another task. Examples might be printing a batch of checks, carrying them to a check imprinter, and imprinting them; or cutting a piece of metal, carrying the piece to another location, and polishing the cut. Analyzing the movement of the work is an important part of identifying the causes of nonvalue-added activity. Movement is a nonvalue-added activity. Movement, like handoffs, usually results in at least one wait—another nonvalue-added activity.

The most valid measure of movements would be the number of movements per value-added step. The number of movements the work makes in relation to the number of value-added steps is a measure of how well connected the process flow is. The more disconnected the process, the more moves there are. The less connected the process flow is, the less likely it is to be synchronized. Lack of synchronization leads to lack of responsiveness to the customer and lack of flexibility. So, movements point to causes of nonvalue-added steps that should be eliminated and to disconnects with the customer that could be important in maximizing value to the customer.

The movement ratio is calculated in the same way as the handoff ratio, but they are not necessarily the same value. The movement ratio is calculated by the following formula:

$$\text{Movement Ratio} = \frac{\text{Movements}}{\text{Value-Added Steps}}$$

Charting Work Flow

Ideal work flow through a process is continuous, balanced, and synchronized. Creating this flow, or coming as close to it as possible, requires reducing batch sizes until they approach one unit of work. Any movement of the work is impractical in small batches if the move distance is very great.

To determine move distances, the flow is plotted on a floor plan of the work area. The flow is drawn as accurately as possible, showing all movements and locations where steps take place. The result is a process flow diagram such as that shown in Figure 7-8. This diagram is sometimes called a spaghetti diagram. You can see why!

The distances the product moves can now be measured. The greater the distance, the more disconnected the flow is likely to be. It is not just the moves, but the distances involved in the moves that

Figure 7-8. Process flow diagram showing movements.

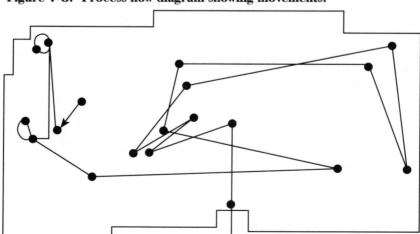

contribute to the disconnects in flow. Distance limits communication. Greater distance means more time is taken in accomplishing the move—nonvalue-added time. Greater distance and longer move times usually result in larger batches, causing longer waits. The implications multiply for redesigning the process!

This is shown graphically in Figure 7-9. The flow starts out the way it was shown in the process flow diagram in Figure 7-8. Then, it is straightened out. Move distances are added, and then the value-added flow analysis steps related to movement are added. The number of nonvalue-added steps is obvious.

Many of these steps exist only because the operations are remote from one another. If the operations could be relocated so that they were adjacent to each other, eliminating distance and allowing the work units to flow one at a time, many of the nonvalue-added steps would be eliminated and the work flow would be much more connected.

Physical relocation to close proximity is not always the whole answer to the problems caused by moves and distance. There may be other issues that have to be addressed at the same time in order to reduce batch sizes and balance and synchronize the flow: the rate at which work flows through individual operations, errors and rework issues, setting up to do an operation, supply shortages. But physical relocation is a major step in the right direction.

Uncovering Problems in Work Flow

The value-added flow analysis begins to bring to light some of the problems that have an impact on how flow is going through the process. Examples are loops of nonvalue-added steps designed to do rework, to correct errors, or to deal with imbalances.

Other problems may have to be uncovered by deliberate inquiry designed to search them out, although our experience is that team members familiar with the process are bursting to tell you about them. They are often the problems employees have been complaining about for years but have been unable to solve. Employees may even have told their supervisors about some of them, but nothing happened. Everyone has accepted the process as it is and just works around the problem.

We will explore some of these problems, how to identify them, and how to analyze them. Once they are identified, many will be candidates for the problem-solving methodology of Chapter 8.

Figure 7-9. Streamlining the process flow.

Original Flow

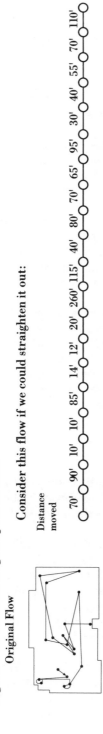

Consider this flow if we could straighten it out:

Distance
moved

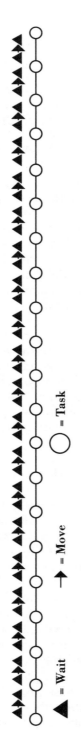

70' 90' 10' 10' 85' 14' 12' 20' 260' 115' 40' 80' 70' 65' 95' 30' 40' 55' 70' 110'

and add symbols to show all the steps:

○ = Task

▲ = Wait   ➤ = Move

The waits and moves exist because the steps are remote from each other. Moving them close together eliminates many steps.

Completely linked, the process would be:

Correcting Long Changeover Times

Have you ever stood in a line at an airport and waited while a ticket agent spent fifteen minutes getting her computer terminal up and running? Have you ever waited in a bank line while one teller closed out and another opened his drawer? Have you ever been unable to run work because the only available computer printer was set up to run the wrong form? Have you ever had to stop in the middle of a printing run and put additional paper in the reproduction machine?

These are all examples of changeover problems. People have a tendency to think of changeover times as machine setup times in manufacturing operations. Machine setups are certainly excellent examples of changeovers, and the times involved are often very long, measured in hours. But changeovers occur in many other processes, sometimes as a start-up activity and sometimes to change the work the process is able to handle. Not all are dramatic time losses, but they all interrupt the work flow. All are nonvalue-added activities. All limit flexibility and responsiveness. And all can be improved.

The longer the changeover time becomes, the greater its impact on the work flow. Longer changeovers, whether in manufacturing or administrative processes, have the same results:

- Desire for larger batch sizes
- Desire for longer times between changeovers
- Inflexibility in operations
- Unresponsive processes
- Larger piles of work in process

The solution is to reduce the time involved in making the changeover. If the time could be reduced 75 percent, you could make four changeovers in the time it now takes you to make one. You could make more frequent changeovers, reduce batch sizes, increase flexibility and responsiveness, and reduce the piles of work that build up in the process—with no increase in cost. In fact, costs almost always go down.

Changeover time reduction can be approached as a problem using the problem-solving techniques discussed in Chapter 8, but with the advantage that there are some proven approaches to the problem that work. Many of those applying to manufacturing machinery are highly technical and would require more space than is appropriate here, but there are some common guidelines that apply to redesign of all changeovers:

- Make it possible to perform as many steps as possible without shutting down the process (i.e., make the steps external to the process).
- Ensure that the person making the changeover has a detailed procedure to follow that clearly describes repeatable steps.
- Make sure all necessary supplies and tools are readily available before beginning.
- Eliminate as many adjustments, tests, approvals, and inspections as possible.

A significant reduction in time for most changeovers can be accomplished just by following these simple guidelines. If a changeover time in a process is leading to delays and large batch sizes, the reduction of the changeover time leads to reduced cycle time and fewer piles of work in process. Flexibility and responsiveness are improved.

Assessing Those Piles of Work

There is a close correlation between piles of work in a process and the cycle time for that process. Those piles of work are not moving. They might as well be in storage—in fact, they are in storage. Piles of work are evidence of long cycle times and flow problems. The bigger the piles, the longer the cycle time.

The best measure of the significance of piles of work in the process is the number of days of supply. This measurement can be made for the process as a whole or for one step in the process that has an associated pile of work. The measure is determined by dividing the number of work units in the piles by the typical daily output:

$$\text{Days of Supply} = \frac{\text{Work Units in Piles}}{\text{Daily Output/Work Units}}$$

The number of days of supply tells you how long the typical work unit spends waiting in the piles on its way through the process. This is a measure of wait time. For example:

An insurance claims office averaged twenty-six days to process and pay claims once they were received in the office. This measure applied only to those routine claims that had no significant problems requiring special review. Management could not understand why it took twenty-six days, since the amount of work involved in processing one claim was about three hours. A simple measure of daily output and the number of work units in the process provided the explanation. The daily output was about 350 claims. The number of claims in piles somewhere in the process was over 9,000. Dividing the number of units in the process by the number produced daily indicated that the average claim would wait about twenty-six to twenty-seven days before its turn came for the three hours of work necessary to process it.

Dealing With Process Imbalances

In the case of the claims process just discussed, management decided that the problem had to be corrected because customers were complaining. Handling the complaint calls was adding to the work load that already wasn't working out well. It should have been possible to keep up with the daily input of claims, since they averaged about 340 per day, just a bit less than the daily output. Of course, the claims did not arrive in a regular drumbeat of 350 each day—they averaged that amount over a two-week test period.

To correct the problem, management made an all-out assault on the piles of claims stuck in the process. Temporary help was brought in, overtime was authorized, and managers went to work processing claims. No efforts were spared.

The results were spectacular. Errors went up. Confusion reigned. Tempers flared. But gradually the piles were reduced until one Saturday, the office was clear of all claims in process.

Management celebrated. Employees were relieved. Customers were astonished.

Well, the good news lasted about a month. Why?

First, the work did not arrive in nice uniform daily drumbeat quantities. The earlier study showed it arrived in quite different quantities depending upon the day of the week. This is shown in a line graph in Figure 7-10.

Another way of looking at these data is a technique called a Pareto chart, which is shown in Figure 7-11. The Pareto chart is constructed by determining the percentage of claims received on each day of the week. The data from the two-week test were used for that purpose. These percentages are then graphed on a typical bar graph with the highest percentage, the most frequent occurrence, on the left. Other bars for each day are added in descending order of importance. You can quickly see the relative importance of each day. (This technique will be used again later in this chapter in another,

Figure 7-10. Daily claim receipts.

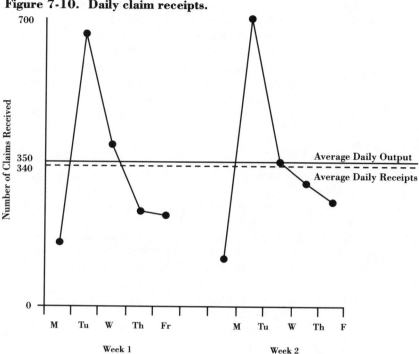

more complicated example where the details of construction will be discussed again in a less obvious situation.) When the daily claim receipts were analyzed, it was found that 40 percent of the claim forms were received on Tuesday, 22 percent were received on Wednesday, 16 percent were received on Thursday, and the balance were divided between Friday and Monday. Apparently, clients filled out their forms on the weekend and mailed them on the way to work the next week.

The results showed that the inputs to the process were out of balance. If the process was capable of processing and paying 350 claims per day, it was overloaded some days and underutilized others. It was inevitable that piles of work would build up during certain periods.

Further study of the process showed that it was also out of balance. There were four basic steps in the process, but they did not all produce at the same rate. Since employees worked as fast as they could, piles of work built up behind two of the processes. In their

Figure 7-11. Pareto chart of claims received.

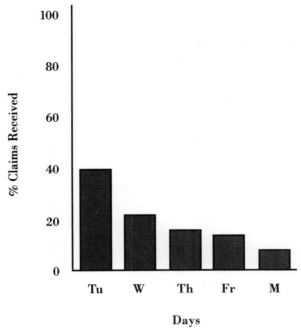

effort to keep up, the employees at these two operations began to make mistakes, creating additional work for correction of errors. The piles built up even more as time was lost on error correction (to say nothing of the stress on the employees). Figure 7-12 shows the effect of imbalance in the process.

Ultimately, the combination of imbalance in the rate of inputs, imbalance in the process steps, and the increasing error rate resulted in the original situation repeating itself and large piles of claims in process building up. It again took over twenty days to get a claim processed.

The situation was corrected by using some of the tools discussed so far: balancing the process, cross-training employees so that those whose output was faster could help those whose work took longer (an organizational solution), and reducing separations so that employees could communicate need for assistance. Problem solving, which is discussed in Chapter 8, was used to find some of the causes for errors. As a result, it was soon possible to process claims routinely in four days or less.

Figure 7-12. The effect of process imbalance.

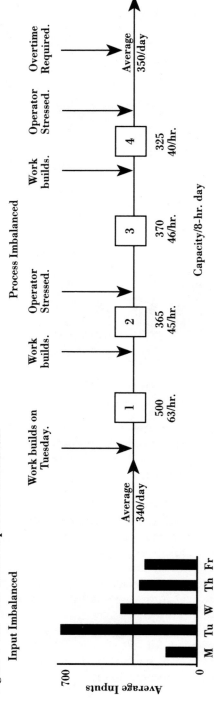

With everybody working as fast as he or she can:

- Work builds up on Tuesday in front of Operator #1.
- Work builds on Tuesday and Wednesday in front of Operator #2 and lasts until Friday.
- Operator #3 has steady flow.
- Work builds up in front of Operator #4 continuously. She works overtime to push out 350 units per day.
- As run, the line is capable of 325 units/day.
- With cross-training and full utilization of people to balance the line, it is capable of about 385 units per day without overtime.

Discovering Process Variabilities

Variations are inevitable in almost any process. Variations are caused by some of the conditions and problems we have been discussing. But sometimes the cause of the variation is not readily apparent and should be the subject of a problem-solving effort to find the root cause and permanently correct the problem.

Variations in processes are not easy to find. They are one of the problems that almost always takes digging. Things to look for that signal problem variations include:

- Significant variations in cycle time from batch to batch
- Significant variations in output quantity from time period to time period
- Large variations in usage of materials or supplies for similar output quantities
- Large variations in number of work units in process

Any significant variation in data that would normally be expected to be consistent should be explored further. Look at more data. Look for reasons for variation that might be deliberate. Analyze the variation to find data points that look abnormal. Then see what was different about the situation that produced that data point.

When significant variations are found, they should be analyzed to see if they point to process problems that need to be solved. For example:

In reviewing cycle time data for a manufacturing process, it was noted that there was a wide variation in the five or six cycle times we looked at to get an estimate of average cycle times. We decided to dig a little deeper and uncovered data on cycle times as measured by production order opening date to production order closing date for a large number of batches. The cycle times varied from a few days to several weeks. These data were plotted on a scatter diagram (see Figure 7-13). Clearly, a problem existed. Examination of other data available on the batches led to a problem-solving effort that corrected the wide swings in cycle time and stabilized the process.

Data from process variations can be displayed and studied using a variety of techniques: scatter diagrams, Pareto charts, line graphs, conventional bar graphs, etc.

Figure 7-13. Scatter diagram of batch cycle times.

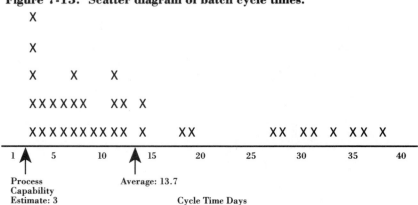

Dealing With Quality Problems

All processes are originally designed to produce 100 percent perfect work output 100 percent of the time. Few achieve this design goal. We seldom look at a process that does not have errors, scrap, or rework. The yield—the percentage of work that goes through the step or process without defect—is less than the 100 percent design goal.

Analyzing Defects and Errors

Yields less than 100 percent suggest that the process is not working as it was originally intended to work. If the process is not working as expected, one or more problems are sure to exist. The problem-solving methodologies discussed in Chapter 8 are intended to help deal with these problems.

Measuring the frequency of the quality problems is an important part of analyzing a process. Scrap, rework, error correction, inspection, and checking in a process all point to quality problems. Quality problems waste time and lead to nonvalue-added activities to rework or correct the defects and errors. They also increase scrap and inspection costs.

Two straightforward measures of quality are the number of work units scrapped and the number of work units that must be reworked to correct errors and defects. These measurements can usually be made directly at each work step. If they are not being measured and errors or defects are occurring, a simple measurement system should be put in place to track the data. These data can then be analyzed by type of defect or error using a Pareto chart similar to the one constructed in Figure 7-11 when we discussed the insurance claim process.

In this case, though, the development of the Pareto chart is less obvious. It is necessary to go through several steps before a chart of any value is created. For example:

1. You need to identify several likely types of defects or errors so that data can be collected in categories suitable for analysis. If you do not know enough about the defects or errors to determine those categories, you may need to gather some preliminary data to help determine them. Usually team members close to the process are helpful in establishing categories.

2. Four to six categories probably need to be established. They should be understandable to those who will record the data. If possible, an "Other" category should be avoided. If it cannot be avoided, look at it with suspicion if it contains more than 3 to 5 percent of the defects or errors. That suggests that you may not have identified all of the right categories in which to track data or that your data recorders are "dumping" data in the "Other" category.

3. Sufficient data should be collected to provide a respresentative sample to evaluate.

4. The data can then be analyzed and presented on a Pareto chart similar to that shown in Figure 7-14. The data are presented to show the most common defects or errors on the left, ranking them to the lowest on the right.

Generally, the top one to three categories include about 80 percent of the defects, making it possible to focus problem-solving efforts on those defects for maximum benefit.

Analyzing Process Yields

The yield of work product from a process is the net result of the yields of the individual steps in the process. Solving the problems requires addressing the issues at each step. But process yields are a good measure of how well the process is working and measure its ability to continually meet its requirements.

The percentage of units of work product that pass through a

Figure 7-14. Pareto chart of claims processing errors.

Error Type	Number	%
Coding	312	30%
Invalid Policy	19	2%
Agent Identification	63	6%
Waiver Signature	492	48%
Calculation	116	11%
Other	23	2%
Total	*1025*	*99%*

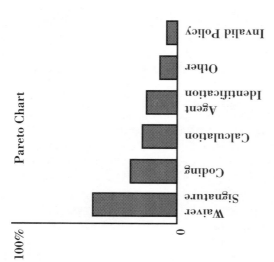

Pareto Chart

Process Steps
1. Identify categories by team.
2. Gather data at each station for two weeks.
3. Summarize and analyze data.
4. Make Pareto chart.
5. Target waiver signature error for problem solving.
6. Follow by problem-solving coding errors.

Observations
• Waiver signature and coding errors account for 78 percent of errors. Solving those problems would be a breakthrough improvement.
• "Other" category is low, so all significant problems must have been identified.

process step without having to be reworked or corrected is the first pass yield of that step. The first pass yield of the entire process is the percentage of work units that pass through the entire process without rework or correction. An example will help clarify this concept:

Suppose a process has four steps, and suppose 100 units of work enter the process at Step 1. Then suppose the four steps have the following first pass yields:

Process Step	Yield From Step	Units Moving to Next Step
Step 1	100%	100 units
Step 2	95%	95 units
Step 3	80%	76 units
Step 4	90%	68 units

Then the first pass yield of the entire process is calculated by compounding the first pass yields of the individual steps:

$$1.00 \times 0.95 \times 0.80 \times 0.90 = 0.68, \text{ or 68 percent}$$

If 100 units enter the process, only sixty-eight will pass all the way through without rework or correction.

A process with a first-pass yield of 68 percent may produce more than sixty-eight units out of 100 that start the process. It may even produce 100 units. But it does so by reworking and correcting some and putting them back into the process. The rework and correction is nonvalue-added work and should be eliminated.

The first-pass yield on the process is a good measure of the quality of the process because it:

- Identifies the presence of problems that can be addressed to improve the process.
- Indicates the extent of nonvalue-added activity expended in the process for rework and correction of errors.

Evaluating the Results of Analyzing the Process

Through the value-added flow analysis and the analytical tools discussed in this chapter, you have a very complete picture of the process being studied and its problems and opportunities. You can now pull all of these data together and begin solving the problems and implementing changes to redesign the process.

The best place to start is with the nonvalue-added steps that have been identified in the value-added flow analysis. Rank them from the highest to the lowest on the basis of the amount of time they consume out of the total cycle time. Attacking them in that order gives the most dramatic results. The steps with the longest times are usually waits. These are also usually the easiest to correct. So by attacking them in order of importance, you get the most dramatic breakthrough results quickly.

Using the analysis tools found in this chapter, you can analyze the flow and determine the reasons for the most time-consuming nonvalue-added steps and eliminate them. Typically, the top items are:

- Unlinked process steps, resulting in:
  —Unbalanced process
  —Extra piles of work in the process
  —Lack of communication
  Which can be solved by:
    • Bringing steps closer together
    • Running steps at the same rate
    • Eliminating waits between steps
- Batches larger than necessary, resulting in:
  —Piles of work in the process
  —Waits between steps
  —Uneven work loads
  Which can be solved by:
    • Reducing batch sizes
    • Reducing changeover times
    • Addressing problems
- Long changeover times, resulting in:
  —Large batch sizes
  —Long runs between changes
  —Inflexibility
  —More piles of work in the process
  Which can be solved by:
    • Reducing the changeover time
- Low first-pass yields, resulting in:
  —Rework, error correction
  —Scrap, waste

—Extra piles of work in the process
—Extra checking and testing
—Extra time
Which can be solved by:
  • Using problem-solving methodologies
• Unpredictable processes, resulting in:
  —Extra piles of work in the process
  —Extra process steps
  —Extra time

Figure 7-15. Value-added flow analysis: summary list form.

Operation	Time VA	Time NVA	Move Distance	Handoff	Days Work Waiting	Change-over Time	Error Rate
Operation 1	10 min			*	.2		–
Wait		4 hrs.			1.3		
Move		10 min.	13 ft.				
Operation 2		20 min.			–		–
Operation 3		5 min.			.4		–
Operation 4	5 min.			*	.2		6.5%
Move		5 min.	68 ft.				
Operation 5		18 min.		*	–		–
Operation 6		3 min.			–		3.1%
Wait		6 hrs.			2.1		
Move		10 min.	112 ft.				
Wait		4 hrs.			1.9		
Operation 7		1 hr.		*	.1	4 hrs.	1.0%
Operation 8		2 min.			.3		–
Operation 9	5 min.			*	.1		–
Wait		3 hrs.			1.7		
Operation 10		10 min.		*	–		1.0%
Operation 11		15 min.		*	.6		2.3%
Move		5 min.	6 ft.				
Operation 12		2 min.			.1		–

% Value-Added Steps:	4/20 = 20%	Changeovers:	One, 4 hrs.
% Value-Added Time:	20/1205 in. = 1.7%	First Pass Yield:	86.7%
Total Move Distance:	199 ft.	*Total Ft^2 Occupied:	96 ft^2
Ratio Moves/Value-Added Step:	4/4 = 1	*No. people involved:	27
Ratio Handoffs/Value-Added Step:	7/4 = 1.75		
Total Days Work in Piles:	9	*Determined elsewhere.	

Which can be solved by:
• Using problem-solving methodologies

As you continue to work down the list of nonvalue-added steps, you encounter the need for problem solving and more detailed implementation. But the data you have developed will lead you to the solutions.

Wrapping Up the Data

Figure 7-15 presents a brief section of a value-added flow analysis that has been expanded to include some of the data developed by using other analytical tools from this chapter. You can see how the value-added flow analysis in list form is a convenient way to summarize and present complex process data in concise form. Used with a process map enhanced by some of the time-based mapping discussed in this chapter, a complete data picture of a process can be assembled in a straightforward and understandable way.

All of the data developed becomes a part of the data baseline of the process against which the results of the team can be measured. At the conclusion of the process redesign effort, comparative data should be developed so that the team members, and others, can see the total impact of their work. The impact will go well beyond the two or three measures they have agreed to in their charter. Regardless of the specific measures with which the team is charged, successful efforts usually result in breakthrough improvement in time, quality, distance traveled, handoffs, amount of work in process, space utilized, employee frustration levels, and other factors. The sense of accomplishment of the team will be enhanced by comparing all of the data. It is worth doing.

8

Taking the Mystery Out of
Problem Solving

Joe dropped in to visit the product-development team. Its members
had just completed the analysis that shows how many times the
design gets handed off during the process. One team member put it
well: "It's easy to see why so many things go wrong. Having twenty
different handoffs makes it almost impossible for anything to go
right. And, do you know that we hardly ever involve the customer in
this whole process? It's a wonder that we have introduced any new
widgets that sold. We also found that the widget-making department
is brought into the process so late that the people there can't have an
impact on the design so it is easier to make. This process isn't black
magic. It just seemed that way because none of us understood what
happened outside of our area."

Joe left the room thinking, "Wow, they're really going to make
their goal of reducing the time it takes to develop products. Imagine
what that will mean for sales!"

Next, he went to the widget-making team. Its members were
adding up how many feet the widget travels to get made. Their flow
diagram looked like a maze. They wondered how the flow had gotten
so mixed up, but Joe could relate stories about how they just had to
put stuff where there was room. Finally, the team member with the
calculator exclaimed, "Wow, a widget travels two miles to get made."
Everyone was astounded. No wonder it took two weeks to make a
widget.

Another team member said, "At least we don't have quality
problems. Our yield is 99 percent." Another said, "Well, that's the
final test yield, but the work that I do has a 96 percent yield." The
team decided that the first-pass yield measure should be calculated

after all. The result was a 92 percent first-pass yield. The team no longer discounted quality improvement as an opportunity.

Finally, Joe visited the financial closing and reporting team. The week before, one of the team members had left the meeting very upset. The time analysis had shown that her step in the process was very long and always caused the process to be out of balance. Everyone had assumed that she was just too slow. After all, what else could be wrong?

As Joe walked in, the team was completing an analysis of process imbalances, and it turned out that this step just had more work associated with it. The imbalance was not a people problem at all. Joe thought, "These tools really do help identify the real problems, don't they? But some of the solutions aren't apparent. We are going to need some additional help with this one."

As you baseline and analyze a process and begin to identify opportunities for improvement, tools beyond those discussed in Chapters 6 and 7 may be needed to realize the gains from innovative process redesign. Since each situation is a little different, we will provide a methodology as well as a guide to the most commonly used tools. Our methodology of problem solving is a step-by-step guide, including the outcome from each step and the tools that will most likely be needed. This is not an attempt to provide advanced quality tools; in fact, you don't have to know anything about statistics to follow our straightforward and simple methodology.

We have found that most problems identified during process redesign can be solved using the tools described in this chapter. However, if you have a very technical quality issue, you may need to add more advanced tools. The purpose of this chapter is to introduce you to the six-step problem-solving methodology and many of the most commonly used tools. First, let's clarify how problem solving fits into the scheme of process redesign.

Anytime a process isn't doing what it's intended to do there is a problem. For example, some flow problems may be due to unexpected time-consuming moves or delays in the process, while others may be due to quality problems that cause rework or scrap. In either case, the process analysis uncovers a number of opportunities to make improvements through the elimination of problems. Thus, this problem-solving methodology can be used effectively whether you are proactively improving something that's not really broken (it works, just not very well) or frantically trying to fix something that is broken. Figure 8-1 shows when problem solving is most often applied as a part of process redesign:

- After process analysis to determine what to implement for improvement
- After implementation as you monitor your improvements for additional changes
- After you have monitored the process to determine adjustments

Business problems fall into one of three basic categories:

1. Systems problems (procedures, methods, traditions)
2. Technical problems (machines, engineering, chemical)
3. People problems (skills, training, hiring)

The six-step problem-solving methodology is equally appropriate for all three. In fact, many problems are combinations of the three areas.

Using the Methodology to Really Solve Problems

The advantage of using this six-step methodology is that the problem really gets solved—for good. The temptation for all of us is to use a quick "shoot from the hip" approach to find solutions to problems, thinking that we are too pressed for time to take certain steps and use tools or that the answer seems obvious. The idea is just to try something to at least solve the problem temporarily. Longer term, this "quick" approach actually takes longer because the problem isn't really solved the first time.

The six-step problem-solving methodology is outlined in Figure 8-2. Notice that solutions are not considered until after the root cause of the problem is found. We will introduce some of the most useful tools as each step is described. Some tools are used at almost every step of problem solving, like a basic hammer is used when building a house. The hammer is used to pound the stakes into the ground to mark where the foundation goes, to pound heavy nails into large pieces of wood for framing, and to fine-finish the staircase. However, other tools are needed only at certain stages of the process. For instance, you might use a large power saw for the framing boards,

(Text continues on page 170)

Figure 8-1. Innovative process redesign by applying problem solving.

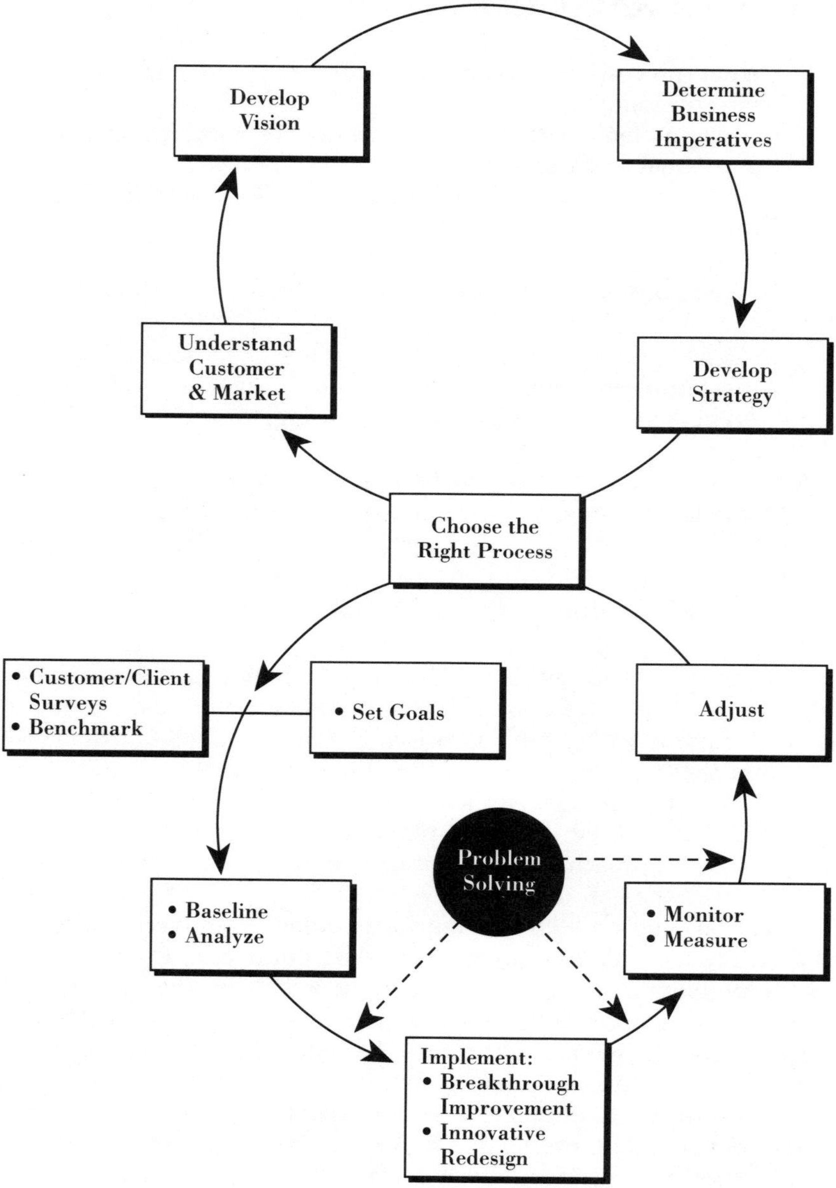

Figure 8-2. The six-step problem-solving methodology.

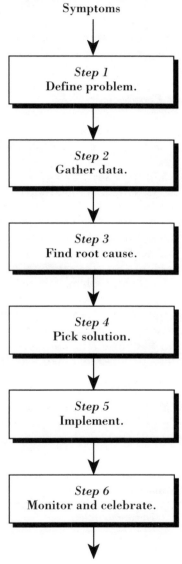

but you would need a smaller, more precise saw for finishing the staircase railing.

We will begin by describing each step along with the outcome expected and the tools most commonly used. An example will be used from a recent client experience to illustrate how the tools can be used.

Step 1: Defining the Problem

Step 1, defining the problem, seems simple enough. After all, we wouldn't be talking about problem solving if we hadn't identified a problem—or would we? More often than not, we do know we have a problem. But clearly defining exactly what that problem is may not be as easy as it seems. Many teams have started on problem solving and discovered during the process that each member had a slightly different problem in mind that they were solving. You can imagine the confusion. Eventually, they had to go back to Step 1 to define the problem completely and begin again.

As you can see in Figure 8-3, the outcome of Step 1 is a problem statement. In order to create a problem statement, it is necessary first to discuss the situation in general. Then identify the business imperative that is not being met because of this problem, and next list all of the symptoms present. The problem statement should be detailed, clear, and to the point. Let's use an example—which we will follow throughout this chapter—to illustrate how a problem statement might be developed.

> *THE SITUATION:* The product has been on the market only nine months. To make the product, a series of plastic tubes are glued to various plastic molded parts and expandable rubberlike

Figure 8-3. The outcome and tools of Step 1.

Step 1:	Define problem.
Outcome:	Problem Statement
Tools:	Brainstorming Problem Statement Worksheet

material. The product is tested for leaks in these bonding locations, since the product does not work properly if it is not airtight. The yield rate is only 55 percent, and the company is losing money on the product, which was supposed to be very profitable. The best engineers have been working on this problem for about six months, going out to various suppliers and research foundations searching for a better bonding material (glue, in lay terms). All tests with various new glues have yielded about the same results: a 55 percent average yield.

As part of the process redesign effort, a team has been formed to reduce the cycle time for the product and improve the yields. Engineers are on the team as well as employees who build and inspect the product, those who plan and schedule the product, those who purchase the material for the product, and the product manager from marketing. During the process analysis, it was obvious that this technical problem needed to be solved.

THE BUSINESS IMPERATIVE: To produce this product as the customer needs it at a cost that supports a competitive price while making the planned profit.

THE SYMPTOMS: At this point, the team used a tool called brainstorming to list all the symptoms. Guidelines for brainstorming are listed in Figure 8-4. Brainstorming is one of those multiuse problem-solving tools, like the hammer for building a house. Many ideas are generated quickly, bringing out data that would be lost otherwise.

Symptoms are those indicators that alert you that there may be a problem: those outward notifiers. Symptoms listed during the brainstorming session on the product included:

- Too much rework
- Frustration among employees
- The fact that leaks occur regardless of wait time
- The fact that leaks are irregular, not all occurring at one location
- The fact that costs are high and that there is no profit

The problem statement should include all the specific data available about the problem so that clear measures can determine if, in fact, the problem was solved. Only state the problem: Do not slip into causes or solutions in the problem statement. For example:

Figure 8-4. Brainstorming guidelines.

There are a few simple rules for a brainstorming session:

1. Set a time limit, and have a timekeeper. Usually five to fifteen minutes will be enough time to generate a number of good ideas and will not use all of a group's productive time or energy.
2. Generate as many ideas as possible. Even if ideas seem silly or off target, it is important that people get them out; there will be plenty of time to analyze them later, and sometimes a solution that doesn't seem appropriate at first has within it the kernal of an important idea.
3. Suspend criticism. Again, this is a time for getting ideas out, not taking potshots at ideas or those who have them.
4. Do not evaluate ideas, and don't problem solve. Evaluation comes after all ideas are aired.
5. Do not discuss, except to ask for clarifications.
6. Piggyback ideas on a previous idea.
7. At the end of time, ask for one more idea.

The next step is to try to reduce the list to one or two handfuls of ideas. This can be accomplished by asking for clarification or elaboration of ideas and by grouping like ideas. Creating a more coherent concept from a group of similar ideas often occurs, with the result being a more powerful suggestion. Also, when you ask for elaboration, a lot of ideas deflate, and there isn't much there beyond the initial words.

Once the list has been cut to a manageable size, the problem-solving team can begin doing a more rigorous analysis.

PROBLEM STATEMENT: 45 percent of the product fails the leak test after bonding. A 90 percent yield is required to make profit goals.

Step 2: Gathering Data

You learned many ways to gather and analyze data associated with processes in Chapters 6 and 7. Hopefully, it is apparent by now that data-based improvement is much more effective than opinion-based improvement. Many of the same tools already mentioned can be used in Step 2 of problem solving. However, one difference may be that now you are gathering data around the particular problem statement. So, for instance, these data may be focused on one piece of the process where a particular problem has been identified.

The outcome of Step 2 is a data picture: a compilation of data relevant to the problem statement. (See Figure 8-5.) An example of a data picture for the bonding problem is shown in Figure 8-6. This data picture includes a process map, descriptors about the process and the employees who run the process, as well as quality analysis data.

Each data picture is a little different depending on the nature of the problem. The goal is to create a display of all relevant data for the problem. Often, the team members gain a better understanding of the process and the problem by developing this picture together.

Again, brainstorming can be used to ensure that all data are listed. You can first brainstorm categories of data that may be appropriate, such as employee information, equipment utilized, or quality data. Then it may make sense to brainstorm each category for all the data available. For instance, a brainstorming session on employee information might include length of service, skills, training, or rotation of jobs.

You can move on to Step 3 when the team agrees that all relevant data for the problem are displayed in a data picture.

Step 3: Finding the Root Cause

Step 3, finding the root cause, is one of the most important and most often skipped steps in problem solving. Every problem has a cause. The principle is that if the root cause is eliminated, the problem will go away. The temptation is to begin discussing solutions at this stage,

Figure 8-5. The outcome and tools of Step 2.

Step 2:	Gather data.
Outcome:	Data Picture
Tools:	Process Analysis Tools Brainstorming

Figure 8-6. Product data picture for bonding problem.

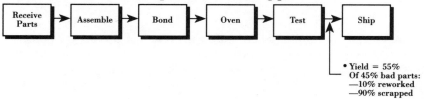

Receive Parts → Assemble → Bond → Oven → Test → Ship

• Yield = 55%
Of 45% bad parts:
—10% reworked
—90% scrapped

• Controlled environment (cleanliness and humidity)
• Four employees equally trained
• Rotate positions
• Four different glues tested—each averaging 45 to 65% yield

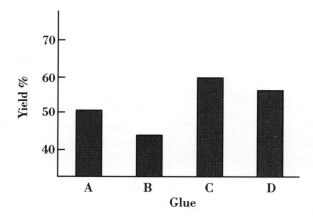

• Schedule requires 30 good products per day. Output has varied from 10 to 45 per day:

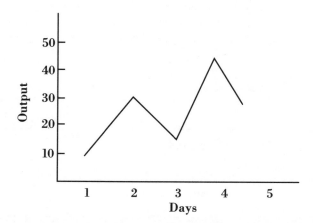

so there has to be a well-understood ground rule that team members will not discuss solutions until the root cause is identified.

Figure 8-7 shows the outcome of Step 3 as the root cause statement. This statement clearly describes what has to be eliminated or changed to solve the problem. Again, no solutions yet.

Brainstorming is also used in this step. In addition, there are two other tools particularly suited to this step: five whys and the fishbone chart. First, we will give you an example of the five whys and then go back to the bonding problem and show how these tools can be utilized together.

The Five Whys

You will find the five whys tool useful not only as a stand-alone tool but also in conjunction with the fishbone chart for more complex problems. By continuing to ask "why," you are led down the cause-and-effect chain until you discover the root cause. It may actually take more or less than five whys to get to the root cause, but five is an average. Here is a simple example using the five whys from a home builder:

Problem:	Complaints have risen concerning water standing in the crawl space under houses.
Why?	Water is not draining to the pump area.
Why?	Crawl space is not graded so the pump is in the lowest point.
Why?	Crawl space is graded before the location of the pump is known.
Why?	The drawings were not available, and the production schedule had to be maintained.

Figure 8-7. The outcome and tools of Step 3.

Step 3:	Find root cause.
Outcome:	Root Cause Statement
Tools:	Five Whys Brainstorming Fishbone

Why?   It takes two weeks to do the drawings.
Root cause: The cycle time to create drawings is two weeks
                  and needs to be no more than one week.

An appropriate root cause statement clearly states the cause of the problem, or what you would eliminate to make the problem go away. When first confronted with the water problem, the builder assumed that either the pumps were not working properly or there were serious leaks that created water beyond the capacity of the pumps. You can see how continuing to ask "why" can help get to the end of the cause-and-effect chain until the root cause is found.

One caution about this tool is in order. If you begin to ask someone "why" again and again without an explanation, he or she may punch you in the nose or at least feel very frustrated. To avoid this reaction, explain the five whys tool and root cause before beginning the exercise.

Now let's get back to our bonding problem and discuss how to use a fishbone chart to determine the root cause for a more complex problem. As you recall, the engineers had made an assumption that the problem was related to the type of glue being utilized in the bonding process. This explains the massive search for a different glue. Now that every function is represented on the team—not just the technical experts—we will use a fishbone chart to identify the root cause of the problem.

The Fishbone Chart

The Ishikawa Diagram, better known as a fishbone chart, simply provides a way to organize possible causes for the stated problem. A standard fishbone chart generally has six categories of causes: (1) methods, (2) machines, (3) material, (4) people, (5) measurement, and (6) environment. These categories can be changed to fit the particular problem situation.

Brainstorming can be utilized to list all the possible causes within a certain category, or you may brainstorm all possible causes and then place them into categories. The brainstorming list for the bonding problem included:

- Training insufficient
- Employees rushed
- Not enough time for glue to harden
- Temperature

- Humidity
- Particles
- Glue
- Plastic material
- Rubber material
- Process not well defined
- Oven
- Test equipment
- Glue adheres unevenly

As you can see in Figure 8-8, these possible causes have been placed on the various spines of the fishbone chart. The problem statement always goes at the head of the fishbone and the category headings at the end of each spine. To go on with our example:

Once the brainstorming list and fishbone chart were completed, the team reviewed each item to determine which ones seemed most likely to be possible root causes. They did not choose test equipment because the equipment had been calibrated weekly during the nine months and they felt this was an unlikely cause. The oven had also been tested regularly, and variation in temperature did not seem to affect the bonding problem. Environmental factors were well within the specifications of the glue manufacturers, so they decided to leave those for later as well. The three categories chosen for a closer look were people, methods, and materials.

The five whys could now be applied to each possible cause in order to move closer to the root cause. Each answer to "why" appears on a connecting spine until there seem to be no more logical answers without additional data. Notice the additional branches in Figure 8-9.

Sometimes asking "why" leads to a dead end or a circle, like "employees rushed" under the people category. If asked why employees are rushed, a logical answer would be that there is too much rework and scrap. Of course, this can bring you right back around to the problem statement. "Employees rushed" may be a result of the problem or a symptom rather than a cause.

The possible causes that seemed most viable to the team are highlighted in Figure 8-9. They seem to center around the process itself, or *how* the parts are glued, and around the plastic material, which leads to some ideas about the surface of the

(Text continues on page 180)

Figure 8-8. Fishbone chart for bonding problem.

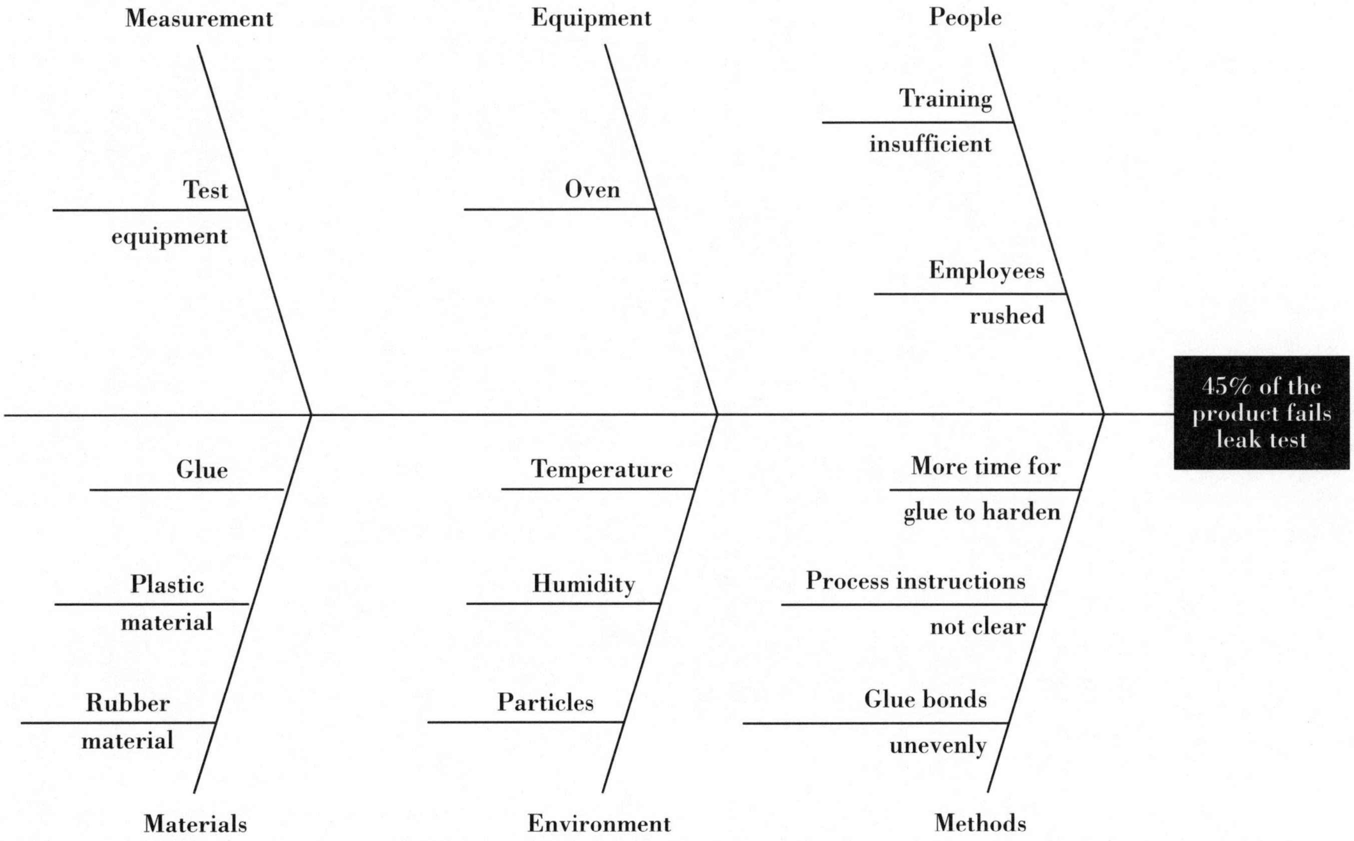

45% of the product fails leak test

People
- Training insufficient
- Employees rushed

Methods
- More time for glue to harden
- Process instructions not clear
- Glue bonds unevenly

Equipment
- Oven

Environment
- Temperature
- Humidity
- Particles

Measurement
- Test equipment

Materials
- Glue
- Plastic material
- Rubber material

Figure 8-9. Amplified fishbone chart for bonding problem.

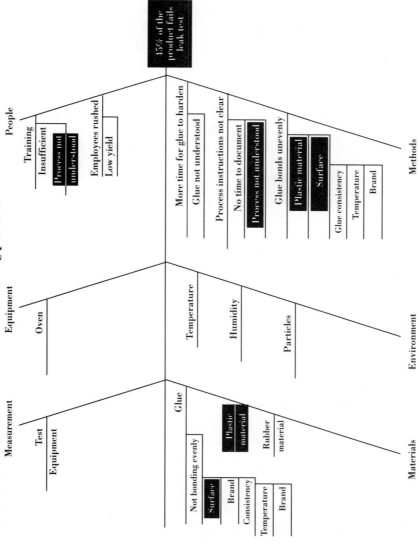

plastic. The conclusion at this stage is that more data are needed focusing on the relationship between the plastic material and the gluing process as the probable root cause. Thus, the root cause statement is: *The root cause of a 55 percent yield is the gluing process as it relates to the plastic material.*

The team was able to utilize the tools of brainstorming, the five whys, and the fishbone chart to collect and organize additional data that would not likely have been discovered without the involvement of all functions associated with this product.

Step 4: Picking a Solution

Finally, it is time to pick a solution in Step 4. As you can see in Figure 8-10, the outcome of Step 4 is to pick the best solution based on the selection criteria agreed upon. Brainstorming is again utilized, along with a new tool called a rating chart.

The first step in picking a solution is, once again, not jumping to your favorite solution. Instead, it is important to brainstorm all possible solutions based on the root cause identified. To illustrate, let's go back to the team working on the bonding problem once again.

The team used brainstorming to develop the following list of possible solutions associated with the identified root cause of the gluing process as it relates to the plastic material:

- Try more new glues.
- Heat at different temperature.
- Leave in oven longer.
- Change surface of plastic.
- Try a new plastic material.

Figure 8-10. The outcome and tools of Step 4.

Step 4:	Pick solution.
Outcome:	Best Solution Based on Criteria
Tools:	Brainstorming Rating Chart

The team created a shorter list of solutions through some additional data gathering. Utilizing the engineer's experiences in testing different glues, the team members decided that trying more glues was not a good idea; they would stick with the four that had been identified. The buyer checked with the suppliers of the glue and the plastic, who recommended against changing the temperature in the oven, so that idea was eliminated as well. They also rated their ideas using a rating chart.

Using a Rating Chart

A rating chart is a straightforward way to rate different ideas against criteria required. It's likely that you have purchased a car at some point in your life. Examples of criteria for a car purchase might include a certain payment amount, good in the snow, five speeds, and a sporty style. This set of criteria would automatically eliminate some models from your list of cars. It would at least narrow the choices down from many to a few as you began to rate each choice against the criteria. The team also developed criteria for selecting possible solutions.

The criteria list was developed by utilizing brainstorming to generate the list and to develop the short list of:

- Quick implementation
- Low cost
- Probability of solving the yield problem

The team set up a rating chart similar to the one in Figure 8-11 including their short list of solutions and the three criteria for selecting possible solutions.

It is very important always to include the rating scale on the rating chart and to ensure that the criteria are stated in such a way that consistency exists in the rating system. For example, in Figure 8-11, the criteria of "low cost" is used instead of "cost." If "cost" had been used, then a high rating (a 3) could mean high cost instead of highly preferred. This rating chart was designed so that a higher score would be more preferred.

It is also possible to weight certain criteria more than others. In our example, solving the yield problem would be most important and weighted more strongly.

Figure 8-11. Rating chart for bonding problem.

Rate 1—3 1 = Not preferred 3 = Preferred	Quick Implementation	Low Cost	Probability of Solving Yield Problem	Total
Leave in oven longer.	3	2	1	6
Change surface of plastic.	2	2	2	6
Try new plastic material.	1	1	3	5

As you can see in Figure 8-11, two possible solutions tied as most preferred: "leave in oven longer" and "change surface of plastic." Since it was not certain that either would solve the yield problem, experiments would have to be designed to test different combinations of the solution ideas. "Design of experiments" is a common problem-solving tool used to test ideas carefully at different stages of the problem-solving process.

The team designed some test lots, each containing ten parts. One of the employees who builds the product happened to mention in a team meeting that she had noticed that when she roughed up the plastic surface with a file, the glue seemed to spread more evenly. Otherwise, she had noticed that it seemed to run in blobs. The team immediately started test lots with each of the four glues already identified, using the employee's method of filing the plastic surface before the glue was applied in some of them and using longer times in the oven for others. Data were carefully recorded on each lot.

An exciting result occurred: All four of the test lots with filed surfaces passed the leak test! One part was rejected for another reason, and all the rest were good. Additional testing validated that it didn't matter which glue was used; it was the process of applying it that mattered. The oven time did not affect the test results either. Thus, the best solution is: *To develop a process to rough up the surface of the plastic.*

Step 5: Implementing the Solution

The next step is to implement the chosen solution. You may think that you are home free now; however, Step 5, implementation, may be the most difficult of all. Actually implementing changes requires careful and deliberate planning and execution. In the early stages of innovative process redesign, it still may not be the norm for a team of employees to find solutions to problems, much less implement them. Usually, changing the process is up to the managers and technical experts. There may be uneasiness and even resistance at first, but you will find that most employee teams are actually more careful planners than many managers have been in the past. As you can see in Figure 8-12, the outcome of Step 5 is to complete the implementation of the solution. The planning tools used are a milestone chart and an action plan.

A milestone chart is calendar-driven and shows the key steps of an implementation plan. The relationships between different steps should be noted, so if one step is not on schedule, it is simple to determine other required adjustments to the plan. Figure 8-13 shows the milestone chart from the team implementing the solution to the bonding problem.

An action plan is a more detailed step-by-step plan showing exactly what each step is, who is responsible for completing it, and the exact date completion is required. Figure 8-14 shows a part of the action plan for the bonding problem-solving team.

More detail will be provided in Chapter 9 on other considerations for implementation. However, we cannot overemphasize the advantage of visual measurement of progress as the implementation progresses. It is critical that everyone involved be informed of progress as well as issues that may arise during implementation.

Figure 8-12. The outcome and tools of Step 5.

Step 5:	Implement.
Outcome:	Implementation Complete
Tools:	Milestone Chart Action Plan

Figure 8-13. Milestone chart for bonding problem.

Step	Week Ending					
	4/30	5/7	5/14	5/21	5/28	6/4
1. Design process.	■—	—■				
2. Order tools.		■				
3. Revise documentation.		■—	—■			
4. Documentation approval.				■		
5. Test tools.				■		
6. Train employees.					■	
7. Revise capacity plans.					■	
8. Implement.						■

Figure 8-14. Action plan for bonding problem.

Task	Responsible	Due Date
1. Design process.	Design Engineer	5/5
2. Source tools, price, get approval, and order.	Buyer	5/6
3. Meet to approve new process and develop documentation.	Quality Engineer	5/14
4. Meet with V.P. to approve documentation.	Team Leader	5/19
5. Receive tools and run tests.	Process Engineer	5/20
6. Develop training and train employees.	Training Manager	5/28
7. Review schedule and revise capacity plans.	Scheduler	5/26
8. Implementation review meeting.	Team Leader	6/4

Step 6: Monitoring and Celebrating Results

It is critical to monitor a process when changes are made for several reasons:

1. To determine if the solution solved the problem—for good.
2. To identify additional opportunities to make improvements.
3. To quantify the team's accomplishments and boost energy for additional process redesign teams.

Step 6 in the problem-solving methodology is to monitor and celebrate results. As you can see in Figure 8-15, the outcome is that the problem is solved and that there is increased energy to solve additional problems. The tool of visible measures is a broad description of just how important it is to measure your success. We will discuss measurement in more detail in Chapter 9.

This step may seem natural, and you may assume that it's hardly worth mentioning. However, we believe that most of us have a tendency to lose interest in an effort right at the finish line. Once we can clearly see success, we may tend to move on to the next challenge. It takes extra effort and a certain amount of diligence to continually monitor, measure, and adjust improvements. The second outcome from Step 6, increased energy to solve more problems, is closely tied to making it all the way across the finish line. When people have clear, quantifiable measurements for accomplishments, energy is increased to do even more.

Celebration can come in a number of ways. The way to ensure that the team members feel they have had an opportunity to celebrate is to involve them in the process of deciding what the celebration will be like. Many times, managers have "given" the team a celebration designed for the managers, not the team members. One group may

Figure 8-15. The outcome and tools of Step 6.

Step 6:	Monitor and celebrate.
Outcome:	Problem Solved Increased Energy
Tools:	Visible Measures

think that an ideal celebration would be to go out to dinner at a fancy place with friends or spouses. Another may think that the ideal would be to just sleep late one morning and come in late. A third might choose an informal picnic with only people from the company and an afternoon off. You need to set boundaries on what the team members can and cannot do, but then let them brainstorm their own ideas.

Conclusion

The six-step problem-solving methodology described in this chapter will become a habit if the entire organization reinforces use of the steps and the tools for all problems: large and small, group and individual, technical and nontechnical. The process works. It may take fifteen minutes for an individual to complete the six steps on a simple problem or six months for a team to solve a more complex, technical problem. In either case, the mystery is gone.

9

Implementing Innovative Process Redesign and Measuring for Success

Brenda, the order processing manager, burst into Joe's office and said, "I've had it, Joe. We had another order from that sales rep in Georgia with the wrong widget number on it. The order was shipped incorrectly, and now we have another unhappy customer, plus we have to pay for the returned goods. I can't believe that sales rep makes so many mistakes! I think it's time to let him go."

Joe called Bill, the sales manager, and described the situation. Bill said, "It's hard to believe that this sales rep is just being careless. He's one of our best guys. Let me look into it."

A week later, Bill and Joe got together with the sales rep by conference call to discuss the high incidence of incorrect widget numbers. Bill and Joe had recently been to problem-solving training and decided to use some of the tools. The first assumption had been to blame the sales rep. However, when Bill and Joe asked the sales rep why the widget numbers were often wrong, the sales rep replied, "Well, I do the best I can, but I have to identify my samples by memory about half the time. The labels are often missing." Joe exclaimed, "I can't imagine that. The widget-making department is responsible for samples, and they double-check the labels. Why are they missing?" All three answered the question: "They must be falling off." Joe wondered why it was only the sales rep in the south who had this problem. They realized that the south is much more humid than their part of the country. Joe volunteered to call the supplier of the labels. He found that the widget label specification did not specify that the label had to stick in very humid climates. So the reason the labels weren't sticking was because the specification was not complete. When they asked *why* one last time, the answer was that the specification writing process needed to be improved.

As they were leaving the meeting, Bill said, "Wow, I'm sure glad we learned how to get to the root cause of problems. I could have lost one of my best sales reps."

Now that we have discussed the mechanics of innovative process redesign, it is time to step back and determine what it takes to get full benefit from the methodologies and tools described in this book—in other words, how to make them really work for the long haul! Success with innovative process redesign takes:

- A focus on maximizing customer value
- Results that are tied to the business imperatives
- Breakthrough improvements
- Teamwork as the norm
- An innovative organization with entrepreneurial spirit
- Leadership from the middle as well as from the top

We have shown how the process redesign tools can yield breakthrough results in any process regardless of the business that you are in. You now have guidelines on how to choose processes, get organized, and charter teams that achieve results focused on customer values and business imperatives.

This chapter will discuss three additional key topics: high-performing teams, keeping enthusiasm and motivation high, and using measurement to drive success. Chapters 10 and 11 will focus on leading innovative process redesign from the middle management level and developing an innovative organization.

High-Performing Teams

In Chapter 5, we discussed forming the Steering Committee, selecting a driver/coordinator, and chartering innovative process redesign teams. The way that these teams are formed, supported, and managed has a significant impact not only on the shorter term results but particularly on your ability to make breakthrough improvement a way of life. The teams must be high-performing to achieve breakthrough results and create an organization focused on the customer and innovation.

Communication—There's Never Enough

One of the most important keys to success is communication. Success is affected by the degree to which all employees understand what innovative process redesign is, why you are doing it, what your plans are, what is happening now, and what the results are. There are at least three levels of involvement in this effort to consider: (1) all employees of the company, (2) those employees closest to the effort or affected by the changes, and (3) those directly involved in process redesign teams.

Communication should be done in many ways. Don't expect everyone to understand and buy in just because a memo was sent. Some respond best to written communication, others to verbal communication. Written communication can be expanded beyond memos to include letters sent to all employees' homes, letters enclosed with paychecks, articles in the company paper, and information on bulletin boards. Verbal communication can include awareness sessions with groups of employees, small or departmental group discussions (e.g., brown bag lunches), large celebrations for team achievements, company meetings, and simple one-on-one discussuions. Videotapes for companies with many remote employees can be helpful if the video is made with extreme care. This should be a last resort, however, since the video cannot react to the audience and answer questions. This requires the video to be made with an accurate assumption of how the employees will react and what they would ask if they could.

Many companies make the mistake of communicating well when the process redesign effort begins, but of not continuing to communicate. You must realize that communication never ends—it goes on forever. Get your most creative and energetic employees focused on communicating, and the results will speak for themselves.

Communication and Teams

Communication is a very important step as teams are chartered and team members are enrolled. First, the managers of team members need to be enrolled. After all, being a team member takes time and energy: The manager's support is necessary. Then, each team member should be enrolled or invited to be on the team. This is best done personally, in order to explain the purpose of the team and answer any questions or respond to concerns the potential team member may have. The enrollment process is an excellent opportunity to generate excitement and buy-in for the process redesign effort.

As teams progress through training and implementation, communication should continue, in both ways: management to employees *and* employees to management. One ideal approach is to have the teams report to the Steering Committee regularly, maybe once a month. Nothing fancy, just a summary of accomplishments, decisions, results, learnings, issues, and those items that they need help with. This process works best when all team members participate and when several teams participate during the same meeting. This gives teams the opportunity to hear what other teams are doing well. Good ideas can be exchanged, and a little healthy competition won't hurt!

Now that we have discussed the importance of communication as a part of having high-performing teams, let's describe teams that are high-performing.

What a High-Performing Team Is

The best way that we have found to describe a high-performing team is to ask any group of people to think of past team experiences that they would consider successful—an experience that they would like to have again. They can use any type of team experience from their past—sports, music, school, or work-related. As the individuals in the group describe these experiences, the following descriptors always appear:

- Clear and common goal
- Challenging
- Clear roles
- Well-defined procedures
- Respect for each other
- Balanced participation
- Excellence
- Success

It has been said that a well-functioning team can accomplish more than the sum of the individuals. Advantages of teamwork include:

- *Encourages participation.* Employees are more secure participating as a team than as individuals.
- *Generates more ideas.* Team members get ideas from each other and expand on them.
- *Generates better ideas.* With input from team members, ideas are thought through more thoroughly.
- *Encourages risk taking.* Team members do not feel "out on a limb." If a new idea doesn't work, team members provide support for each other. They are more willing to try new things.
- *Fosters feelings of empowerment and influence.* The principle of power in numbers applies here. A group usually feels that it can have more influence than an individual.
- *Improves quality of worklife.* Employees experience more pride and fulfillment as a member of a team. People are happier when they feel that they can make a difference.[1]

There is little controversy about the value of teamwork. The struggle since the early 1980s in organizations has been how to develop high-performing, results-oriented teams that just keep on going. This book is not intended to be a complete guide on teamwork. However, we have identified seven attributes of high-performing process redesign teams that ensure success:

1. *Clear and measurable breakthrough goal.* Team members align themselves well to achieve a challenging goal. Breakthrough goals force innovative ideas and a competitive spirit to emerge. Teams are not able to accomplish breakthrough goals by just working a little faster and harder; they are forced to break paradigms to reach breakthrough goals.

2. *Well-defined roles and procedures.* The role of the team as well as each individual on the team is clear. Procedures concerning how the team will operate, such as decision making and planning, are clear and agreed upon.

3. *Teams that are allowed to flow through the stages of development.* The stages of development for all teams include form, storm, norm, and perform. These stages are not necessarily in sequence, and every team repeats stages. Storming is not avoided but managed.

4. *The right members and leader with strong support from the top.* Attitude, experience, and knowledge are all considered in choosing

the right team members and leader. Team members require support and encouragement from management for success.

5. *Diligent meeting management and facilitation.* Meeting management guidelines are consistently followed. Even though there is usually a designated facilitator, every member takes responsibility for good facilitation.

6. *Regular and honest self-evaluation.* If you don't measure it, you can't improve it. This rule applies to how well a group works as a team. High-performing teams evaluate themselves during every meeting, carefully noting what they need to do differently to improve. Figure 9-1 is an example of an evaluation form used by many teams.

7. *Continuous training in both technical (methodology and tools) and teamwork skills.* Training only begins in the classroom, and it never ends for the life of the team. Training can be in the form of a structured training session, or it can be ongoing as the team works together.

Never-Ending Training

As we have indicated, training for process redesign teams includes the process redesign methodology and tools described in this book as well as teamwork skills. Yes, teamwork can be learned! We have found that there are six skill areas of teamwork that are needed for process redesign teams.

1. *Appreciating diversity.* Different team members bring different strengths to the team. For instance, some team members may have endless new ideas, whereas others may be very good at gathering and analyzing data. The outcome of training in this skill area would be to understand the strengths that each team member brings to the team and how to utilize the diversity of team members to the greatest advantage.

2. *Understanding how teams work.* The team development model shown in Figure 9-2 clearly describes not only how teams work but also what to do when they don't work. This is a sound diagnostic tool for all teams. The model shows the hierarchy of goals, roles, procedures, and interpersonal relationshpis. The principle is that first, the goal must be clear. Then, roles can be defined. Once roles are defined, then procedures can be decided. Finally, if the top three

Figure 9-1. Team meeting evaluation form.

Rating Scale 1—5
1 = Poor
5 = Excellent

Weekly Chart

	1	2	3	4	5
1. Preparation			I	⊮	I
2. Listening		I		⊮	I
3. Participation		I	I	IIII	I
4. Agenda				II ⊮	
5. Progress			I ⊮	I	

Notes:
1. On the weekly chart, mark each team member's rating.
2. Discuss reasons for wide variations, such as Listening and Participation. It may be a sign of one team member having a problem.
3. Discuss how to improve where necessary, such as Progress.
4. Transfer scores to summary chart for tracking.

Summary Chart

	Week											
	1	2	3	4	5	6	7	8	9	10	11	12
1. Team members prepared.	4											
2. Team members listened to each other.	4											
3. All team members participated.	4											
4. Agenda was followed— stayed on track.	4											
5. Progress made— accomplished meeting objectives.	4											
Total	4											

Figure 9-2. Team development model.

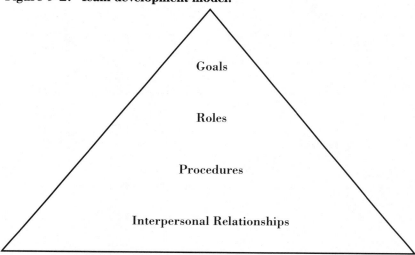

Source: Irwin Rubin, Mark Plounick, and Ron Fry, *Task-Oriented Team Development* (New York: McGraw-Hill, 1975).

are done well, interpersonal relationships will not be an issue in the team.[2]

Let us give you an example of how this powerful model can serve as a diagnostic tool. If role clarity is problematic in the team, the goal is likely unclear. Once the goal is clarified, the team will be able to define roles. The same is true of procedures. If procedures are not working well (such as making decisions), it's time to revisit the role definitions. This is a simple model that works.

3. *Making decisions.* One of the most important skills needed by a process redesign team is to be able to make decisions. The different decision-making procedures are described in Chapter 10. Let us just assume for now that most team decisions are ideally made by the group as a consensus, so that each team member can live with the decision and support it. Teams require training and practice in making group decisions.

4. *Having effective meetings.* Meeting management seems so simple, and yet it is so difficult to get groups to follow the straightforward guidelines: prepare an agenda, plan and manage the time, stay on track, use a flip chart, record actions and asides (those items that are

not on track, but that you don't want to lose), take minutes, evaluate the meeting, review the actions, and develop the agenda for the next meeting. The guidelines can be taught, but lots of practice is required for effective meetings.

5. *Developing the Team Charter.* The development of the Team Charter by the Steering Committee was described in Chapter 5. The outcome of this training is for the team to understand and support the charter. The team may modify the original charter or develop questions for the Steering Committee if the expectations are not clear. A meeting should be held with the Steering Committee to agree on the Team Charter. Doing this step correctly saves weeks of confusion concerning just what is expected of the team.

6. *Learning facilitation skills.* Facilitation is the skill to unleash the abilities of others—in this case, as they work in process redesign teams. Facilitation skills training is essential for the team leader and team facilitator. It is also desirable for every team member. Facilitation skills training is helpful for anyone who is facilitating a group, especially managers. We have found that attendees benefit far more from this training after they have had some experience with facilitating a group. With three to six weeks' experience, they are very clear about exactly what they need to learn to be more successful.

How to Get the Training Done

You should develop the ability to train with internal resources even if you begin innovative process redesign by using external help. The most effective trainers for process redesign are not those who train full-time but trainers who also work in a job in the company 70 to 80 percent of the time. These are the employees out there living the business day-to-day; they can provide the best insight on how to get results from process redesign in your organization. Train-the-trainer sessions can provide the needed training to become a trainer.

Natural Work Group Teams

Innovative process redesign emphasizes cross-functional teams formed to get breakthrough results. It is more difficult (but not impossible) to get breakthrough results with a departmental team. However, since teamwork is the norm in this "new" environment, it is important to acknowledge that there is another type of team that we call a continuous improvement team, usually made up of departmental groups. We sometimes refer to these groups as natural work groups, since they work together day in and day out. Training for these teams differs from that provided for breakthrough teams, and the improvements are generally in the 10 to 40 percent range.

Sustaining the Enthusiasm

Generating the enthusiasm and motivation for an improvement effort is usually easy. If the communications guidelines mentioned earlier in this chapter are followed and the teams are trained in both the technical aspects of innovative process redesign as well as the team-work aspects, they get off to an enthusiastic start. The challenge is to keep that enthusiasm alive and make it contagious throughout the organization. Success seems to be the single largest contributor to enthusiasm. So, our first ideas on this issue have to do with ensuring success of the team effort.

Identifying Stakeholders

Stakeholders are those people who may have an impact on or be impacted by the team effort. These are the people who could block the team if they are not well informed and involved in what the team is trying to accomplish. A supervisor or manager of a team member is a good example of a stakeholder; so is a manager who would receive a different set of reports once a financial process was redesigned. It is important to do a stakeholder analysis early in the team process to ensure that these people are not left out until it's too late.

A stakeholder analysis consists of a list of stakeholders that includes a description of the impact involved and actions to ensure that these people are kept informed and involved to the extent required. Figure 9-3 shows a simple form that can be used by the team.

Finding Potential Barriers Early

Good planning requires not only determing the steps to be taken and the outcomes to be expected but also considering the potential barriers for success. By going through an exercise early in the effort to identify potential barriers, there is time to work at eliminating these barriers. One tool to help in this barrier identification and prevention process is called a force-field analysis. Figure 9-4 shows a format often used.

Figure 9-3. Stakeholder analysis form.

Stakeholder Analysis					
Stakeholder Name	Position or Department	Impact: t = on team s = on stakeholder	Describe the Impact	Action Plan	

The object is to strengthen the helping factors and eliminate the hindering ones, moving the present condition toward the goal. By brainstorming a list of each factor and then discussing and clarifying each one, the team members can begin to classify hindering factors according to how much control they have over each one. For instance, an "A" item would be one that the team has control of or that could be a top priority, whereas a "C" item might be in the hands of top management or a corporate entity and be more difficult for the team to impact. We're not saying to ignore these items, only to categorize the hindering factors in terms of influence, since more time may be required to impact them.

By using this tool, teams can develop a proactive plan to prevent barriers from occurring as they identify opportunities for improvement and begin the implementation of their ideas. For example, a training plan could be established quickly to address lack of training, the "A" item in Figure 9-4.

Recognizing the Gains

Rewards and recognition were discussed briefly in Chapter 8. Giving consistent attention to the positive gains from innovative process

Figure 9-4. Force-field analysis.

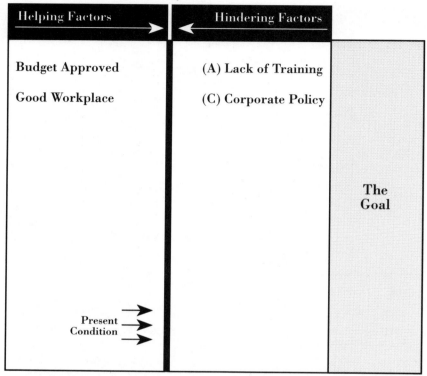

Object: Move center line to the goal.

redesign is extremely important. Recognition can be as simple as a pat on the back for a job well done or a letter from the leader thanking a team for a specific accomplishment. Team recognition days are becoming increasingly popular as a way to celebrate and give teams an opportunity to present their wins to the company. They also give teams the opportunity to hear what other teams have accomplished.

A critical issue is that the performance management system be consistent with innovative process redesign. All the enthusiasm in the world will quickly disappear if the formal measures for employees conflict with or don't support their involvement in the improvement effort.

Supporting Like Crazy

In the early stages of most change processes such as process redesign, empowerment is low, and many feel something on the order of "They won't really let us make decisions and change things, anyway." This attitude from many team members is well-founded and confirms their past experience. They'll believe it when they see it.

This issue requires overt support of the team until it has some successes of its own. So if you are a person who could block changes being made by the team, don't do it unless you are certain that serious consequences would result if the team went ahead. It's not the time to nitpick a team solution.

Driving Success With Measurement

There are at least three reasons for measurement:

1. To measure what happened in the past (history).
2. To prepare for or sustain improvement (baseline and focus).
3. To get what you measure by driving breakthrough improvement (set goals).

Our focus for the purpose of innovative process improvement is on numbers 2 and 3. If you measure it, it will improve. The concept has been proven time and time again. This emphasizes the extreme importance of making the decisions about what and how to measure in a thoughtful way. Getting breakthrough results focuses on the third reason. Later in this chapter, we will discuss the second reason to measure as a way to prepare for or sustain an improvement effort. We will leave the first reason for the stockholders and the accountants.

That Fear of Measurement

Why do we as humans resist measurement? Maybe it goes back to memories of bringing home a report card from school. The grade was everything, and if you didn't make it, there were unpleasant consequences. Far more emphasis has been placed on the grade instead of what is being measured. This experience has resulted in a nation focused on measuring (only if we have to) in a way that makes us look good, rather than in a way that identifies the most opportunities for improvement by uncovering the greatest number of problems. You can see the issue by now. When new measures are implemented to drive breakthrough improvement, you won't look so good at first!

So the first step is to begin to create a different mind-set about measurement that goes something like this: *"Measurements are created to get you"* must change to *"Measurements are created to help you identify opportunities for improvements."*

Principles for Measuring Innovative Process Redesign

• *Make measures visible.* Visible measures should be displayed prominently. They do not have to be fancy; in fact, flip charts or bulletin boards are fine. Just make sure that they are noticeable and in locations where the people who are affected by the measures can easily see them. One reaction to visible measures would be "It's bad enough to have to measure this; why do I have to put it out for the whole world to see? Can't I have some time to improve it first?" This is the "created to get you" reaction. In contrast, the "created to help you" reaction would be "Maybe if I put these measures out for everyone to see, they will focus on the problem and share ideas on how we might solve it."

The most progressive companies have their walls covered with measurements. Don't worry about format and formality. Just get people sharing their measurements publicly.

• *Make sure the measures are meaningful to those who can make a difference.* Ensure that measures translate into action for improvement. The people who have the most impact on the issue being measured need to be able to relate to the way it is measured. Otherwise, they will not believe or trust the measure.

Recently, we had a client who set an aggressive goal for scrap reduction. The finance manager took responsibility for baselining the scrap. In the process of having a computer program written to calculate the dollars, the standards changed and the program didn't work anymore. The entire team did not trust the numbers and lost a lot of enthusiasm because this measurement was not meaningful to the members. They could tell you story after story of how scrap should have improved, but they could never "prove" it with the measurement.

• *Select only the few right measures.* More is not better in this case. A few good measures provide a focus that supports process redesign.

Lots of detailed measures only confuse the issue. Look for the few that give the whole story. For instance, time has been mentioned throughout this book as one of the best, most compelling measures for process redesign. There are at least three reasons why:

1. If the cycle time in a process is decreasing, this is a valid indicator that other measures are also improving. For instance, non-value-added steps are surely decreasing as cycle time decreases. Piles of work are getting smaller as the cycle time is reduced, because there is less waiting in the process and better flow. Quality always gets better as cycle time goes down because there is quicker feedback for problems leading to quicker resolution. And customer service should improve: As cycle times goes down, you can respond more quickly to requests and changes from the customer.

2. The nice thing about time is that people like to reduce it. They all feel pressed for time and they want more of it for something else.

3. Time is usually easy to measure. You can get data on the time it takes work to go through the process regardless of the characteristics of the process. Just measure it like a race: the elapsed time between the start line and the finish line.

• *Measure consistently and on a regular schedule.* There's nothing more telling about a business than having outdated measures posted. These may do more harm than good. (It's like not "walking the talk"—it's better not to say it at all than to say it and then not do it.) When a measurement is defined and made visible, an update schedule should be agreed upon and followed.

• *See that measurement is done by people closest to the process.* Since the primary purpose of measurement is to uncover opportunities for improvement in an organization implementing innovative process redesign, measurement should be done by those closest to the process. It is not very helpful for people working in a process to get a monthly report from another department to tell them about problems. There's really not much they can do to determine the cause of a problem that occurred a month ago. In addition, the people closest to the process can measure it best.

• *Remember that quantitative measures are best.* Measures that can be stated in exact terms are most meaningful. The clearer the measure, the more believable it is. Number of hours, dollars, and late customer deliveries are examples of quantitative measures. However, it is also important to measure the climate of the organization or, as described in Chapter 3, to measure what the customer values. These measures may be less quantitative, but the data are still very important.

Stating Measures in the Right Terms Can Drive Breakthrough Results

The way that measures are set can help drive breakthrough improvement along with the right goals. For instance, choosing a defect measure that is stated in percentage rather than parts per million may produce a less compelling result. Working on reducing one defect in 100 has a different impact than reducing 10,000 in a million. Breakthrough goals require solid and consistent measures to ensure results.

Another example would be inventory turns for the company versus days of inventory on hand for a particular department. The first is too general to work on; the second provides information specific enough to drive the focus.

Laying the Groundwork Through Measurement

As we mentioned earlier in this chapter, another good reason to measure is to provide a baseline and a focus for processes. Establishing measures throughout the organization by following the principles for measuring innovative process redesign can lay the groundwork for breakthrough improvement. You may be pleasantly surprised to discover that improvements in the continuous improvement range may result just because of the measures and that the attitude about measurement may begin to change. The process of establishing certain visible measures involving every department in the company begins to provide a focus on measurement and improvement.

We are not suggesting that departmental teams be formed but that these measures be established around the business processes. Many teams could be departmental, measuring a particular department's piece of the overall business process. Of course, this requires that these measures collectively drive the organization forward to satisfy business imperatives, not that they be focused internally by department.

We are reminded of an example of an internally focused measure from a client's customer service department:

> One of the company's key measures was the number of phone calls per customer service representative per day. The idea was

that more calls per person represented an improvement in productivity and possibly even responsiveness to the customer. (More calls answered = fewer not answered?) This measure makes sense from the customer service department's standpoint.

However, if you get what you measure, what do you get with this one? As calls were monitored on a random basis, the manager noticed that the representatives no longer took the time to chat with the customer—you know, the common courtesy behaviors. They no longer seemed to take the time to really solve the customer's problem; the goal was to just get the customers off the phone and go on to the next call. So what this customer service manager got in the end was a higher number of calls from more frustrated customers!

The process of establishing measures throughout an organization needs to be collaborative, involving all functions. The goal is to establish one or two key measures for each primary business process and determine how to break down these measures into meaningful pieces. Usually, this is predominantly departmental. The process for establishing these measures is:

1. Identify key managers who would represent the departments associated with the key business processes for your company.

2. Hold a meeting with these managers to clarify the process and goals of the effort and to identify the key business processes.

3. Have each manager complete the quality measures questionnaire shown in Figure 9-5.

4. Interview each manager using the questionnaire. Interviews are best done by someone who is experienced in process redesign. These questions lead the manager through a thought process that should result in sound decisions about what to measure. The manager develops a short list of possible measures during this interview.

5. Determine which of the measures from the short list make the most sense to pursue by holding a meeting with each manager and his/her department, explaining the principles of measurement and getting input from each member of the department.

6. Hold a second meeting of all the managers. Each manager presents his/her proposal for measures including a full explanation of the measure, the expected result from the measure, and exactly how the measure would be implemented and maintained. By having all managers determine the chosen measures as a group, those measures

Figure 9-5. Quality measures questionnaire.

1. What are your company's overall key business imperatives (must do's for success)? _____

   How can your department have an impact on satisfying these business imperatives? _____
   _____
   _____

2. Who are your customers (external)? _____

   What do they value? _____
   _____

   How does your department have an impact on your customers? _____

   Who are your clients (internal customers)? _____

   What do they value? _____
   _____

   How does your department have an impact on your clients? _____
   _____

3. What are the top two or three issues or problems facing your department? _____
   _____
   _____
   _____

4. What would you like to see improved in your department? _____
   _____
   _____

5. Make a list of all possible measurements for your department. Don't hold back—list anything and everything! _____
   _____
   _____
   _____

6. Which of the above will "pull" your department to address Question #3 and/or #4 and be of value in satisfying your customer and client(s)? _____
   _____
   _____
   _____

that are internally or departmentally focused are eliminated, and only those measures that drive the company toward the business imperatives (and, therefore, the customer) survive. This process also provides some peer pressure to follow through with the measurement plan.

7. Once per quarter, have these managers meet to present the results from their measures, to propose possible changes in the measures, and to share what has been learned about the process by measuring it in a different way.

This process of implementing measures throughout the organization that are visible and maintained by the people closest to the process does not require that goals be set. The first step is just to begin measuring. Benefits of this process include:

- Continuous improvement occurs because of the focus resulting from the measure and the identification of problems in the process.
- The attitude about measurement (remember the fear?) begins to change, preparing the organization for breakthrough improvement efforts.
- Opportunities for breakthrough results from innovative process redesign are identified.

This process is a rather low-key way to begin to pervade the organization with measurement.

Sustaining the Improvement Effort

Another way to ensure enthusiasm in a team process redesign effort is for the team to implement solutions and improvements as they identify them. On an ongoing basis, improvement will then be measured, providing encouragement for the team (and management!). This would oppose another point of view that suggests identifying all ideas for improvement, creating an implementation plan, and implementing it all at once. This approach expects all ideas to work and save the day. A more gradual implementation not only provides encouragement but also an opportunity to learn what ideas provide the best results as the implementation progresses. The team will be able to make better informed decisions as a result of this

Figure 9-6. Measuring results with different implementation approaches.

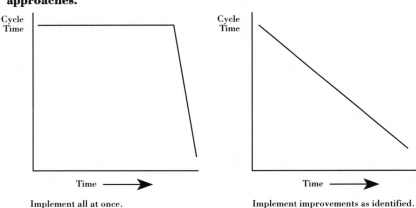

Implement all at once.   Implement improvements as identified.

learning. The measurement for cycle time would look like Figure 9-6 depending on the implementation approach chosen.

Conclusion

In this chapter, we have discussed three key topics for the implementation of innovative process design: high-performing teams, keeping motivation high, and using measurement to drive success. To complete the discussion on how to make the methodologies and tools of process redesign really work, Chapters 10 and 11 focus on how to lead innovative process redesign from the middle and how to develop an innovative organization.

Notes

1. Charlene B. Adair-Heeley, *The Human Side of Just-In-Time* (New York: AMACOM, 1991).
2. Irwin Rubin, Mark Plovnick, and Ron Fry, *Task-Oriented Team Development* (New York: McGraw-Hill, 1975).

10

Leading Successful Process Redesign From the Middle

Joe came in early. This was the day for the teams to celebrate their success. They had all reached their goals and had chosen a companywide celebration as their recognition. It would be an exciting day.

Soon, it was 10 A.M. All employees filed into the cafeteria. The three teams were ready. The president spoke first: "We are here today to celebrate our employees. I'm not going to make a speech today—this is your day. These three pilot teams have proven that all of you have tremendous abilities yet to be unleashed. Congratulations to all of you for your success!"

Joe thought, "That's the shortest speech he has ever made. What a change."

Joe was the emcee. He began by introducing each team member, who proudly came down to the makeshift stage. Everyone applauded. Each team presented what it had accomplished and some of the things that it had learned. The overarching message was: "We never thought that they would let us do this. We've had ideas about how to change these processes for years—they just didn't listen until now."

The widget-making team reported zero back orders, as a result of the ability with its redesigned process to make widgets as the customer ordered them and still ship the next day. No quality problems had been reported for one month. The financial reporting team reported that it now produced reports in two days instead of ten and that its internal clients had confirmed that the information now distributed was much more useful in running the business. The product-development team had redesigned its process, trained everyone involved, and begun to form product teams with all the right functions represented on each team. The first product using the new process was scheduled for release in one-third the previous time.

After all the team reports, a full buffet lunch was served, and all employees seemed to feel good about being involved. Many were discussing other projects and how they might help form a team. Well, almost everyone. Joe noticed Tom, the widget manager, back in a corner looking worried. He would talk to Tom later.

Joe returned to his office feeling great. He couldn't wait to call Sally at the ABC Customer Company and tell her the good news. After all, she had introduced him to the power of process redesign. Just as he was about to pick up the phone, a special delivery envelope was placed on his desk. Inside was a check from ABC—only five days after the invoice date—with a note from Sally: "We're down to three days and counting. You should budget our 10 percent discount into your sales numbers!"

Middle management plays a pivotal role in integrating the organization's process redesign efforts with customer and business imperatives. It is middle management that keeps the learning and improvement flowing from the top of the organization to all levels for practical applications. General Electric's CEO, Jack Welch, put it well when he said, "Leaders have to find a better fit between their organization's needs and their people's capabilities. . . . Middle managers can be the stronghold of the organization. But their jobs have to be redefined."[1]

The purpose of this chapter is to describe the issues faced by middle managers in organizations embarking on improvement efforts; to discuss the leadership role that middle managers play and how decision-making changes evolve; and to determine the benefits of these changes for middle managers.

Alan L. Frohman and Leonard W. Johnson's extensive research on middle managers found that organization structure and procedures must change as middle managers are given more responsibility. Integration was also an important factor in at least two ways:

1. Inside the organization, as the number of levels flatten and the departmental and functional barriers begin to disappear
2. Outside the organization, as networks are formed with suppliers, customers, and even competitors in order to keep the pace on new technology and the business in general[2]

Two conclusions are clear to us:

1. Middle managers play a critical role in the success of any effort focusing on innovative process redesign and break-through improvement.
2. That role is clearly different from the traditional middle manager role of directing, making decisions, and thinking while running.

Acknowledging the Brilliance and Care of the Employee

Listen in the hallways to your employees' conversations. The general opinion is that managers get in the way. A common theme continues to arise that goes something like this: "We want to do our jobs. We want to do them well. We want to contribute to a successful company. Get out of our way and let us do it."

We have found that employees are innately customer-driven. They want to do a good job and to have the good or service they produce appreciated. Employees generally are not satisfied with the status quo, know where the problems lie, and want a way to fix them. The problem is that often employees lack an understanding of exactly what the customer values and how they can help provide ultimate value. What customers truly value has never been articulated to them; instead, it has usually been locked up in the marketing department, often in jargon completely unfamiliar to the direct production or service delivery employee.

Beginning in the late 1980s and continuing up until today, there has been a lot of talk about employee involvement: having employees solve problems, embracing empowerment, and even instituting self-managed teams. However, not much has been said about empowering middle managers. Middle managers feel left out in the shuffle when they should play a key role in integrating the changes needed for competitiveness. What employees need are middle managers who can take bottom-up input, analyze it, filter it, combine it with top-down decisions and their own experience, and then create tactical plans that line employees can implement. What middle managers need is to feel that they are more of an integral force in the business's success, not just a buffer between senior managers who make decisions and line employees who carry out tasks.

Tapping That Entrepreneurial Spirit

In Japan, the values of discipline, conformity, and identification with the enterprise support the ideas of Total Quality Management well. Duty and obligation to the group and consistency versus variation are naturals in the Japanese culture. However, in other cultures, including that of the United States, the ultimate career objective is not necessarily to become a manager in a company. In fact, many in the United States would choose starting their own business, leveraging their own creative energies, and getting a piece of the action. Think of the many times you have heard employees say, "If I were my own boss, I could do what makes sense here." If that entrepreneurial spirit can be tapped in our middle managers, they will be excited and encouraged to involve employees.

The American work force embraces innovation, entrepreneurialism, individualism, and teamwork. Innovation happens when that entrepreneurial spirit is tapped. Many of the most successful companies today are giving employees complete (end-to-end) responsibility for entire work processes to promote these values.

Middle Management's New Role in the Entrepreneurial Organization

The Issues

Middle managers get many mixed messages as a company makes the transition to employee empowerment:

- Manage for the long term, but make the short-term goals.
- Serve the customer, but make the internal numbers.
- Decide what's best for your piece of the business, but do what top management says.
- Think strategically, but fix problems fast.
- Encourage innovation, but make sure it's right the first time.
- Know the answers when asked, but let employees develop the answers.
- Train and be trained, but don't miss a beat.
- Jobs are secure as long as you do the right thing, but make the numbers.
- Utilize employee expertise through facilitation, but be the technical expert.

- Ensure breakthrough improvement, but don't spend time and money on training.
- Work across functions to get the job done, but make your departmental goals.

With all of these mixed messages, it's no wonder that middle managers can face conflicting goals and roles that are totally unfamiliar and seemingly have nothing to do with past experience. In addition, they often see procedures, measures, and systems that are inconsistent with creating an entrepreneurial and empowered organization. These are some of the issues facing middle managers. But they also face what they can perceive as a threat to their jobs and positions.

Empowerment of Employees: A Threat to Middle Managers?

Many middle managers feel they are being told to "let go" as employees become more involved. The typical reaction is "I will give up power if employees are truly involved and make more of the decisions." This reaction assumes that there is a discrete and limited amount of power available, so if employees have more, managers must have less. There is usually also an assumption that top management will not give up any of its power, so all of the management power given up will be given up by middle managers (see Figure 10-1). The middle manager who envisions power sharing this way sees him or herself as inextricably caught in a cross fire of empowered employees and senior managers who still wield real power and control.

Figure 10-1. Empowerment distributed.

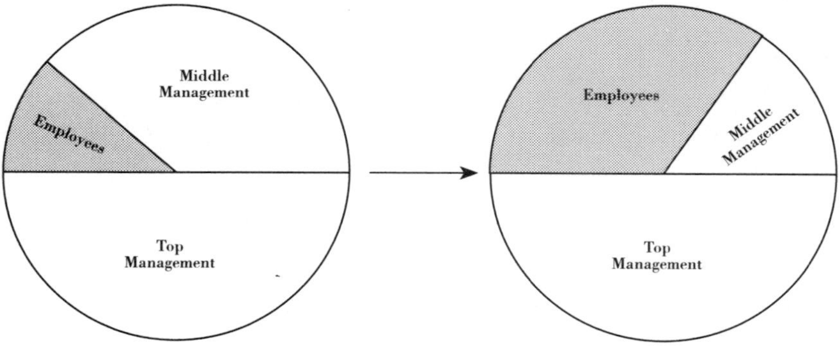

We suggest that the involvement of every employee in innovative process redesign increases the total power in an organization and redistributes it so everyone gets all he or she can handle. If the effort is organized correctly, middle managers don't lose power; rather, they play a key role in ensuring and integrating the new and greater power throughout the organization. They become the center of the power gird, constantly fine-tuning, balancing, coaching, and brokering the flow of power, as seen in Figure 10-2.

Changing the Organization

In an empowerment workshop for organizations, David Gershon, co-author of the book *Empowerment: The Art of Creating Your Life as You Want It*, defined organizational empowerment as an atmosphere in which:

Figure 10-2. Empowerment unlimited.

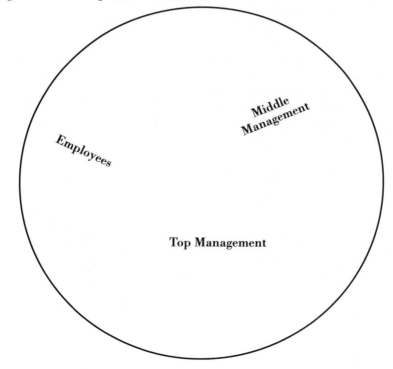

- People are "enabled to realize their full potential in creativity, productivity, and personal fulfillment."
- A feeling of empowerment develops by doing powerful and challenging things to meaningful issues.

Employees will feel that they have real power if they are able to improve a process that has a direct impact on customer service, as opposed to a project, say, to rearrange the company cafeteria.

But empowerment without alignment is counterproductive. The burden on management, especially middle management, is actually increased in order to maintain priorities and focus while building a common understanding of what the business needs are.

In order for individuals to realize their full creative potential, an organization must foster and encourage innovation. In order for individuals to realize their full productive potential, an organization must reward achievement and foster accountability and responsibility. In order for individuals to realize their full potential for personal fulfillment, they need to receive support and encouragement from the organization.

Chapter 11 deals more specifically with the behaviors and skills required for managers to lead innovative process redesign successfully. But it is important here to understand why behavior and skills need to be refined. For that, we can turn to Stephen R. Covey's model for a Maturity Continuum (as discussed in his book *The 7 Habits of Highly Effective People*), which applies to both organizations and individuals. It has particular relevance here to the ideas of increasing empowerment within the organization to tap the entrepreneurial spirit so prevalent in most of us.

Realizing the Organization's Full Potential Through Interdependence

The Maturity Continuum is a model that describes the growth cycle from dependence to independence to interdependence. Dependence puts the focus on *you*—someone else is in control. "There's nothing I can do," "They won't allow that," "I just don't have the time," and "That's just the way I am" are all examples of dependent thinking. It's easy to see that an organization that has a majority of dependent thinkers would not be very empowered!

Independence puts the focus on *I*—I alone am in control. "I am self-reliant and need no one," "I am responsible," "I can do it," and

"I don't need any help" are examples of independent thinking. Covey points out that this state is considered the ultimate by many personal growth movements, as well as in many organizational performance and reward systems. This way of thinking has traditionally been most rewarded in middle managers. This way of thinking fosters acting rather than being acted upon, and it can result in good individual producers. But empowerment cannot be achieved by having individuals think this way.

Interdependence puts the focus on *we*—"the sum of the parts is greater than the whole" thinking. "We can work together to solve this problem," "By hearing all ideas, we can pick the best solution," "We can make the goal as a team," and "Let's tap that team spirit and win" are examples of interdependent thinking. Managers who are interdependent thinkers have a great deal of self-worth, but they also recognize and are comfortable with the fact that their ideas, pooled with the ideas of others, result in a better solution.[3] Wayne Fortun, the president of Hutchinson Technology in Hutchinson, Minnesota, put it well when he recently said to us, "You have to put your ego in your pocket to work here." Interdependent-thinking managers find it natural to empower themselves and others.

Motivating Middle Managers

Now that we have explored a bit about the type of organization that needs to be created in order to get the most from innovative process improvement and about how middle managers play a key role in this process, let's talk about the catalyst, or what motivates people to make the changes described. After all, unless middle managers see some personal advantage in changing, it will be difficult for them to move ahead.

Individual Motivation

Individuals are motivated differently. At least one model uses three motivational factors: achievement, control (power), and affiliation. Many middle managers are motivated by control; after all, that's what they have traditionally been measured on. Some organizations have high motivational needs around affiliation—the ability to make the workplace a social and friendly place. In these organizations, almost nothing is worth "rocking the boat." The most progressive and competitive organizations are motivated by achievement: the ability to accomplish goals (which in the best companies are, of course, tied to providing value to the customer).

To become an organization that taps the entrepreneurial spirit, achievement must grow and control must decrease as a primary motivator. Affiliation is important, since we are talking about a people-oriented organization. Growing both achievement as a primary motivator and interdependence as the primary way of thinking have major implications for middle managers.

The Middle Manager's Dilemma

Frohman and Johnson's research results show why it is so difficult to effect the change noted in Figure 10-3. In surveying many levels within several organizations, they found three distinct differences in middle management compared with levels both below and above them:

1. Most middle managers feel a lack of career development. They comment, "I don't get the job assignments I need to help me

Figure 10-3. Growth in an entrepreneurial organization.

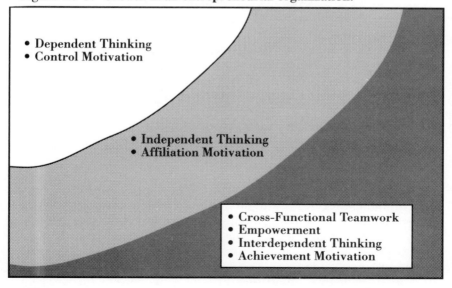

- Dependent Thinking
- Control Motivation

- Independent Thinking
- Affiliation Motivation

- Cross-Functional Teamwork
- Empowerment
- Interdependent Thinking
- Achievement Motivation

Time ⟶

develop my career" and, "We need to have more management development training to help us broaden our skills."

2. They give cross-functional teamwork a low priority. They complain, "People in other departments often stand in the way of what we're trying to accomplish in my area" and, "There is a lot of tension and rivalry between departments in this company."

3. They view communication from top management as incomplete. "They don't really keep us well-informed about what's going on and the changes they're making" and, "A lot of times, the information just doesn't seem to filter down to our level. There seems to be a block just above us," are popular refrains.[4]

These middle managers truly feel trapped between senior managers above them who seem to have high mobility and tangible rewards, and an increasingly trained and skilled line work force below them. The lack of a clear career path makes them feel vulnerable and locked in. The tendency when faced with this situation is to let control motivation and independent thinking take over. Many middle managers become experts in one or two areas and feel that by controlling that area of expertise, they can command respect. With middle managers in various departments all creating little fiefdoms of expertise for themselves, it's no wonder that cross-functional teamwork is low.

We believe that most companies today do not put enough emphasis on moving managers around to different functions and positions. Our most competitive clients regularly move managers to new functions, and it pays off in at least two ways:

1. The manager has a major development opportunity.
2. Cross-functional teamwork and understanding are increased manyfold.

Incomplete communication from top management certainly does not promote a feeling of empowerment in middle managers. At the same time they are thinking independently in order to assert control, they are thinking dependently, feeling that they don't know enough about what is really going on to control anything that is truly important.

To prevent this, companies have to look actively for ways for senior managers and middle managers to communicate regularly, in both directions. One of the most effective processes for excellent communication and focus is found at Hutchinson Technology. Every Monday afternoon, all levels of management get together for a customer focus meeting. Customer issues and success are discussed along with what the customer will value in the future.

In order to keep the company's day-to-day activities on track, every two hours, output and problems are logged in every department. Problems are rolled up into daily and weekly summaries, along with solutions and plans to avoid the problem in the future. Every Tuesday morning, all levels of management meet to present their summaries of the previous week. A manager will not likely stand up too many weeks in a row without solutions and plans! Two important outcomes of this process are apparent:

1. Problems get focused on and solved quickly.
2. Management is informed about the priorities for focus as well as the accomplishments.

In addition to having just met on Monday to engage in the more far-reaching strategic thinking, managers get fresh ideas from the Monday meetings about how to deal with the tactical problems and solutions they will talk about on Tuesday. The key to this process is the rigorous measurement of parameters that everyone in the organization knows, understands, and agrees are important. One of Wayne Fortun's favorite axioms is "You can't improve it if you can't measure it."

In many organizations, lack of cross-functional teamwork, often brought on by middle managers who feel trapped, inhibits empowerment and interdependent thinking and further encourages control as a primary motivator. The middle manager is inevitably measured on departmental goals and control within his or her department. But entrepreneurial spirit requires cross-functional teamwork, since no business is a single department but is instead a combination of many functions working together to accomplish a common goal.

An effort that recognizes cross-functional teamwork is a way to begin to break the vicious circle of bad practices leading to the need to control, which in turn lead to more bad practices, which in turn lead to a still stronger feeling of a need to control. During a tour of Hutchinson Technology, you can't miss the many thank you notes and banners displayed on the walls everywhere, from one department to another department, thanking them for some special effort.

Now that we have discussed the importance of the middle

manager's role in process redesign and many of the issues faced as employees become more empowered, let's discuss how to lead such an effort.

Discovering the Meaning of Leadership

The most effective leader in an organization that is aligned to deliver maximum value to customers by fostering innovation leads others to lead themselves. This idea is captured best by Lao-tzu, sixth-century B.C. Chinese philosopher:

> A leader is best
> When people barely know he exists,
> Not so good when people obey and acclaim him,
> Worse when they despise him.
> But of a good leader, who talks little,
> When his work is done, his aim fulfilled,
> They will say:
> We did it ourselves.

Leadership is not just for the CEO or the president. The most influential and wide-reaching leadership should come from middle managers. Therefore, it is appropriate to understand the differences between leadership and management, since the attributes of leadership may be those most needed to address the issues faced by middle managers. Middle managers are very rarely trained in leadership skills and usually don't think of leadership as their role.

Leadership compels the organization to be drawn toward a vision and goals, almost like a magnet. Management, on the other hand, provides the policy, procedures, and systems to push the organization into alignment. Both leadership and management are required to move an organization forward, as shown in Figure 10-4. Although most, if not all, of the emphasis in the middle managers's job has been put on management in the past, leadership has been saved for those at the top.

As employees become empowered and innovation is emphasized, a new leadership model needs to emerge. The new model measures a leader's strength, in the words of Charles C. Manz and Henry P. Sims, Jr., as:

> One's ability to maximize the contributions of others through recognition of their right to guide their own destiny, rather

Figure 10-4. Leadership and management moving an organization forward.

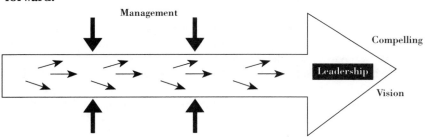

than the leader's ability to bend the will of others to his or her own. The challenge for organizations is to understand how to go about bringing out the wealth of talent that each employee possesses.

The emphasis shifts from conformity and adherence to leading others to lead themselves.[5]

Manz and Sims describe four types of leaders: (1) the strong man, who commands and uses fear-based compliance, (2) the transactor, who rewards and uses calculative compliance, (3) the visionary hero, who visions and uses emotional commitment, and (4) the superleader, who shares power by focusing on self-leadership and uses commitment based on ownership. The strong-man type is the typical authoritative leader of the past: "Do what I say and keep quiet." The transactor type struggles between being authoritative and becoming a leader. Their ineffectiveness comes from their inconsistency.

Visionary leadership has gained much attention at the top of organizations, and self-leadership is a newer concept that complements the creation of an innovative organization aligned by customer value. Such leaders unleash the abilities of the employees who surround them.[6]

Leaders reinforce the kind of organization being created by:

- What they pay attention to, measure, and control
- Their reactions to critical issues in the organization
- The way that they model the role, teach, and coach
- Their criteria for rewards, promotion, and hiring
- Most of all, the questions they ask

Of course, organizational structure, systems, procedures, design of physical space, and formal statements of mission, vision, and strategy will only be effective if they are consistent with the leadership thinking on these five criteria. When there is a lack of consistency, employees often ignore what is said by the leader and defer to the old behaviors; in this case, conflicts are likely to occur.

If middle managers are locked into a strong man type of leadership, which reinforces their controlling behavior and independent thinking, many employees will be buffeted between the top leaders' words and the middle managers' supervisory actions. To employees, this looks like another "flavor of the month" effort from senior managers, while they are still being judged by old criteria. To middle managers, this looks like "being set up as the bad guy" again by senior managers who give them little flexibility and no training to lead, only to manage.

Making Decisions in an Empowered Organization

Decision making gets pushed down to the employees closest to the process as individuals become empowered. Middle managers feel particularly threatened by this trend, since one of their primary roles has always been to make most of the decisions (except for those their own managers made!). In the minds of middle managers, authority is tied to who makes decisions.

But the development of an empowerment model throughout the organization does not necessarily remove authority from middle managers. In fact, it is still appropriate for managers at any level to make unilateral decisions. Authority of management does not decrease; it is just exercised differently. Let's discuss three different modes of decision making and determine the criteria for choosing the best decision-making process for the situation.

The first decision-making process involves unilateral decisions made by one person. The decisions are quick. The quality of the decision is good if the one person is the expert. But buy-in from the organization may be low.

The second decision-making process involves consultative decisions made by one person after getting input from other people. This process takes a little longer than unilateral decision making, may increase the quality if the right people are consulted, and usually increases buy-in for the decision. One caution, though: Always tell the people with whom you are consulting that you will be making the final decision. One common way to destroy the buy-in is to get input from people on a certain decision without telling them that the final decision will be made by one individual. By asking for input, people may assume that they will be involved in the decision-making process; when they hear that the decision was made without them, their support is difficult to gain. Therefore, it is important to be clear about who will make the final decision.

The third decision-making process is consensus, or group decision making. This is not a voting process; instead, everyone must be able to live with and support the decision made by the group. Consensus requires that everyone feels heard and that group members not agree unless they can sincerely support the decision; in other words, each member has the opportunity to hold out until he or she can live with the decision. Obviously, this process takes longer than the other processes. The quality of the decision may be better, but only if the experts are in the group. Group decision making has the highest buy-in, since members have been involved in the process.

Moving decision making lower in the organization is evolutionary. Figure 10-5, done by Sondra Ford, a principal at Rath & Strong, shows the evolution from decisions being made by management up to encouraging decisions at the level where the work is done.

A tool that can be used in group decision making is responsibility charting. Not every member of the group must be included in every group decision. Some decisions are best made by only a portion of the group. For instance, if a team is making a very technical decision about how to proceed on a new product design, it may be more practical for that decision to be made only by those who have the technical expertise required. Responsibility charting is a simple way to determine who should make the decision, who should just be informed about the decision, and who does not care to be involved at all.

In a recent workshop involving all managers from a client company, the managers shared data that they had been collecting in preparation for the workshop. Their assignment was twofold:

1. To keep data on every decision that each of them was involved in, including who was involved in the decision and the subject matter for the decision itself
2. To keep data on how they spent their time in several categories

The conclusion was that many of the decisions could involve employees to a greater extent. More of the decisions could have been

Figure 10-5. The evolution of decision making as empowerment grows.

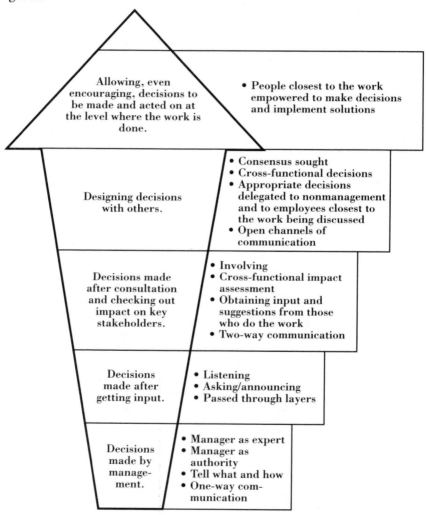

consensus and consultative rather than unilateral. Figure 10-6 shows the results of decision making after empowerment was begun. The time data were also surprising to the group. As you can see in Figure 10-7, 13 percent of the managers' time was spent just making decisions! Only 16 percent of the total was spent in what we might

Figure 10-6. Decisions made by management group.

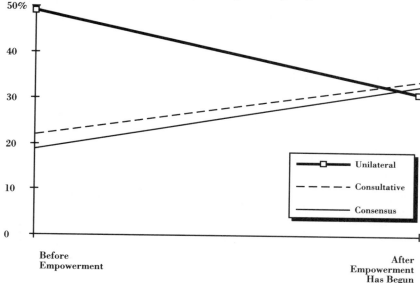

consider proactive activities (planning/strategy, employee development, and self-development) versus the remaining 84 percent in
reactive activities (work tasks, solving problems, performance man-
agement/information sharing, and discipline).

To support innovation through empowerment, the managers
attending the workshop developed plans to transition their time
usage to more proactive activities associated with leadership, as in
Figure 10-8.

Reaping the Benefits

Leadership is an important attribute for middle managers to succeed
in an organization placing high value on innovation and process
redesign with the customer in mind. Chapter 11 will discuss more
completely the behavioral changes and skills required. The benefits
for middle managers as employees are empowered include:

- Time to plan ahead for the future
- Ability to act instead of just to react
- Opportunity for career development

Figure 10-7. How one group of managers spent their time.

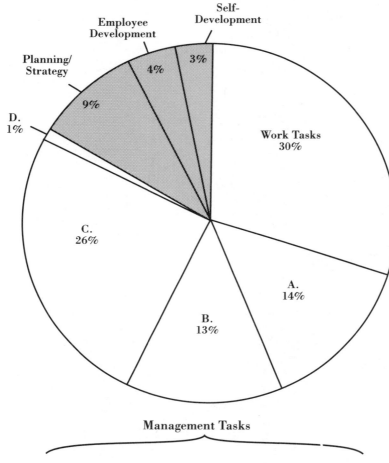

Management Tasks

A. Solving Problems (doing the work)
B. Decision Making
C. Performance Management/
   Information Sharing
D. Discipline

Figure 10-8. How middle management leaders should spend their time.

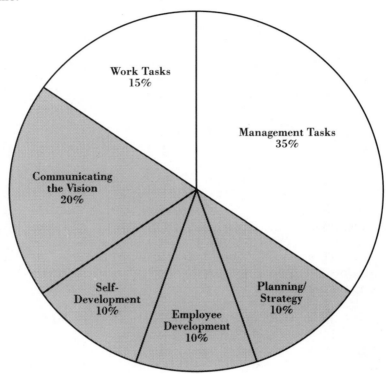

Middle managers will be able to see these and other benefits to this new role given time, training, support, and understanding as they make the transition.

Notes

1. Thomas R. Horton and Peter C. Reid, "What Fate for Middle Managers?" *Management Review* (January 1991).
2. Alan L. Frohman and Leonard W. Johnson, *The Middle Management Challenge Moving From Crisis to Empowerment* (New York: McGraw-Hill, 1993).
3. Stephen R. Covey, *The 7 Habits of Highly Effective People* (New York: Fireside, 1990).
4. Frohman and Johnson.
5. Charles C. Manz and Henry P. Sims, Jr., *Superleadership: Leading Others to Lead Themselves* (Englewood Cliffs, N.J.: Prentice-Hall, 1989).
6. Ibid.

11

How to Become a Leader of Innovation

After everyone had gone home, Joe found Tom in his office. He really looked worried. Joe sat down, propped his feet up, and said, "Tom, you looked a little worried today. Is there anything I can do to help?" Tom sat back and said, "You know, Joe, I've been here in widget making for a long time. It's always been up to me to make all the decisions and give directions to people. I'm good at that. That's why I have this position. When the widget-making team first started, I didn't pay much attention. Nothing like that had ever worked before, and I didn't figure that the people wanted to take on the responsibility. They've always seemed so willing just to go along with whatever I told them to do. But they did make it work. And you know what? They had some darn good ideas. Wish I had thought of them."

Joe remarked, "So, Tom, what's the problem?"

Tom answered rather meekly, "I'm not sure what my job is anymore. They won't really need me out there if they keep going this way. I don't know what my role should be or how I should act anymore. It's always been clear how to succeed in this business: Just make the numbers and keep everything under control. Have plenty of inventory to keep all the people and machines busy to get good measures. Now, it's all about low inventories, short cycle times, and teams. I'm not sure I can succeed. How do I coach and guide the employees without just telling them what to do? It feels like I'm giving up everything I've worked so hard to gain."

Tom continued, "How can I stand by and watch the team make mistakes that I made ten years ago? They don't have the experience that I have." Joe responded, "Well, I guess we didn't realize how process redesign would affect your role, nor did we pay enough attention to the fact that you managers are the key to the success of this effort. Tom, I'm sure you can succeed. I'll look into some training for you first thing in the morning. And let's schedule a weekly conversation about this change process. Now, go home and get some rest. You look exhausted."

We have discussed the issues faced by middle managers in an improvement effort, painted a picture of the leadership required, and described in more global terms how empowerment fosters innovation. At this point, you should have a pretty good idea of the organization we believe is required for process redesign with breakthrough results.

Now it is time to discuss *how* to best succeed as a middle manager in such an organization. This chapter should take the blindfold off (remember the trapeze artist in Chapter 1?) and make it clearer just what you are aiming for and how to gain the skills to get there.

The data and ideas presented here result from experience with many organizations, as well as a specific research project targeting middle managers in companies making the journey described in this book. Interviews were conducted with managers who were in various stages of this process, as well as with those enjoying different degrees of success in making the transition. We were particularly looking for differences between those who were well along the journey and very successful and those who were either early in the transition and/or not as successful.

Again, the transition we are describing is significant and very seldom easy. One way to think about the traditional organization versus the organization that promotes and supports innovative process redesign is to think about each in terms of a picture.

For the traditional company, picture the typical organization chart as shown in Figure 11-1. That is pretty much the way we operate: We communicate up the hierarchy, across the functions, and down again. This way of operating may not make sense as the most effective way to do business, but it is clear and simple.

For the innovative process redesign company, imagine a spider web like that shown in Figure 11-2. Spiders may not be your favorite living thing, but the web can be a work of art! Each strand is there to serve a purpose and, if broken, the entire web may not function for its intended purpose. The design may look confusing, and it's certainly not clear where the "up" or "down," "top" or "bottom," are. In fact, the options and connections are endless. Now, think of the strands of the web as communication lines: multiple directions with

Figure 11-1. The traditional organization.

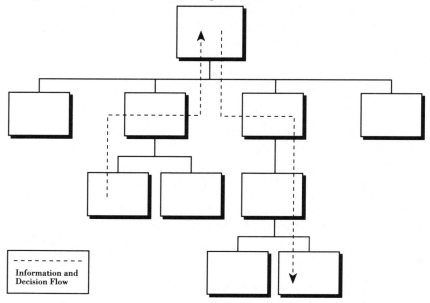

Information and
Decision Flow

many points of contact with other strands of the web. All parts clearly make up the whole, but the design could change tomorrow. The web is more circular than up and down. Being a manager in this "web" environment requires inclusion and does not emphasize hierarchy.

The purpose of this chapter is to describe in tangible terms the competencies, behaviors, and skills found in outstanding managers of innovation, plus key steps for you to take in making the transition. As Figure 11-3 illustrates, competencies describe those core values as well as character traits exhibited by each person; we experience one's competencies through behaviors. Behavior can be modified with acquisition of new skills through self-awareness and training.

We will describe eight competencies. Four are values and four are character traits. For each compentency, we include a description of the manager who demonstrates the competency well. Then, we describe each competency and the behaviors typically experienced from that competency. Finally, we describe how employees generally act, given a manager with that particular competency—in other words, what effect the behaviors resulting from the competency have on the organization.

Having a description of managers who have demonstrated out-

Figure 11-2. The innovative process redesign organization.

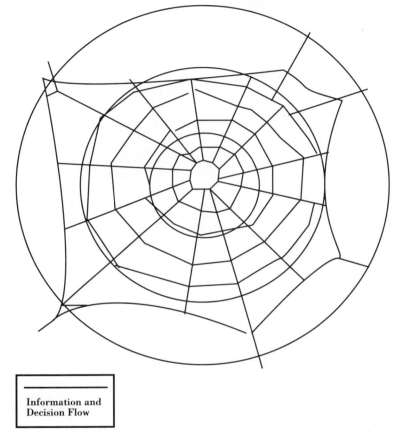

Information and
Decision Flow

standing success in developing innovative organizations should be useful in three key ways:

1. As a self-evaluation and development tool
2. As a tool for evaluating and developing others
3. As a tool for hiring new employees

What Successful Managers Care About

Let's begin by describing those core values that we found most often represented in successful managers. What people really care about is

Figure 11-3. How competencies relate to behaviors.

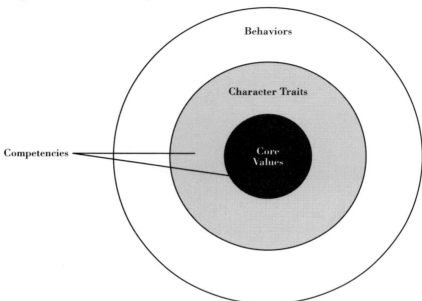

a very personal thing. It is not clear exactly how a person develops these strong core values, and it is not the purpose of this discussion to determine that. What we will say is that through our experience and research, we have found the most successful managers to have strong values around the four following areas: (1) valuing the individual, (2) feeling OK with self, (3) valuing achievement and action, and (4) looking for a better way.

Valuing the Individual

The first competency and first value are to value the individual, shown in Figure 11-4. Successful managers sincerely care about the individual, and it shows. They constantly make the assumption that the individual wants to do a good job and means well. Consideration is given to the "whole" individual—that is, the person's entire life, not just the work part. Using first names and chatting about children or the latest vacation are common in this environment.

Managers who exhibit this competency believe that people are good, even if what they do at a particular time isn't. Development and learning are of highest priority; being too busy is a reason to

Figure 11-4. Competency 1: Values the individual.

- Demonstrates personal care and knowledge of the employee.

- Regularly asks, "How can I help you succeed?"

- Believes empowerment without learning and training is dangerous.

- Empathizes, but doesn't fix problems or discount them as being unimportant.

- Shows confidence in the individual by giving him or her responsibility and letting him or her be accountable for the results.

improve, not an excuse to avoid it. Of top priority for the manager is to walk around regularly to connect with employees at all levels.

In this environment, each employee feels like an individual who has special strengths that are understood and appreciated—not like a number. Barriers and problems are made visible to management along with solutions. Because they feel encouraged to do so, employees make the time for learning opportunities. People feel validated, respected, and trusted.

Feeling OK With Self

The second competency and second value are to feel OK with self, shown in Figure 11-5. Successful managers exhibit an inner satisfaction and peace that regularly say, "Regardless of what happens here, my inner well-being is not at stake. I am OK." Covey's interdependent stage describes it best. These managers do not have to invent solutions in order to support them. They delight in the ideas of others (even if they are better than their own!). Their self-worth is not tied to events or the actions of others.

In this environment, employees freely give management feedback, even if they are pointing out a mistake. When self-development opportunities are offered almost everyone signs up. The spirit is one of learning and growing, piggybacking on each other's ideas, with direct and honest feedback as an important tool in the process.

Valuing Achievement and Action

The third competency and third value are to value achievement and action, shown in Figure 11-6. Successful managers get most excited

Figure 11-5. Competency 2: Feels OK with self.

- Demonstrates clarity about beliefs and is willing to take a stand.

- Constantly evaluates self and asks for feedback from peers and employees.

- Regularly learns more through reading, seminars, training, and self-development.

- Encourages and gets open and honest feedback from employees.

- Readily admits mistakes and learns from them.

- Takes responsibility for behavior and self-reflects about it.

about achieving a meaningful goal, particularly one reached by the people they manage. The process of working together is highly valued along with action. These managers are likely to say, "Do something. If it doesn't work, learn from it and try again."

In this environment, employees accept responsibility for action to achieve goals. They do what they say they will do and really worry if a goal is not achieved on time—without prodding. People are happy to go the extra mile because they know that their extra effort will be noticed and appreciated. Persistence and determination prevail.

Looking for a Better Way

The fourth competency and fourth value are to look for a better way, shown in Figure 11-7. Successful managers are always looking for a better way to do something, even if they created the present process. In fact, they are looking not only for better ways but *radically* better ways. They assume that opportunities to take giant leaps forward surround them, so having more people looking for them creates a greater possibility for success. In other words, the manager talks constantly with others about new ideas and does not hesitate sharing and receiving "wild and crazy" ideas.

Employees feel free to question anything; in fact, they are rewarded for looking for improvement opportunities by constantly questioning the status quo. They regularly go back to management regarding an idea that was not approved with additional data if they

Figure 11-6. Competency 3: Values achievement and action.

- Refuses to take "we can't" for an answer: "If we don't do it, someone else will."

- Demonstrates a winning attitude: "If others can do it, we can do it better!"

- Regularly notices and rewards achievement.

- Encourages people to stretch, but not until they break.

- Sets clear and measurable goals for self and others.

- Teaches employees to take responsibility for their own performances and solve problems themselves.

really believe in the idea. "Thinking outside the box" and radical ideas are the norm.

Character Traits for Managing Innovation

Character traits of an individual seem to be more discernible than core values; often they manifest themselves clearly in behaviors. Again, the traits discussed here are most often found in managers in organizations that are successful innovators focusing on customer value. We will describe four character traits: (1) communicating a clear vision focused on customer values, (2) unleashing the abilities of others, (3) generating positive energy to win as a team, and (4) demonstrating initiative and adaptability.

Communicating a Clear Vision Focused on Customer Value

The fifth competency and first character trait are to communicate a clear vision focused on customer value, shown in Figure 11-8. Successful managers understand that if it's worth saying once, it's worth saying 100 times in 100 different ways. It is not by chance that these managers regularly communicate, always emphasizing to each employee how they contribute to the customer; they deliberately plan time to walk around out where the action is. They always have time to talk. Employees stop them in the cafeteria and hallways regularly. Employee meetings focused on the customer are planned

Figure 11-7. Competency 4: Looks for a better way.

- Manages innovation and change—it's not a haphazard event.

- Challenges his or her own ideas publicly and is constantly curious.

- Asks for and values feedback and ideas from all employees equally.

- Demonstrates an impatience with the status quo and has a passion for change.

- Is willing to receive and analyze new data and change directions if necessary.

- Thinks of ideas that failed as learning experiences.

often, and it doesn't take weeks to get on the manager's calendar: He or she plans open-door office time every day.

Consistency is important to avoid misunderstandings and confusion. These managers talk a lot about the vision and ask employees to fill in their piece of the vision. Boundaries for authority and power are clarified, but employees feel free to ask if they don't understand what is expected of them. Impatience with a purpose is pervasive in these individuals.

In this environment, authentic communication with minimal jargon is the norm. Employees never wonder about the focus and priorities. Resources are deployed in an effective and nonfrantic way, always with the customer in mind. No one forgets that it is the customer who defines value.

Unleashing the Abilities of Others

The sixth competency and second character trait are to unleash the abilities of others, shown in Figure 11-9. Decision making is encouraged through a facilitative management style. One manager put it aptly: "I realize the people I manage are just as smart as I am. They just needed the opportunity. When a problem arises, I ask what they would like to do. Before, I felt I always had to give the answer."

Making decisions can be turned into learning experiences for employees. Allowing decisions that fail can speed the learning process for teams; sometimes these managers let groups or individuals fail rather than take the learning experience away from them. The

Figure 11-8. Competency 5: Communicates a clear vision focused on customer value.

- Emphasizes the customer in getting everything done.

- Communicates constantly, deliberately, and consistently.

- Keeps the vision alive by relating it to everything.

- Shares a broad scope of information with employees.

- Communicates expected outcomes in terms of quantitative results and the process used to get there; expects to leap forward, but appreciates small steps.

- Insists on clear measurement of everything.

role of manager does not require all the answers but instead the ability to unleash the answers from others.

In this environment, employees at all levels are valued, fully utilized, and challenged. Managers delight in the excellent work done by their employees and recognize them regularly. Employees feel empowered to make decisions and implement ideas. They reach out for more involvement as their skills develop.

Generating Positive Energy to Win as a Team

The seventh competency and third character trait are to generate positive energy to win as a team, shown in Figure 11-10. The reaction of one manager summarizes this competence: "It's far nicer to coach, encourage, and motivate rather than to manage, push, and shove. It becomes more like play."

One tool that is frequently mentioned is that of meeting management. Effective meetings are contagious in any organization. There's nothing like an ineffective meeting to sap all the energy for the day!

Successful managers encourage new thoughts and ideas even if they disagree. Conflict is managed, not avoided. A wide range of resources and contacts are used to get the job done. The sphere of influence goes beyond employees managed to peers and upper management.

In this environment, employees enjoy a high level of team spirit as they understand the goal and each member's role. Departmental

Figure 11-9. Competency 6: Unleashes the abilities of others.

- Explores alternatives with employees realizing their high potential.

- Encourages maximum influence of all employees by facilitating.

- Distributes responsibility for decision making and implementation to lowest level.

- Listens effectively and checks for understanding.

- Recognizes that the employees are the experts; managers don't have to have all the answers.

- Gives credit to others: "It amazed me what good ideas they had!"

boundaries are almost nonexistent; they are overshadowed by teaming up to provide maximum value for the customer. Celebrations occur regularly as everyone learns and succeeds.

Demonstrating Initiative and Adaptability

The eighth competency and fourth character trait are to demonstrate initiative and adaptability, shown in Figure 11-11. Successful managers find a way to make things happen. These are the people who do not wait for resources or opportunities to be handed to them: They go get what they need. They "walk the talk," realizing that their actions model the behavior most likely to occur within their influence. They go out of their way to recognize initiative in others as being positive and appreciated—even when it results in a mistake.

Individuals in this environment value flexibility and the ability to "go with the flow," but always with a purpose. Things change—it's inevitable in today's competitive world. Readiness to react is more important than being the best at one thing.

Employees go out of their way to serve the customer, demonstrating ownership and responsibility to get the job done. They feel 100 percent supported by management as they do what it takes. Recognition is high that an organization may not survive if it depends on stability and making what worked in the past work for the future. Instead, energy is focused on creating an organization that quickly adapts to markets that are changing at breakneck speed. People feel secure in their ability to initiate and adapt.

Figure 11-10. Competency 7: Generates positive energy to win as a team.

- Motivates and inspires through coaching, guiding, and cheerleading.

- Creates an exciting, challenging, and fun atmosphere.

- Encourages and models teamwork within department and cross-functionally.

- Views employees as most important asset and sees teamwork as a way to maximize results and energy.

- Sets high standards, gives clear expectations, and focuses on outcomes.

- Celebrates successes from wins and learnings from losses.

Moving From Competencies to Behaviors to Skills

Figure 11-12 shows the evolution of development to become success-ful as a middle manager promoting and achieving innovative process redesign. The competencies are more easily described in terms of behaviors, because that is what we experience as we work with individuals. Also important are the skills obtained and utilized by the individual. Skills development can occur quite quickly, and behaviors can be changed or modified relatively quickly if the new behaviors do not conflict with the individual's core values (we believe that core values do not change) and possibly character traits (we believe that character traits can be modified, but not altogether changed).

It is important to emphasize that an individual can take multiple trips through this evolution: It's not a onetime shot at change. In other words, a manager may work on modifying one character trait through behavior modification and skills training. Later, the individual may select other developmental challenges to work on in the same way.

It is difficult to determine when one moves from a value to a character trait to a behavior and, therefore, a skill. These attributes usually blend, particularly at the transition points.

We will describe the skills that seem most important in leading successful process redesign from the middle. Keep in mind that this is not a comprehensive discussion on management development but a focused discussion on how to make innovative process redesign

Figure 11-11. Competency 8: Demonstrates initiative and adaptability.

- Recognizes a responsibility to make things happen and assumes a certain control over destiny.

- Creates circumstances as well as chooses responses to circumstances.

- Demonstrates an interdependent attitude: "Let's look at alternatives."

- Accepts ambiguity and lack of structure.

- Recognizes changing needs and reprioritizes activities accordingly.

- Adapts behavior to new demands.

---

really work. Therefore, we have selected those skills most relevant within our scope for discussion.

Using the Methodology and Tools of Process Redesign

A manager who exhibits strength in all eight competencies still needs a methodology, or a step-by-step process, and tools to get the job done. For example, a manager may have values that naturally align around the individual and may be self-confident, always achieving and looking for better ways. He or she may be an effective leader, generating energy and excitement in others. If that is true, all the right stuff is there to utilize the methodology and tools in the most effective way possible, applying the competencies as described earlier in this chapter.

As you know, there are other ways to apply the process redesign methodology and tools. Recently, we visited a company whose managers assured us that they knew all about mapping processes. It turned out that the company had hired a consultant to come in and map the processes by talking with a few people who worked in the area under study. Individuals at the company didn't have time to get together and develop the map themselves! Of course, you can imagine the missed opportunity. All of the conversations and ideas that typically occur when people closest to the process develop the process map were lost. The result was a process map that probably resembled the process as individuals saw it, with a consultant who

Figure 11-12. Evolving as a manager.

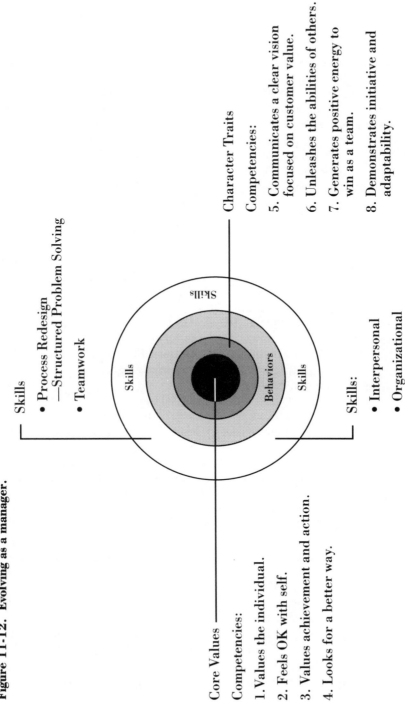

Skills
- Process Redesign
  — Structured Problem Solving
- Teamwork

Character Traits
Competencies:

5. Communicates a clear vision focused on customer value.

6. Unleashes the abilities of others.

7. Generates positive energy to win as a team.

8. Demonstrates initiative and adaptability.

Core Values
Competencies:

1. Values the individual.

2. Feels OK with self.

3. Values achievement and action.

4. Looks for a better way.

Skills:
- Interpersonal
- Organizational
- Management

Skills

Skills

Behaviors

Skills

learned about some of the challenges and problems associated with that particular process. The employees did not necessarily agree with the consultant on the improvement ideas, and nothing significant happened to improve the process. However, the methodology and tools were probably applied in a technically correct way.

The point is that the most successful managers exhibit the eight competencies through their behaviors and in the way that they apply their learned skills. These managers understand and apply the process redesign methodology and tools, including structured problem solving, as well as the teamwork skills described earlier in this book. They coach and guide employees to always take a data-based, logical approach to improvement. If they find that employees are not using the methodology and tools, they can teach them how to do it.

We are reminded of a manager who dropped in on a team meeting to find the team struggling with a particular problem that it was trying to solve. The group had so much data that it didn't know how to organize the information to get to the next step. The manager was able to step in and facilitate a discussion of the different problem-solving tools available and help the team choose and utilize the preferred one. The team felt supported but still had ownership of the process and the solutions that were later implemented.

This manager exhibited a number of the eight competencies, including valuing the team members by taking the time to teach them how to discover solutions themselves (unleashed the abilities of others), generating positive energy, and exhibiting initiative. He did this by applying the skills that he had gained on using problem-solving tools. Without the tools, he would have been much less effective in this situation. A more traditional manager would have probably just given the team the solution to the problem.

Using Teamwork Skills

Another skill exhibited by this manager is teamwork. Now, you may say, "What is there to learn about teamwork? That's pretty simple. You just get a group of people together to work on something." Not so. Teamwork is hard work, and there are specific skills that can be learned to make successful teams.

Let's return to the team meeting. This time, the problem faced by the team members is that they are unable to make a consensus decision. The manager stepped in to facilitate the process by ensuring that everyone had been heard and that each point of view had been clearly communicated. By understanding how teams operate and having the tool of consensus decision making, he was able to help the team not only learn more about group decision making but also make the decision.

Applying Interpersonal, Organizational, and Management Skills

Other particularly important skills are interpersonal, organizational, and management skills. Interpersonal skills include skills such as listening and facilitating. Yes, listening can be learned! There are some tools that help increase listening skills. Facilitation skills training is essential for those people who are facilitating groups. Other examples include influence skills and how to communicate more effectively.

Organizational skills involve issues related to the organization, such as organizational structure, empowerment, and how to plan and manage change effectively throughout an entire organization. Another way to think about this is to be able to determine how certain changes may have an impact on an entire organization.

Management skills cover a wide variety of issues. We will mention only those most affected by innovative process redesign. This is not to ignore skills such as how to discipline an individual or follow the laws of equal opportunity, but we consider these very basic and of importance in any company. Those management skills most relevant to our scope include strategy and planning, performance management, goal setting, and reward and recognition.

Training, Training, and More Training

A pervasive trait of every company that is consistently competitive by constantly innovating and always focusing on the customer is that there is training all the time. In today's fast-changing world, employees require and deserve the opportunity to constantly learn new skills while working on the eight competencies and modifying behaviors.

It is critical that middle managers are not just included but are in the center of this activity. Specific training can occur for each of the skills that we have listed. This is a good place to begin. As you get involved in this change process, other needed skills will be identified to continue the learning process.

We believe that training is most effective when "pulled" by the organization. Let's see if we can explain. Training is more effective if there is a well-understood need for the new skill being taught. Take again the manager who dropped into the team meeting. If he had not known about problem-solving tools, he would not have been as helpful. That experience could cause him (if he has the initiative competency) to search out training that would provide those tools and skills in the future. His training experience in this situation could be somewhat different than that of another manager in the class who has not perceived a need for problem-solving tools. In fact, she may sit there thinking, "This is interesting, but when will I ever use it?" This reaction would be particularly prevalent if that manager does not look for better ways of doing things but instead just keeps things running as they always have. In the latter scenario, she probably has all the answers for the problems that may arise, anyway!

Let us emphasize once again that formal training is just the beginning in learning a new behavior or skill. Ongoing training with continuous feedback during implementation is necessary to complete the learning process.

The Steps for the Transition

In summary, middle managers have the greatest impact on success with innovative process redesign, given that top management has signed up to lead the change process in a supportive way. It is critical that they be involved as drivers of the process, not as victims. This requires "taking the blindfold" off early to give middle managers the opportunity to understand how their role changes in this different organization as well as to develop the behaviors and skills to succeed.

Awareness training for middle managers can provide a picture of the new environment being created. These individuals need to understand the common vision and how they fit into it. The performance management process may need to be modified or redesigned to provide measures of performance that support the vision and how middle managers are to operate in the future. As we have said, skills training is essential and ongoing. Forming support groups of middle managers who meet regularly to discuss challenges and issues they may be facing has proven valuable time and time again. The key is that involving middle managers early in the change process will develop into ownership, and ownership will develop into commitment. You will be empowered and confident in your new role leading innovative process redesign.

Beginning the Journey

The foundation of maximizing customer value is a focus on the business processes that drive the business along with creating a climate that values innovation. We have provided step-by-step methodologies and tools to use in planning and implementing innovative process redesign for breakthrough results. To ensure success, the critical role of middle management has to be redefined, including how to develop the behaviors and skills that will be required in the future. Good luck as you begin this most fascinating journey!

Appendix

Assessing the Organization's Readiness

There are two issues to consider in determining the readiness of your organization to undertake a breakthrough process improvement effort:

1. Is the character of the organization receptive to such an effort?
2. Where should the organization enter the process?

This Appendix is intended to help you think through those questions and reach some conclusions about your own organization. It will not give you an absolute answer—there really is no absolute answer.

You might begin by asking the question "Why does it take a special effort in the first place?" That's a very valid question and one that a lot of people ask. It leads directly to the assessment of readiness.

Understanding the Inertia

The reason a special effort is required in the beginning is that the organization is bogged down with inertia. That's the whole point of the effort. You want to overcome that inertia and change the character and culture of the organization. The goal is to make the organization one in which breakthrough and continuous improvement efforts *are* the culture.

The organization's culture is a product of the values, thoughts, and feelings of the individual employees. You can get a good feel for the culture of an organization just by talking with a small number of employees about how the organization works. Ask them about what happens between two departments—i.e., during an interaction. What are the conversations like? How are the decisions made? What are employees told or not told by their supervisors?

Another way to get an assessment of how the organization would respond to breakthrough improvement efforts is to ask employees about what they can do to drive improvements. Their limiting beliefs are a good assessment of the degree of inertia to be overcome. A limiting belief is almost the opposite of a driving vision. It is a negative sort of vision that says "I can't do that because—." Some typical limiting beliefs that often surface when talking with employees are:

- I don't have the time to work on problems. I'm too busy fighting fires and trying to get my job done.
- Someone else works on that. It isn't part of my job.
- That problem is too big for me to handle, and nobody will join me to work on it.
- This organization is so messed up it's hopeless to try to fix anything.
- I can't make a difference on that. It's too big, and there are too many high-level issues for me. I don't have what is needed to solve it.
- People don't want to change anything. They are happy the way it is. Or if not happy, they don't have the energy to change.
- I'm afraid to come out with any ideas because I don't know whom I can trust here. If it isn't a good idea, some people will use it against me.
- I could lose my job or my chances for promotion by making waves. I'd better just keep quiet.

We hear statements like these often. They tell us that a spontaneous change to innovative breakthrough improvement is unlikely to happen.

On the other hand, we recently worked with a client where the roots of a total turnaround of a division with sales of several hundred million dollars lay in a hallway conversation between two people. One had read a book about process improvement and the other had worked at a company with a well-developed breakthrough improvement effort. That hallway conversation led to other conversations, which eventually led to a group of about a dozen middle managers visiting a series of companies with successful efforts under way. After a few months, the group members approached top management with a proposal that an effort be launched in their division. Top management was supportive, largely because of the quality of the study work done by the middle management group totally on its own. Top-division management took the proposal to the corporate board, and funds were approved to support a major effort to launch a break-through improvement program that is now paying big dividends. Ultimately, the turnaround spread to two other major divisions of the corporation, totalling almost a billion dollars in sales. All from a hallway conversation between two middle managers who discovered they shared an interest in doing something.

This organization had a culture with few limiting beliefs. Time was an issue, and there was some fear of risk taking. But the overwhelming beliefs were:

- I'm confident in my abilities.
- I'm confident in my management's ability to recognize a good idea, well researched and well presented.
- The job of improving the company belongs to all of us.
- I'm sure that action will improve my career.
- My actions alone make a difference to the company.
- This is my company, and I am dedicated to making it better.

These might be called affirmative beliefs.

A place to begin assessing your organization would be to make a list of the limiting beliefs and affirmative beliefs. These might be put on a force-field analysis chart that you learned about in Chapter 9. Figure A-1 is an example.

Then, consider those limiting beliefs and determine which ones absolutely must begin to change if a breakthrough improvement effort is to succeed in your organization. What is going to be required to change the limiting beliefs? Can awareness and training begin to make a change? Will working through pilot teams change the doubters? At what level do these limiting beliefs appear in the organization? Are they at the very top, or low in the organization? Is the issue going to be leadership or willingness of others to follow?

You might also ask yourself what strengths are on your side from the affirmative beliefs you have identified. How will they help you? How can they be used to counter the limiting beliefs? Where in the organization are the affirmative beliefs strongest? What do they predict about leadership?

Figure A-1. Using the force-field analysis to assess the organization.

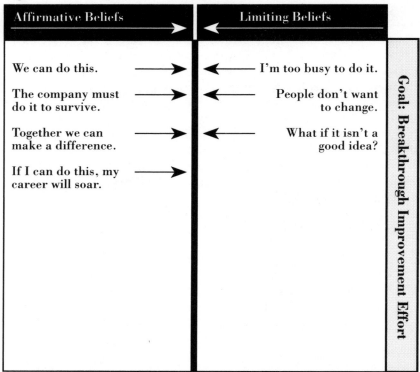

Determining Where to Begin

The second major step in assessing the readiness of your organization is to evaluate where you would enter the improvement model if you were to begin the process. The upper loop of the model shown in Figure 3-1 is reproduced here as Figure A-2.

As we said in the text, companies might enter the loop at different points depending upon how far they have evolved in getting close to and understanding their customers, how well focused they are on a common vision of where they are going, how well their business imperatives are identified, how clear their strategies are, and how well these things have been communicated to the organization. We acknowledged that some organizations (a turnaround situation was used as an example) might have some critical imperatives and needs that are so strong that the other steps should be deferred

Figure A-2. Where to enter the improvement model.

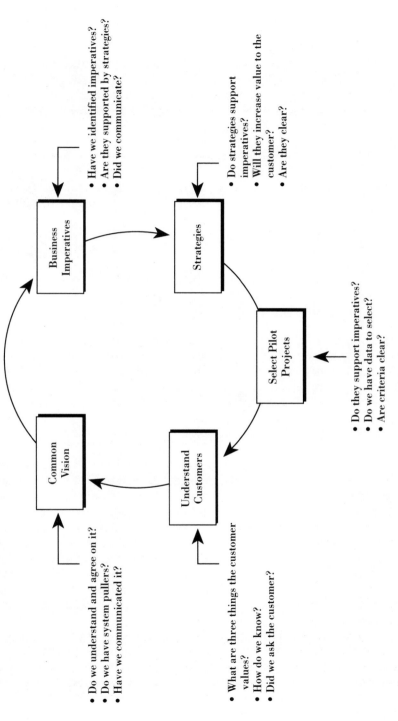

until later and all effort should be focused on breakthroughs that will allow the company to survive. But barring a crisis situation, you can make a logical journey through the model and ask yourself some questions that will help you determine where you might enter the process.

Testing Customer Understanding

To test the extent of how well your organization understands the customer and the validity of that understanding, ask the following questions:

- What are three things the customer values highly in making buying decisions?
- On what do we base this belief?
- Have we tested this belief by asking the customer?
- If so, how long ago?

You might write these answers down and review them with others to see how commonly held your perception of customer values is. If it is not commonly held, or if the perceptions have not been tested recently with the customer, you may want to consider doing work to determine what is important to the customers in your market.

Confirming the Common Vision

Confirming that there is a common vision helps you understand whether or not efforts in the organization would be directed toward a common goal. If there is risk that efforts may not be directed toward a common goal and that people do not understand a common vision, work may be required to create and communicate a common vision for the organization that can be a driving force for the improvement effort. Many times, there is a semblance of a common vision, but it has not been articulated and refined. Steps should be taken to communicate the vision throughout the organization. A fuzzy vision becomes even fuzzier the lower it gets in the organization and the further it gets from the originators.

Write down what you believe the vision of the organization to be. Ask others to do the same, and compare the results. If you do not see a common picture and key characteristics of the visions in common, work is necessary to develop a better understanding and to communicate it to all. System pullers may help you do so.

Creating System Pullers

In many organizations, the vision will be articulated and pulled into the way work gets done as a set of affirmations, e.g., "We are—." Few organizations that have not gone through formal common vision development workshops have system pullers. They need to be developed from the common vision even in an organization that has a well-developed and well-communicated common vision. The system pullers are an important part of instilling the vision in the organization. If you do not have them, you may want to do some specific work to develop some.

Looking for Business Imperatives

Look at what you believe to be your business imperatives. Are they really business imperatives designed to achieve the common vision, or are they strategies? If they are strategies—which is commonly the case when we ask for a list of what the company believes to be its business imperatives—you may need to do some serious thinking about developing business imperatives.

Again, write down what you believe to be the business imperatives of the company. Test them with two or three people and see how much agreement you have. A word of caution here: Do not just write down what was listed in the last management memo on important projects. Write down what appear to be the imperatives according to where people are devoting their efforts and where resources are being allocated. That list would be interesting to compare to the last management list of important projects to see how they tie together.

Examining the Strategies

By this time you should have a loose chain tying together key customers values, the common vision, system pullers, and business imperatives. Examine the key strategies of the company against that chain, focusing again more on where resources and effort are devoted than on the key project list. Are all imperatives adequately supported? Are there strategies that do not relate to key imperatives? Are the strategies aimed at creating more customer value, either directly or indirectly? What needs to be done to clarify strategies and make them more meaningful to the organization?

Evaluating Project Selection

If you are at the stage of choosing pilot projects, it may be time to take a hard look at your first candidates to see if they meet the criteria for pilots described in Chapter 3. Even if you have already begun projects, you probably want to look at how well your selection fits these criteria.

If you have not chosen projects, you may want to discuss whether or not your situation is one in which the requirements are so clear that you should charter and launch teams immediately, or whether you should begin gathering data for future project selection. Determine what the criteria are going to be for targeting areas for data gathering. Evaluate whether or not you know enough to make choices now.

Taking a Hard Look at How the Organization Works

In our earlier discussion of limiting beliefs, we described some attitudes in the company that, if they represent the character of the company, could be obstacles to quick and successful implementation of a breakthrough improvement effort. We also discussed an example of a company with strong affirmative beliefs. Assessing the attitudes of employees and the character of the company is one way to measure the obstacles. Another way to assess readiness of the organization and determine strengths and issues that might affect success is a more detailed look at how the company actually works. This is often called a climate survey.

There are many ways to do a successful climate survey. The brief general review we are doing here is designed to stimulate your thinking about issues that need to be considered in making decisions about an improvement effort. This is not a substitute for a full-scale professional climate survey in any sense. It does not take into account organization functions, strata, or even all of the factors that might be of interest in a full climate study. But it does serve to heighten your awareness of some of the things about how the organization works on a day-to-day basis that affect the launch and successful conduct of a breakthrough improvement process.

The questions that follow have been categorized into topics to aid your thinking. Score these questions on the following scale:

1 = Almost always
2 = More than half the time

3 = About half the time
4 = Less than half the time
5 = Almost never

In reviewing your answers, keep in mind that both the score of individual questions and the composite score for the topic are of interest. Lower scores are more positive than higher scores. If a question is scored higher than 3, try to think of examples of situations that have occurred that made you assign a value higher than 3. Think through those situations to try to determine what impact the behavior exhibited would have on the breakthrough improvement process from your understanding of leadership skills requirements and the process required to succeed. For entire categories that have composite scores higher than 3, give some serious thought to what that says about your organization with respect to implementing the improvement effort.

Your Personal Assessment of Your Organization

Strategy and Direction

1. The company has established a strategy and direction that will keep it competitive in the future. __
2. Most work units have a definite direction and purpose; they know where they are going and how to get there. __
3. I have a clear understanding of the mission of my organization and how the products and services contribute to the mission. __
4. I have a great deal of confidence in the business judgment of the management of this company. __
5. I have a clear understanding of what I am expected to accomplish this year as a manager. __

Problem Solving

1. Problems get solved the first time. They are not repeated. __
2. My work group has fewer problems than one year ago. __
3. Members of my work group spend a lot of energy to solve problems. __
4. Management corrects problems. It does not rationalize them away or spend time blaming people. __

Decision Making

1. In this company people who make decisions know what is going on at my level. __
2. I am often asked to participate in decision making. __
3. Changes are well thought out and carefully implemented. __
4. Circumstances of employees are considered when decisions are made that will affect them. __
5. Decisions are made on the basis of long-term strategy rather than short-term results. __

Organizational Structure

1. My work group is organized in such a way that we are able to function in an efficient manner. __
2. Very little falls between the cracks in this organization. __
3. The number of management levels in the company is never a problem in getting things done effectively. __
4. Supervisors know how to organize resources and get things done. __

Employee Empowerment

1. My opinions are solicited and utilized by my manager. __
2. People are encouraged to express ideas and innovate. __
3. I am a part of departmental problem-solving activities. __
4. Frank and candid expression of feelings is the norm in the company. __

Conflict Resolution

1. Complaints are dealt with promptly and openly. __
2. When a difference of opinion occurs, management does not assume it is right and employees are wrong. __
3. Conflicts between departments are always resolved, never ignored. __
4. Employees who challenge the way things have always been done are appreciated and encouraged. __

Communications

1. In my work group, good communications are the norm. __
2. Other departments respond quickly and cooperatively and never give me the runaround. __
3. Ideas are expressed openly and freely at all times. __

4. Employees receive advance notice from management when changes are to be made. __

Collaboration

1. There is a lot of incentive for groups to work together. __
2. Management encourages groups to work together and recognizes success. __
3. Company resources and money are used effectively because of the way different groups cooperate with each other. __
4. Different departments are not competing with each other for money, people, or recognition. __

Customer Service

1. Customers can depend on this company to meet deadlines and fulfill commitments. __
2. We all go out of our way to make sure customers and clients are satisfied. __
3. Employees are well enough informed to provide correct answers to customer inquiries. __
4. Customers trust and rely upon us. __

Innovation

1. Employees are encouraged to innovate and are rewarded for "thinking outside the box." __
2. We are constantly trying to improve our products and services. __
3. The way to get ahead here is to take risks and try things when the situation calls for it. __
4. People are not afraid to make mistakes. __

Openness to Change

1. The company adapts well to changing circumstances. __
2. The company does not stick to one strategy; strategies are adjusted in response to changing conditions. __
3. People are enthusiastic about learning new things. __
4. Ideas and suggestions are well received. __

Company Values

1. Company values are clearly communicated to all employees. __

2. Doing the right thing for customers comes ahead of making short-term profit goals. ___
3. We believe in providing products and services that are clearly the finest in our industry. ___
4. Results are honestly reported without distortion or rationalization. ___
5. The company believes in providing opportunities for its people to grow and excel. ___

Index

visible measures, 200
vision
    based on customer values, 43
    combining individual, 34–36
    communication of, 39–42
    concept of, 33
    confirmation of, 250
    customer value focused, 233–234, 235
    description of, 33–34
    development of, 33–37
    examples of, 34–35
    failure to invest in, 9
    integrating organization through, 36
visionary hero, 219
visioning session, 28

waits, 115
    elimination of, 129–130

with handoffs and batches, 146–147
Welch, Jack, on leadership, 208
whys, five, 175–176, 177
work flow
    charting of, 148–149
    uncovering of problems in, 149–157
    see also flow
work group teams, 195–196
work movement analysis, 147–148
work piles, assessment of, 152–153
written customer/client surveys, guidelines for, 79

yields
    analysis of, 159–161
    first-pass, 161